LANDSCAPES OF WISDOM

In Search of a Spirituality of Knowing

Jonas Barciauskas

University Press of America, ® Inc.
Lanham • New York • Oxford

Copyright © 2000 by
University Press of America
4720 Boston Way
Lanham, Maryland 20706

12 Hid's Copse Rd.
Cumnor Hill, Oxford OX2 9JJ

All rights reserved
Printed in the United States of America
British Library Cataloging in Publication Information Available

Library of Congress Cataloging-in-Publication Data

Barciauskas, Jonas Vladas
Landscapes of wisdom : in search of a spirituality of knowing /
Jonas Barciauskas.
p. cm.
Includes bibliographical references and index.
1. Metaphysics. 2. Spirituality. 3. Wisdom. 4. Buddhism. I. Title.
BD111.B13   2000   110—dc21   00-030286 CIP

ISBN 0-7618-1731-X (cloth: alk. ppr.)
ISBN 0-7618-1732-8 (pbk: alk. ppr.)

∞™ The paper used in this publication meets the minimum
requirements of American National Standard for Information
Sciences—Permanence of Paper for Printed Library Materials,
ANSI Z39.48—1984

For Katie Lee, Joel, and Aimee

Contents

Preface		vii
Acknowledgments		xi
Introduction		xiii
Chapter 1	Alpha: An Ascent to God	1
Chapter 2	Alpha: The Wisdom of Being	21
Chapter 3	Zero: A Journey into the Interior	57
Chapter 4	Zero: The Wisdom of Emptiness	77
Chapter 5	Omega: Discovering the Human Adventure	107
Chapter 6	Omega: The Wisdom of Becoming	131
Chapter 7	Omega: The Becoming of Wisdom	159
Conclusion		193
Bibliography		201
Index		207

Preface

Wisdom and books of wisdom. If we think of wisdom, we may imagine its embodiment in an older person made wise by experience, or perhaps younger and "wise beyond his or her years." We are drawn to such figures if we feel a deep desire to grow in wisdom, and if our good fortune brings us into contact with them at a time when we have the ears to hear and eyes to see. We may also explore books of wisdom: scriptures, philosophies, teachings of spiritual masters. When Augustine first read Cicero's *Hortensius*, his reaction was dramatic: "All my empty dreams suddenly lost their charm and my heart began to throb with a bewildering passion for the wisdom of eternal truth."[1] He had experienced a kind of conversion, an awakening to the reality of the inner life. Whether it be the spoken word of a spiritual guide or the printed word on a page, wisdom's message can speak to us in a way that profoundly changes our understanding of the world and ourselves.

The book before you is not a book of wisdom but about it. More accurately, it is an attempt to look for wisdom in contemporary thought. My approach throughout is to assume the role of seeker as well as scholar. As scholar, I read and study books on religion, theology, literature and science. As seeker, I have spiritual practices in two different spiritual traditions, Christianity and Buddhism. The two are similar in many ways but also different, and both are struggling with the challenges of the modern world. In the intellectual realm, the challenges come from many directions, but perhaps most significantly from the sciences. The significance of the challenge arises from the influence of modern science on everyday modes of thought and perception. How we think about nature, society, history, the mind, even religion itself has often been determined by the rules governing the physical sciences. But can we attain wisdom through science?

My initial response is no. While its successes have been considerable, science has clearly led to disastrous results in its applications. Apart from its remarkable discoveries, the scientific enterprise has contributed greatly to the development of thought and learning. It represents a commitment of the human mind to explore the world with careful attention and perseverance in a way that has never been pursued before. Its way has required participation in a global community of researchers which must validate claims made by any of its members before the claims are accepted. Scientific findings must be universally verifiable. This is a stark contrast to the faith claims of individual religions, which often are tolerated but rarely believed to the same profound degree by those outside the community making the claims.

Yet it remains to be proven that science has the capacity to shape and heal the whole person in the way of the great spiritual traditions. Indeed, it has shied away from dealing with matters of the inner life. A great spiritual teacher in the Christian tradition, Thomas Merton, has written that when God touches us, "you are more yourself than you have ever been before. You have only just begun to exist. You feel as if you were at last fully born." Our mental life is transformed: "Our mind swims in the air of an understanding, a reality that is dark and serene and includes in itself everything."[2] The task before us is to see if there is a spiritual way of knowing accessible to the modern mind, an intellectual path meeting the challenge of science with an equally universal message that speaks of the world and its workings, but also of transcendence and the deepest core of human experience.

My effort has been to write a book about wisdom which draws on the insights of others. While the following chapters are in large part a discussion and commentary, they are filled with excerpts from poets, philosophers, and theologians. Their various insights are much like the scattered divine sparks of kabbalist teachings which must be gathered together in a cosmic process of restoration, *tiqqun*, of the Godhead, or in our case, the restoration of wisdom. But the recovery of wisdom cannot be accomplished by thought alone. It is also a matter of love and compassion.

In a story by Isaac Bashevis Singer, *The Spinoza of Market Street*, a life-long student of the Jewish philosopher interprets all that he sees and experiences in terms of Spinoza's metaphysical system. An older man living alone in a garret overlooking the bustle of everyday life, Dr. Fischelson returns again and again to the *Ethics* because Spinoza's great work appears to have explained so much and with such great profundity. Fischelson is, however, deathly ill, and eventually comes under the care of his neighbor, Black Dobbe, who is a spinster "tall and lean, . . black as a baker's shovel. . . . [with] a broken nose and . . . a mustache on her upper lip."[3] The weeks pass and interpersonal barriers begin to fall; each questions the other about the past. Eventually, Fischelson's deteriorating health takes a marked turn for the better, and they decide to marry. The passions which arise during their wedding night "could be called a miracle." At midnight, his new bride asleep behind him, Fischelson reflects on the universe as divine substance, a basic notion in Spinoza's teaching, and murmurs "Divine Spinoza, forgive me. I have become a fool."[4]

Throughout this book, much of our attention will be directed toward the ways in which we can imagine and know ultimate reality, exploring what various wisdom doctrines have to offer. Love as a theme is raised at critical moments in the discussion, but what I am aiming for is not wisdom of the wise but of fools, fools like the miraculously revived Dr. Fischelson. For wisdom is empty doctrine if not vivified by a miraculous love both human and divine.

Notes

1. St. Augustine, *Confessions*, III, 4, trans. R.S. Pine-Coffin (Harmondsworth, Eng.: Penguin Books, 1961), 58.

2. Thomas Merton, *New Seeds of Contemplation* (New York: New Directions, 1961), 227.

3. Isaac Bashevis Singer, "The Spinoza of Market Street," in *The Collected Stories* (New York: Farrar, Straus, Giroux, 1982), 86.

4. Ibid., 92-93.

Acknowledgments

To practice a spirituality of knowing is to practice a spirituality of gratitude. As the book's title suggests, landscapes have an important role in its text. Imaginary and real, poetic and metaphysical, they are the worlds through which our souls journey toward transcendence. I am grateful to the landscapes which shaped my spiritual and intellectual growth: the worlds of poets and mystics, philosophers and theologians, and the real worlds of nature and city, the surroundings which influenced me in ways I cannot fully understand. My initial thoughts came while driving through the wooded hills of West Virginia. Chapters were written in a variety of locations: Ghana, the Côte d'Azur, a medieval village in Provence, London, and several New England towns. I give thanks to all the scenes of natural beauty and human community that have provided me with a larger sense of the world we seek to know.

My debt to my teachers is considerable. Ewert Cousins, my doctoral mentor at Fordham University, introduced me to the Christian mystical tradition. Eido Shimano Roshi splashed me with the cold water of living Zen practice. Huston Smith deepened my appreciation of perennial philosophy. Thomas Berry introduced me to the writings of Pierre Teilhard de Chardin and a new vision of an ecological global community. Their voices are still vivid in my mind, continuing to speak to me across the miles and years.

The National Endowment for the Humanities Summer Seminar program enabled me to work with Huston Smith and a group of scholars exploring the metaphysical theme of the Great Chain of Being and its occurrence in religious traditions; it was during those wonderful summer months in Berkeley, California, when I carried out most of the initial research for the ideas behind the book. Mary Cronin, University Librarian at Boston College during the first phase of my project, gave me the opportunity to go on a research leave at a period when free time was essential. Robert Jonas' critical reading of the chapters on Buddhist thought were most helpful. Joseph Bracken's encouragement got me through a rough patch when I was seeking a publisher, and I have learned much from his scholarship in process thought.

And how can a writer do anything without the loving support of family and friends? In the last and most difficult phase of my project, Katie Lee Crane's unfailing encouragement helped me get to the finish line. Perhaps, as loving wife she could do no less, but anyone who has lived with a writer possessed with the need to "get it all down" learns to share the daily loneliness of writing. Her willingness to do so was a gift for which I can't give thanks enough.

Introduction

The Physicist and the Cardinal

People seeking wisdom can take different paths. Some may begin with an examination of their own lives, others with the study of sacred texts. Let us begin with two men, separated in time by more than 500 years, each trying to understand the origin of the universe.

In 1988, the British theoretical physicist Stephen Hawking published *A Brief History of Time*, a survey of the history of physics that became a best-seller and the basis of an award-winning film. In its concluding chapter, he admits having a desire to know life's meaning: "We want to make sense of what we see around us and to ask: What is the nature of the universe? What is our place in it and where did it and we come from? Why is it the way it is?"[1] According to Hawking, we have always formed some version of a "world picture" which answers such questions, but theories of the universe no longer rely on the kinds of myths and beliefs created by earlier societies. Instead, contemporary models of the universe rely on the latest scientific theories, including Hawking's ground-breaking work on black holes and the Big Bang. His involvement with physics and mathematics has led him to believe in the possibility of a "Theory of Everything" which would satisfy the human need for ultimate meaning:

> However, if we do discover a complete theory, it should be understandable in broad principle by everyone, not just a few scientists. Then we shall all, philosophers, scientists, and just ordinary people, be able to take part in the discussion of the question why it is that we and the universe exist. If we find the answer to that, it would be the ultimate triumph of human reason - for then we would know the mind of God.[2]

Hawking's high claim that God is ultimately knowable through science may not be universally shared in the scientific community, but it expresses a hope harbored by many since the dawn of our scientific era.

Nicholas of Cusa wrote during a period of transition in European thought between the scholasticism of the Middle Ages and the advent of humanism and modern science in the Renaissance. A German by birth, he was appointed cardinal after years of diplomatic service for the Roman Church. In 1440, he wrote the mystical and speculative work, *De docta ignorantia (On Learned Ignorance)* in which he rejects the Ptolemaic universe with its series of concentric spheres and a single physical center. Cusa argued that centrality requires equidistance and "precise equidistance to different points cannot be found outside God, for God alone is infinite equality."[3] In place of the Ptolemaic model, he proposed a universe of multiple centers which in reality are only one center, the One who is God. According to Ernst Cassirer, Cusa's cosmology is "new" compared to the medieval picture of concentric heavens, and significantly Cusa's insight has "at once a natural and an intellectual sense, a physical and a 'spiritual' sense."[4] Cusa believed that the human mind wants to know as much as possible about the world but also about the divine mystery behind it all.

> In the creation of the world God made use of arithmetic, geometry, music and astronomy which we also use when we investigate the proportion of things, including elements and motions. . . . It is also God's will that we should come to admire so marvelous a machine of the world, but the more we admire it the more God hides it from our view, for God alone wants to be sought with our whole heart and purpose. . . .
> But to one who in learned ignorance inquires what they are or how they exist or to what purpose they exist, all things reply: "Of ourselves we are nothing, nor of ourselves are we able to give any other reply than nothing, . . . If you wish to know anything about us, seek it in our reason and cause, not in us. There, while seeking one thing, you will find all things. Nor can you find yourself except in that One."[5]

For Cusa, the practice of reason is primarily a way to wisdom. If an individual's rational faculty is stretched to its limits, it realizes an even higher mode of knowing, learned ignorance. Cultivating learned ignorance means recognizing the absolute difference between rational knowledge and spiritual wisdom as well as their intimate relationship. Frequently, Cusa relies on paradoxical language to describe wisdom's inaccessible accessibility. In the following passage, Cusa plays on the Latin word for wisdom, *sapientia*, derived from *sapere*, to taste:

> Nothing tastes sweeter to the intellect than wisdom. Those men who speak only by way of the word and not by taste ought not to be considered in any manner to be wise. . . . For all internal taste is by, from, and

in that wisdom which is not able to be tasted by any taste. Therefore, it is tasted untastingly because it is higher than anything can be tasted: whether it be sensible, rational or intellectual.[6]

Both Hawking and Cusa believe deeply in our capacity to "investigate the proportions of things," and proposed innovative theories about the structure of the universe. But where Hawking focuses on reason, Cusa speaks of a wisdom beyond reason's grasp. If each is in some way mirroring the intellectual world of his time, then a question arises: has wisdom declined as a universally recognized value? Can we arrive at ultimate truths only through rational inquiry and scientific method or is there another, higher way of knowing?

Posing the Question

Religious and philosophical traditions have regarded wisdom as a major goal in life. As a special kind of knowledge, wisdom has been familiar to ancient and medieval thinkers in Western culture, as well as sages and mystics in other religions. As a term in the English language, wisdom has been used to translate *prajna* in Buddhism, *paravidya* or *jnana* in Hindu Vedanta, *hokhmah* in Judaism, *'irfan* in Islam, *sophia* in Greek texts and *sapientia* in Latin. In the Judeo-Christian tradition, wisdom literature in scripture provides a view of reality, praises the mysteries of creation, and portrays wisdom as a feminine divinity. Cusa's theological forebears considered wisdom central to their relationship with God. Augustine, for example, emphasized "the right distinction between wisdom and knowledge, that the intellectual cognizance of eternal things belongs to wisdom, but the rational cognizance of temporal things to knowledge."[7] Dionysius the Areopagite began his influential *Mystical Theology* with a prayer to the Holy Trinity: "Thou that instructeth Christians in Thy heavenly wisdom!"[8]

Common usage accepts wisdom as a knowledge of life and its complexities that can only be gained through experience. For some, a wise person is one who follows a life of moderation and observes practical principles about personal, social, and material well-being. The project of this book, however, is not to examine this kind of "worldly wisdom" but to explore a spiritual understanding of the term. The challenge for us today is to find ways of talking about a spirituality of knowing within a modern context. The book's central question is: How can we understand wisdom? How can we talk about a higher mode of knowing when the dominant modes provided by science and reason seem, for many thinkers, to be the only ones possible?

The intellectual climate proves to be quite unfavorable to any discussion of this sort. Gabriel Marcel has spoken of a "decline of wisdom."[9] Jerome Miller notes that "philosophers do not say much about wisdom these days" and believes their reticence to explore the topic is "because the pluralism of postmodern culture makes this cardinal virtue of our intellectual tradition seem impossible to achieve and therefore irrelevant to us."[10] If we are to talk about wisdom, two major obstacles arise immediately. The first is the fundamental mysteriousness of wisdom. How will we able to talk about something that often eludes language? The second is the postmodern suspicion of anything identified as a fundamental truth or idea. How can we consider wisdom seriously when such notions as self, truth, and God have seemingly crumbled in the withering glare of deconstructive analysis? The book's basic premise is that a serious examination of wisdom within a contemporary intellectual context is possible despite these two considerable challenges, and it is in fact occurring within particular groups of writers and thinkers.

I have selected three contemporary schools of wisdom to explore. My names for them are Alpha, Zero, and Omega. All three schools are well acquainted with the Western philosophical and theological tradition and are deeply committed to preserving or exploring spiritual modes of knowing. The Alpha school bases its teachings on a perennial philosophy which claims that a sacred wisdom tradition lies at the core of all the great religions. The Zero group is composed of Buddhist philosophers from the Kyoto school. The Omega school is still developing its understanding of wisdom, but its foundation is process thought and the writings of Teilhard de Chardin.

I have several reasons for choosing these three schools. First, each has an identifiable metaphysics. Alpha presents us with a metaphysics of being, Zero with a metaphysics of nothingness, and Omega with one of becoming. As wisdom's most intellectually developed mode of discourse, metaphysical language has come under heavy fire in contemporary discourse for using abstract terms which no longer carry the weight of generally accepted meanings. In defense of this intellectual enterprise, Huston Smith has defined metaphysics as a "worldview that provides a sense of orientation." Wisdom's ability to describe place as a path, the *topos* where we struggle toward redemption and light, is sorely missed in our contemporary world. Metaphysics, wisdom's *scientia*, performs precisely this function of providing a map for the soul's journey. In Smith's words, ". . . the landscape that metaphysics opens onto and spreads before the mind's eye is a topography, a lay of the land," and its value is to direct us in our journey, "for orientation always includes a sense of what is important and what is not."[11]

Smith's thoughts on metaphysics inspired my usage of the word "landscape" in the book's title and its text. I want it to mean something more than the usual sense of a stretch of scenery; rather it should include the full environment of the human spiritual journey in all its intellectual, emotional, imaginal, and physical dimensions. In this sense the natural world plays an important part, but not the only part. Furthermore, the phrase "landscape of wisdom" attempts to evoke a holistic rather than analytic form of knowledge. Wisdom requires a viewing of the whole; its etymological roots connect it with *videre*, the Latin "to see," and vision.

Second, each of the three metaphysical systems - Alpha's being, Zero's nothingness, and Omega's becoming - has the potential for stimulating the imagination, and their intellectual themes can be illustrated by works of narrative art. I have chosen three works which offer narrative and poetic versions of the three schools' teachings. They are Dante's *Divine Comedy* (Alpha), Basho's *The Narrow Road to the Deep North* (Zero), and Goethe's *Faust* (Omega). These literary masterworks have succeeded in incorporating a culture's most potent images of self, society, cosmos, and God into a single vision of the spiritual journey of its time. I will summarize and discuss each work as a literary introduction to an examination of the corresponding wisdom school.

Third, each of the schools has views about time, history, and science that are central to its wisdom teachings. Each metaphysical framework brings with it a particular understanding of the temporal and attempts to answer some basic questions. Is time a reality, an illusion, or something that can include both illusion and reality? Does it serve to separate creatures from their Source, or is it the basis of relationship? And what about science? Has it improperly obscured or subordinated the place of wisdom, or does it have a key role to play in spirituality?

When discussing the myths of history offered by the three schools, I use the term "myth" not to criticize their versions of history but to consider them as important elements of their wisdom doctrines. All three schools accept the general facts of history but interpret their significance differently; their interpretations, which are shaped by certain values reflecting their doctrines, are their "myths." Raimundo Panikkar reminds us, "Myth and wisdom go together, as Aristotle had already seen when he affirmed, at the beginning of his *Metaphysics*, that the lover of myth is a sort of philosopher, a lover of wisdom."[12] The "myths/histories" offered by

Alpha, Omega, and Zero are of a piece with their corresponding metaphysics and worldviews, and I approach each one with an openness to the wisdom it may bear.

Much of what the three schools have to say is of course open to discussion and debate, but I also want to respond to their myths and metaphysics from a deeper place than rational discourse. I am less interested in critical analysis and more in finding a vision that grasps my imagination, intellect, and spirit. This approach makes this book something other than just a scholarly monograph. Its purpose is to provide summaries of three contemporary wisdom schools along with some evaluation, but it also serves as a record of a personal search for spiritual knowledge.

One Man's Journey

I have, at one time or another, been deeply involved with all three schools. My own spiritual journey has traced a path through Alpha, Zero, and Omega. Baptized a Catholic and reared a Lutheran, I later found the rich possibilities of spiritual discipline in a Zen Buddhist community. But my experiences in Buddhist meditation halls did not make me want to become a Buddhist. Rather, I felt a desire to find the same richness and depth in the Christian tradition. During my doctoral studies in theology, I was introduced to the writings of Dionysius the Areopagite, Augustine, Bernard of Clairvaux, Julian of Norwich, and other mystics. I wrote a dissertation on Meister Eckhart which helped me interpret my Christian and Buddhist experiences and their interrelationship. I was also introduced to various modern theological figures and schools; among them, Teilhard de Chardin and process thought made the most impact on my thinking. My silent meditative practice continued, now within a Western theological context.

While I have upon occasion taught in a college classroom, the steadiest source of income has been from my work as a librarian. One of my most challenging tasks has been to help people gain the skills required to learn and teach in a world of rapid technological change. The challenge of the job is real, for change is invigorating yet constant, almost relentless. The speed and ease with which we can communicate with one another around the world and gather data to meet research needs are now almost taken for granted, but could be hardly imagined by earlier generations. But can we equate technological advance with real improvement of the human condition? The larger story of scientific discovery and technological innovation over the past several centuries has both encouraged creativity and displaced traditional values. I live in a time of intellectual and moral uncertainty, but this too is part of my spiritual landscape. Like previous eras, our age has its moments of exhilarating beauty and destructive turmoil, but both its darkness and its light have shaped who I am.

My own search for wisdom begins with questions much like those of Stephen Hawking. What is the nature of the universe and why are we in it? What is my role in the human story and the story of the earth? Where is God in all this? My worship community provides opportunities for acting in faith and love, but I also need to know, not just in the academic sense of theological expertise, but in the way of mystics and sages. I have found that my path to wisdom is profoundly shaped by values gained through personal experience and religious and intellectual training. I seek wisdom that illuminates reality as deeply personal, for the ideals of personhood found in the Judeo-Christian tradition and Western political thought are precious values. I seek wisdom that links my story with that of the earth, for nature has often renewed me in ways humans could not. I seek wisdom that makes my work meaningful, and that gives a spiritual context to a society that values creativity and change. These desiderata determine the rightness for me of any particular wisdom school.

The phrase "rightness for me" may seem a narrow criterion for choosing one school over another. Here I admit I am a member of an age of intellectual uncertainty, unable to say what or where absolute truth is, and who speaks it. Instead, I have chosen to listen to conversations that sound promising and that resonate with my own experience. Amid an overwhelming plurality of ideas, thought systems, and spiritual paths, I have found three groups of thinkers whose worldviews engage my deepest attention. Perhaps I can be criticized for choosing three and not one, for wisdom surely has a single vision, a unitary landscape. That is probably so and I am simply wandering in the foothills when the view is better and clearer higher up. But the view down here is fascinating, and the words I hear make me want to keep listening.

A Note on Method

The ways in which I have pursued my project - using literary texts, choosing three specific schools of thought, and introducing a personal dimension to the discussion - are not without some basis in scholarly method. The extensive attention I give to works of literature reflects not only a personal interest in the close relationship between religion and the arts but also my belief in the importance of the imagination. While a great deal of contemporary critical thought has focused on a deconstruction of traditional values and worldviews, the imagination in both popular culture and the artistic community is continually generating visions of life's meaning and the world we live in. At the root of my project is the principle that wisdom and imagination have much in common and that both are experiential realities requiring involvement of the whole person - emotions, the will, even a somatic response - in addition to rational thought.[13]

In my use of literary texts, therefore, I am following the phenomenological method. According to Louis Dupré, the phenomenologist of religion aims at an empathetic understanding of religious experience as well as an interpretation of its symbolic expressions. Experience cannot be studied apart from outer expression, nor can an objective examination of its outer forms yield a fruitful analysis without some inward sense of what motivated or caused religious behavior. Wisdom, like the Chinese notion of the Tao, is fundamentally an experience beyond words. It does not necessarily follow rules of logic, nor is it readily identified by any particular set of intellectual notions. A view that pierces through illusions or an expansive vision beyond the everyday, it is a transcendent insight about life's meaning. As received knowledge (received from God, transmitted from master to disciple, or realized in enlightenment), it cannot be transmitted to another person through normal discourse or persuasive argument but must engage the other totally and without the other's resistance in order to be communicated fully. If wisdom is like a wind, then its expressions are like the movement of the trees and grasses in the wind. In studying wisdom, I will be using the literary texts in the same way I have observed swaying trees. In reading Dante, Basho, and Goethe, I have felt the rushing air of great insight and experienced knowledge as life-giving breath. In other words, summaries of literary texts allow me to articulate how wisdom is experiential before I turn to using intellectual discourse about wisdom's message.

Much of the book is devoted to an exploration of metaphysical systems. To continue my wind metaphor, this stage of the discussion is like an attempt at a more scientific description of the trees and grasses' motions. At this point in my scholarly exploration of wisdom (as I have admitted above, a point most accurately placed in the "foothills" than near any peak of true realization), I have found three distinct schools of thought. In part, I am simply being true to the intellectual climate of our time, an era of pluralism where no one can claim to know truth in a way which defines it for everyone. Disagreeing with this fundamental principle of diversity can lead to a premature blurring of vital differences and isolate one from contemporary intellectual discourse. At the same time, however, by looking for a wisdom teaching that resonates with the values I hold most dear, I am drawn to schools of thought that offer expansive and inclusive visions of cosmos, humanity, and transcendent values. Within the context of intellectual plurality, I seek a single doctrine of spiritual knowledge, one which is the most compelling. My search for a spirituality of knowing eventually leads me to the third, perhaps most personally satisfying approach to wisdom in Omega. Yet by the book's conclusion, I hope that the reader will recognize my abiding respect for each of the three schools.

The book will at times strike a personal note and this aspect of my text also, I believe, follows a particular mode of scholarship. The phenomenological method calls for empathic engagement. In pursuing the definition of a transcendent value, I cannot draw on a set of universally accepted first principles in the manner of patristic and medieval philosophers. My beginning is my personal background, my early influences, my cultural milieu, and those aspects of my intellectual heritage I have found most meaningful. Wilfred Cantwell Smith has observed that the study of comparative religions has moved from an analytical "I-it" relationship between subjective scholar and objective religious data to a relationship between subjects where understanding is achieved by a collective "we."[14] My engagement with all three schools has been more than purely intellectual, and the following chapters form a personal as well as scholarly record of my efforts to recover wisdom for our postmodern world. My project will have succeeded if it stimulates further conversation among the three schools. If it does, I will be listening, learning, and watching carefully to see if a new collective understanding of wisdom is indeed emerging.

Notes

1. Stephen W. Hawking, *A Brief History of Time: From the Big Bang to Black Holes* (New York: Bantam Books, 1988), 171.

2. Ibid., 175.

3. *De docta ignorantia* II, 11, 159; English translation in Nicholas of Cusa, *Selected Spiritual Writings*, trans. H. Lawrence Bond (New York: Paulist Press, 1997), 159.

4. Ernst Cassirer, *The Individual and the Cosmos in Renaissance Philosophy*, trans. Mario Domandi (New York: Barnes & Noble, 1963), 27-28.

5. *De docta ignorantia* II, 13, 175, 179-180; Nicholas of Cusa, *Selected Spiritual Writings*, 166, 168.

6. Nicholas of Cusa, *The Layman on Wisdom and the Mind*, trans. M.L. Fuhrer (Ottawa, Canada: Dovehouse Editions, 1989), 25.

7. Augustine, *De trinitate* XII, 15.25; the English translation is from *The Essential Augustine*, ed. Vernon J. Bourke (Indianapolis, Ind.: Hackett, 1964), 40.

8. Dionysius the Areopagite, *The Divine Names and The Mystical Theology*, trans. C. E. Rolt (London: SPCK, 1940), 191.

9. Eugen Biser, "Wisdom," in *Sacramentum Mundi: An Encyclopedia of Theology*, 6 v. (New York: Herder and Herder, 1970), 6:362.

10. Jerome A. Miller, *In the Throes of Wonder* (Albany: State University of New York Press, 1992), 12.

11. Huston Smith, "The View from Everywhere: Ontotheology and the Post-Nietzschean Deconstruction of Metaphysics," in *Religion, Ontotheology and Deconstruction*, ed. Henry Ruf (New York: Paragon House, 1989), 43.

12. R. Panikkar, *Myth, Faith and Hermeneutics: Cross-Cultural Studies* (New York: Paulist Press, 1979), 4.

13. Louis Dupré, *Religious Mystery and Rational Reflection: Excursions in the Phenomenology and Philosophy of Religion* (Grand Rapids, Mich.: Eerdmans, 1998), 107-117.

14. Wilfred Cantwell Smith, "Comparative Religion: Whither - and Why?", in *The History of Religions: Essays in Methodology*, ed. Mircea Eliade and Joseph M. Kitagawa (Chicago: University of Chicago Press, 1959), 31-58.

Chapter 1

Alpha: An Ascent to God

The Approach

Spirituality and mysticism are attracting a new wave of interest. Popular treatments of once obscure figures like Hildegard of Bingen and John Ruusbroec are finding a readership eager to know more about the lives and teachings of mystics. For many today, new translations of spiritual classics serve as guides to the inner life by supplying images and paradigms for the spiritual journey. An increase in available spiritual texts has been accompanied by a great deal of scholarly activity which provides both students and non-academic readers with the best of current knowledge about the spiritual traditions of the West.[1] It is also true that many have turned to Eastern traditions for teachings they were unable to find in the West. The growing number of available Western spiritual classics is more than equaled by classics from India, China, Japan, and other Asian cultures. Our larger bookstores have sections devoted to Eastern religions offering numerous translations of the Tao Te Ching, Bhagavad Gita, Upanishads, and other great texts as well as books by modern teachers of Eastern religious disciplines. The readership is clearly there and its desire for spiritual knowledge is the stimulus for a thriving section of the publishing industry.

In addition to knowledge, many have sought a spiritual practice. Numerous Eastern centers of spirituality have appeared in cities and the countryside. Spiritual masters from South and East Asia have arrived in Europe and North America to found communities of disciples and to train Westerners to become the next generation of leaders of those communities.[2] Books describing the spiritual experiences of Americans and Europeans in the East, or in monasteries and retreat centers of various

Eastern traditions located in the West, provide fascinating personal narratives about the meeting of East and West. Neglected Western spiritual practices have been rediscovered as well, thanks to the widely-read works of Thomas Merton, Thomas Keating, Basil Pennington and others.

Within this environment of renewed interest in past spiritual greatness, the Alpha school has produced an intellectually sophisticated body of writing that relies heavily on the classic spiritual teachings of mystics and sages. Alpha's persuasive power results largely from its constant reference to texts which carry the authority of tradition. Before we consider the Alpha school, we shall look at a work of a poet recognized by Alpha to be one of the greatest exponents of its adherents' perspective, Dante Alighieri.

The Exiled Poet

The fourteenth century was a turbulent period in European history. Evelyn Underhill described it as the "Golden Age of Mysticism,"[3] because it produced such significant spiritual writers as Meister Eckhart, the author of the *Cloud of Unknowing*, Julian of Norwich, Catherine of Siena, and John Ruusbroec. But it was also a period of widespread suffering and unrest. During the years 1347-51, a quarter to a half of the European population died of the Black Death, while religious, political and social conflicts disrupted a number of regions including Dante's Italy.

A man of intense literary creativity, Dante Alighieri (1265-1321) was also deeply immersed in the political life of his day. An activist in his native Florence, he became involved in the struggles for power between traditional religious authority and the emerging urban guilds. Allying himself with the Florentine commune against the papacy, Dante championed the cause of the laity in the face of the clerical establishment. In works written before *The Divine Comedy*, he expressed his political ideas, and he played a key role as spokesman and emissary for his fellow citizens. But his activism led to disappointment when his party was defeated. During one of his absences from the city, the new Florentine government condemned him to death by burning. Return was therefore impossible and he lived out his life in exile.

During his years in Florence and after, his abilities as a writer grew. Dante proved to have a voracious intellect which absorbed the depth and breadth of the knowledge of his day. By the time of the composition of *The Divine Comedy* (1308-1321, finished just before his death), he had become familiar with the masterworks of both pagan and Christian authors in a number of subjects including philosophy and theology. Upon this foundation of a Western, mostly Latin tradition, he constructed his own masterpiece using a comparatively "new" language: Italian. In the loneliness of separation from his beloved native city, he created a vision of the cosmos as a backdrop for the human spiritual journey and communicated it not in the Latin of the universities but in the more familiar tongue of his countrymen.

Dante's Greatest Adventure

At the beginning of his epic journey, Dante finds himself lost in a dark wood, a dreary and difficult wilderness (*Inf.* I, 4-5).[4] Having spotted a way out of "the valley of evil," he tries to climb a little hill "whose shoulders glowed / already with the sweet rays of that planet / whose virtue leads men straight on every road" (*Inf.* I, 17-18). The planet is the sun and all that it symbolizes. Dante's progress toward the dawn is blocked by three beasts: a leopard, a lion, and a she-wolf, which represent destructive worldly passions and drives. Help appears in the figure of Virgil, the pagan poet whom Dante praises as "that fountain of purest speech" and "my true master" (*Inf.* I, 77-78, 82). Virgil has come to guide Dante at the request of Beatrice, a soul in paradise who as a young girl sparked the fires of love in an equally young Dante. Virgil will act as one of several intermediaries between divine love and the poet-pilgrim. As Virgil explains, Dante cannot escape the wilderness without a journey, a descent into the deep pit of the inferno, followed by an ascent up the mountain of purgatory and through the spheres of paradise.

Dante's first impression of hell is that of a world of darkness:

> I found I stood on the very brink of the valley
> called the Dolorous Abyss, the desolate chasm
> where rolls the thunder of Hell's eternal cry,
>
> so depthless-deep and nebulous and dim
> that stare as I might into the frightful pit,
> it gave me back no feature and no bottom.
> (*Inf.* IV, 4-9)

The inferno is a huge funnel-shaped cave with its widest part just under the earth's surface. At its narrowest is a frozen lake with Satan fixed in the middle, literally at the earth's center. The funnel narrows through a series of circles, each circle containing souls being punished eternally for sins identified with that level. Souls guilty of carnal sins of passion are swept around the second circle by a great wind. Further down, blasphemers, sodomites, and usurers, or in other terms the violent against God, nature, and human labor respectively, suffer in the seventh circle on a plain of burning sand beneath a rain of fire. And in the last circle lies the lake where those guilty of various degrees of treachery are frozen. Those who were treacherous against blood relatives are frozen to their shoulders, but those guilty of the worst treachery (according to Dante), treachery against their masters, are entirely cased in ice.

The landscape of hell includes a number of recognizable terrestrial features: rivers, a waterfall, a marsh, a wood, a frozen lake, as well as structures reflecting human civilization: gates, city walls, a great tower, stone dikes that serve as bridges. This all serves as background to the crowds of souls, both historical and mythical, famous and unknown, pagan and Christian. Individuals are identified by Virgil or recognized by Dante, and the latter frequently engages in conversation with them. At the end of their journey through hell, the Christian poet and his pagan guide climb through the earth's center by grasping onto Satan's hairy flank. Still in utter darkness, they follow the sound of the river Lethe by walking along its banks until they reach the other side of the world "where a round opening brought in sight the blest / and beauteous shining of the Heavenly cars. / And we walked out once more beneath the stars" (*Inf.* XXXIV, 141-143).

The poets emerge on an island with a single mountain, the mountain of purgatory. After climbing to the first ledge, its peak is still too high for Dante to see, and he asks his guide how much farther they need to go. Virgil doesn't respond with a precise estimate but with a description of the discipline necessary to scale the mountain.

> Such is this Mount that where a soul
>   begins the lower slopes it must labor;
>   then less and less the more it nears its goal.
>
> Thus when we reach the point where the slopes seem
>   so smooth and gentle that the climb becomes
>   as easy as to float a skiff downstream,
>
> then will this road be run, and not before
>   that journey's end will your repose be found.
>   (*Pur.* IV, 88-95)

The mountain has two major sections: ante-purgatory and purgatory proper. The first section consists of four ledges or cornices while purgatory itself has seven. Like the circles of hell, each ledge is reserved for a particular failing or sin. Souls on the first four ledges in various ways delayed in desiring God's grace and so they must wait before entering purgatory. Each of the seven ledges of purgatory is a place for purging one of the seven traditional vices. Souls progress up the mountain ledge by ledge by willingly undergoing the kind of suffering appropriate for the vice. Ascent is only possible during daytime when sunlight, a symbol of divine wisdom, illumines the path. At night, under the stars (including a configuration of four stars symbolizing the cardinal virtues), when no active progress is possible and thus it is necessary to rest, Dante has dreams and visions.

On the seventh and last cornice, the lustful are wrapped in flames that cleanse them of their excessive passion. Dante himself, despite his terror, passes through a wall of fire in order to continue his journey. On the other side lies the earthly paradise, in Dante's words a place of "everblooming May" (*Pur.* XXVIII, 36). This is actually the second garden in the *Commedia*, the first being the garden in Limbo or the first circle in hell where souls wander condemned to the underworld because they died sinless but unbaptized. Limbo is characterized as a citadel of light (the light of human reason) with a "sweet brook" and "a green meadow blooming round" (*Inf.* IV, 108 and 111). Between these two idyllic locations stretch the great cave and mountain. The first garden is populated by famous poets and philosophers of antiquity, the second by a procession of figures symbolizing books of scripture, virtues, and certain essential doctrines. The second garden is also where Dante has several visions, having reached a point where he has surpassed human reason. Appropriately, Virgil disappears and is replaced by Beatrice. After having drunk of the two rivers that run through the earthly paradise, the Lethe whose waters cause one to forget evil and the Eunoe whose waters reinforce memory of good deeds, Dante declares himself

> . . . remade, reborn, like a sun-wakened tree
> that spreads new foliage to the Spring dew
>
> in sweetest freshness, healed of Winter's scars;
> perfect, pure, and ready for the stars.
> (*Pur.* XXXIII, 143-146)

As in the conclusion to the *Inferno*, Dante makes a reference to the stars.

In the *Inferno* he simply emerges beneath the firmament. Now, after scaling the mountain and being purified by the experience, he is prepared to enter into the starry heavens.

In the first and second parts of the *Commedia*, Dante's progress required physical effort. An example would be the following passage from the *Purgatorio*:

> Squeezed in between two walls that almost meet
> we labor upward through the riven rock:
> a climb that calls for both our hands and feet.
> (*Pur.* IV, 31-33)

Now, purified of sin, he ascends effortlessly through the spheres of paradise. The necessary lift is provided by his "thirst . . . for the God-like realm" (*Par.* II, 19-20) and by God's grace, personified first in Beatrice and later in St. Bernard. The ascent traverses ten heavens, beginning with the sphere of the moon and continuing through those of Mercury, Venus, the Sun, Mars, Jupiter, Saturn, the fixed stars, the *primum mobile*, and the Empyrean. The last heaven is where the poet has his final visions of God.

The lower heavens from the first through the eighth are populated with blessed souls. The order of their placement in the heavens reflects the degree of their perfection. Those who were both virtuous and ambitious in a worldly sense occupy the second heaven. Theologians are found in the fourth heaven, contemplatives in the seventh, and the highest saints along with the Virgin Mary in the eighth. The movement of each of the first nine spheres is governed by one of the nine orders of angels. The primum mobile is beyond all the visible heavens. It is the source of their movement, the "first moved thing," and therefore closest to God, the First Mover. Seraphs, the highest angelic order, govern its motion.

Although they are imagined realms with fabulous details, the inferno and purgatory are described in terms drawn from earthly existence: rivers, mountains, trees, etc. Paradise is another case entirely. While Dante walked and climbed over the landscapes of the first two parts of the journey, he is now propelled by his desire for more knowledge and divine grace. In paradise, his environment is quite unfamiliar to human eyes, and so his choice of images must be extraordinary. He recognizes the challenge to his literary skills and asks for aid. When portraying what he has experienced, he cannot recreate the experience in its purity, because memory is but a shadow of the real thing. At the outset of the *Inferno* and *Purgatorio*, he invokes the aid of the Muses. In the opening canto of the *Paradiso*, Dante calls upon both the Muses and Apollo.

In the final canto of the *Commedia*, Dante prays to God to help him retell his final vision of the divine essence. His vision has two revelations. The first is of God the Creator and shows how the universe exists within God as pages in a book bound by love. The second is of God as Trinity: as three spheres or circles which have three colors but one circumference (*Par.* XXXIII, 85-87). The second circle is colored with "humanness," thereby symbolizing the Person of Christ (*Par.* XXXIII, 115-132).

When Dante strains to comprehend the wonder of the unity of human nature and the second circle, in other words the mystery of the Incarnation, his mind is irradiated with divine light and his intellect ceases its attempt to fathom the mystery. It is Dante's will, now in complete conformity with divine love and in balance with his intellect, that finds ultimate fulfillment in the closing lines of the poem:

> Here my powers rest from their high fantasy,
> but already I could feel my being turned -
> instinct and intellect balanced equally
>
> as in a wheel whose motion nothing jars -
> by the Love that moves the Sun and the other stars.
> (*Par.* XXXIII, 142-146)

Once again, the stars are the final image as they were in the *Inferno* and the *Purgatorio*. Dante is at one with the whole movement of the cosmos where human will, divine love, and celestial motion are part of a single dynamic process.

Making It All Real

Having thus far summarized the landscape of Dante's journey, we need to add a couple of important aspects of Dante's narrative art in order to appreciate the spiritual landscape or *topos* of the *Commedia* to its fullest extent. First, the cave, the mountain, and the heavens are not the only scenes set before us. As Dante converses with Virgil and the other souls in the three realms, they relate stories set in mythical and historical times which are frequently filled with vivid details. Dante compares a rill which provides him and Virgil a path through a burning plain to European constructions:

> As the Flemings in the lowland between Bruges
> and Wissant, under constant threat of the sea,

erect their great dikes to hold back the deluge;

as the Paduans along the shores of the Brent
build levees to protect their towns and castles
lest Chiarentana drown in the spring torrent -

to the same plain, though not so wide nor high,
did the engineer, whoever he may have been,
design the margin we were crossing by.
(*Inf.* XV, 4-12)

Also, in order to intensify the reality of his imagery, Dante frequently compares it to familiar scenes. A cascade in the *Inferno* which falls from the seventh to the eighth circles is compared to one near the Apennines:

... As that river -

the first one on the left of the Apennines
to have a path of its own from Monte Veso
to the Adriatic Sea - which, as it twines

is called the Acquacheta from its source
until it nears Forli, and then is known
as the Montone in its further course -

resounds from the mountain in a single leap
there above San Benedetto dell'Alpe
where a thousand falls might fit into the steep;

so down from a sheer bank, in one enormous
plunge, the tainted water roared so loud
a little longer there would have deafened us.
(*Inf.* XVI, 91-105)

Another source of earthly imagery are stories told by various souls to Dante. The most memorable, perhaps, is that of Ulysses' last voyage. Ulysses speaks to Dante and Virgil from within a flame:

"When I left Circe," it said, "who more than a year
detained me near Gaeta long before

Aeneas came and gave the place that name,
not fondness for my son, nor reverence
for my aged father, nor Penelope's claim

Alpha: An Ascent to God

to the joys of love, could drive out of my mind
the lust to experience the far-flung world
and the failings and felicities of mankind.

I put out on the high and open sea
with a single ship and only those few souls
who stayed true when the rest deserted me.

As far as Morocco and as far as Spain
I saw both shores; and I saw Sardinia
and the other islands of the open main.

I and my men were stiff and slow with age
when we sailed at last into the narrow pass
where, warning all men back from further voyage,

Hercules' Pillars rose upon our sight.
Already I had left Ceuts on the left;
Seville now sank behind me on the right.

'Shipmates,' I said, 'who through a hundred thousand
perils have reached the West, do not deny
to the brief remaining watch our senses stand

experience of the world beyond the sun.
Greeks! You were not born to live like brutes,
but to press on toward manhood and recognition!'

With this brief exhortation I made my crew
so eager for the voyage I could hardly
have held them back from it when I was through;

and turning our stern toward morning, our bow toward night,
we bore southwest out of the world of man;
we made wings of our oars for our fool's flight.

That night we raised the other pole ahead
with all its stars, and ours had so declined
it did not rise out of its ocean bed.

Five times since we had dipped our bending oars
beyond the world, the light beneath the moon
had waxed and waned, when dead upon our course

we sighted, dark in space, a peak so tall

I doubted any man had seen the like.
          Our cheers were hardly sounded, when a squall

          broke hard upon our bow from the new land:
          three times it sucked the ship and the sea about
          as it pleased Another to order and command.

          At the fourth, the poop rose and the bow went down
          till the sea closed over us and the light was gone.
                              (*Inf.* XXVI, 86-131)

   This example is a complex one, containing a mixture of mythical figures and actual geography. By creating a sequel to the original Homeric narrative, Dante succeeds in weaving together Mediterranean geography and his own vision of the earth. It is an orb whose northern hemisphere is land and the southern hemisphere all water, except for the mountain of purgatory which is the land the crew sights before going under. Known reality (Morocco, Spain, etc.) is fused with a largely unknown but imagined realm (purgatory), thereby lending a substantiality to the landscape of the next stage of Dante's own journey, that of the *Purgatorio.*
   A second aspect of Dante's narrative art is his use of scientific description. Although a medieval man, he stood near the brink of the Renaissance and its accompanying wave of scientific discovery. Moreover, scholarship has shown us that the period of the Middle Ages was not without its own examples of scientific enterprise.[5] Dante exhibits a kind of precision that only a scientific mode of thinking can provide, and he does so as still another way of intensifying the reality of his landscape. His science may at times be inaccurate, as in his explanation of lightning storms being a conflict between fiery and watery vapors.[6] Or it might be largely correct, as in his explanation of how light is reflected (*Pur.* XV, 16-21). Certainly he sided with the right camp when he pictured the earth as a sphere, and a number of passages explore the physical ramifications of that fact during Dante's journey. For example, Dante expresses surprise when he realizes that the sun is to his left when facing east on Purgatory Mountain. Virgil explains that Dante is now in the southern hemisphere, and the sun's path will seem as far north to the viewer facing east at that point in the southern hemisphere as it would seem to be south to a viewer facing the same direction at an antipodal point in the northern hemisphere. Commentators have used diagrams to explain Virgil's extended discourse on this subject.[7]

Dante's epic narrative then, takes place in a highly organized universe. It combines mythical, biblical, and historical elements on a single vast canvas. The order of the universe is a moral one which is structured spatially. The worst sinners are closest to Satan, the most purified souls closest to the peak of Purgatory Mountain, and the most blessed saints closest to God in paradise. Having seen the terrain of the medieval spiritual journey, at least the version presented to us by that period's most celebrated poet, we may know turn to the metaphysics behind it.

Some Metaphysical Basics

When Dante began envisioning the three realms of hell, purgatory, and paradise, he drew upon a number of metaphysical and theological themes. The poem draws us into its world largely because of the vividness of detail. But Dante's greatness also lies in his genius for synthesizing philosophical, scientific, and theological concepts within the scope of his epic story. What follows are some of those concepts which will be relevant to our examination of the Alpha school of wisdom.

Creation as a circulatio: This notion is a Christian adaptation of the Neoplatonic process of *exitus* - a going out, and *reditus* - a return. God or the One in his bounty overflows or emanates his creation, which in turn flows back into God. Christian theologians argued against notions that the outflow was in any way necessary. Rather, it was an act of divine free will and God could have chosen not to create at all. The Creator is at once origin and final destination, the sea to which we all as rivers flow.

> In His will is our peace. It is that sea
> to which all moves, all that Itself creates
> and Nature bears through all Eternity.
> (*Par.* III, 85-87)

Exemplarism: Here Dante is drawing on a Christian Neoplatonic tradition at least as old as the writings of Dionysius the Aeropagite (5th cen.). All things which have been created by God were made through the divine ideas or exemplars which pre-exist creation. As such, created beings are dynamically related to their exemplars, and they participate in their divine *paradeigmata* or paradigms. Dionysius uses the image of the sun and the objects it illuminates:

> . . . if our sun, while still remaining one luminary and shedding one

unbroken light, acts on the essences and qualities of the things we perceive, many and various though they be, renewing, nourishing, guarding, and perfecting them; differencing them, unifying them, warming them and making them fruitful, causing them to grow, to change, to take root and to burst forth; quickening them and giving them life, so that each one possesses in its own way a share in the same single sun - if the single sun contains beforehand in itself under the form of an unity the causes of all the things that participate in it; much more doth this truth hold good with the Cause which produced the sun and all things: and all the Exemplars of existent things must pre-exist in It under the form of one Super-Essential Unity.[8]

The first of Dante's final two revelations of God's essence describes a book and its pages bound by God's love. On the level of the Creator, the book's pages, that is to say the exemplars, compose a unified reality that is one with God's mind. On the level of his creation, the pages (exemplars) have been scattered throughout the cosmos to provide the paradigms by which all things have been made.

> Oh grace abounding that had made me fit
> to fix my eyes on the eternal light
> until my vision was consumed in it!
>
> I saw within Its depth how it conceives
> all things in a single volume bound by Love,
> of which the universe is the scattered leaves.
> (*Par.* XXXIII, 82-87)

Created beings can be thought of as symbols; their symbolic nature is a consequence of their participation in their divine paradigms. All symbols point back to another reality and at the same time participate in the reality. In Neoplatonic thought, effects reflect their causes. Bonaventure articulates this doctrine in *The Soul's Journey into God*:

> The creatures of the sense world signify the invisible attributes of God, partly because God is the origin, exemplar and end of every creature, and every effect is the sign of its cause, the exemplification of its exemplar and the path to the end, to which it leads.[9]

In his *Collationes*, he compares creatures to figures in a stained glass window:

> Just as you see that a ray of light entering through a window is colored

in different ways according to the different colors of the various parts, so the divine ray shines forth in each and every creature in different ways and in different properties.[10]

They are also vestiges or footprints of God:

> Creatures are shadows, echoes, and pictures of that first, most powerful, most wise and most perfect Principle. . . . They are vestiges, representations, spectacles proposed to us and signs divinely given so that we can see God.[11]

The material world is the beginning of the journey for Bonaventure, because it contains examples of the handiwork of God, the supreme Craftsman:

> Since we must ascend Jacob's ladder before we descend it, let us place our first step in the ascent at the bottom, presenting to ourselves the whole material world as a mirror through which we may pass over to God, the Supreme Craftsman.[12]

The entire *Commedia* can be seen as presenting a universe of exemplars marking a path to the divine Origin. Light, scarce in the inferno but dazzling in paradise, shines through the depth and breadth of the Dantean cosmos and is reflected back by creatures:

> Consider then how lofty and how wide
> is the excellence of the Eternal Worth
> which in so many mirrors can divide
>
> its power and majesty forevermore,
> Itself remaining One, as It was before.
> (*Par.* XXIX, 142-146)

The Universe as a Hierarchy: In Neoplatonism, the emanation of the One was a fall from unity into multiplicity, from spirit into matter. According to Patrick Boyde, "three of the most important axioms in medieval debates about causality" are as follows:

> (I) "The cause is nobler than the effect"; (ii) "A first principle does exist, and the causes of things are not an infinite series, nor infinitely various in kind"; (iii) "Nature proceeds from one extreme to another through intermediate stages."[13]

The consequence of these axioms is a hierarchical universe where a descending series of levels range from most to least noble, in metaphysical terms most to least real, or in poetical imagery from dazzling light to deep darkness. In Dante's *Commedia,* the hierarchy stretches from God as the source of goodness to Satan, the source of evil, with intervening degrees of reality, light, or moral perfection. Ontologically, the hierarchy runs from God as Being to the nonbeing of chaos, evil, or formless matter. According to Dante, the hierarchical principle even orders the positions of the blessed souls in paradise. When asked by the epic poet why she is content to reside in the sphere furthest from God, Piccarda Donati explains that she is simply following the divine will:

> Brother, the power of love, which is our bliss,
> calms all our will. What we desire, we have.
> There is in us no other thirst than this.
>
> Were we to wish for any higher sphere,
> then our desires would not be in accord
> with the high will of Him who wills us here;
>
> and if love is our whole being, and if you weigh
> love's nature well, then you will see that discord
> can have no place among these circles.
> (*Par.* III, 70-78)

Boyde describes Dante as accepting fully this hierarchical or scale of being doctrine.

> The whole action of the *Comedy* is conceived as an imitation of the Scale of Being, as it shows the protagonist climbing step by step, canto by canto, encounter by encounter, truth by truth, until he comes into the presence of God.[14]

In this, Boyde agrees with Lovejoy who in his important study, *The Great Chain of Being,* examines the development of this concept from the Greeks down to modern thought.[15]

The Soul's Ascent: The soul, created by God, has a desire to return to its source. The created realm is a forest of symbols, vestiges, or footprints of God guiding the soul to its final resting place. The return is frequently described as an ascent from the mutable to the immutable, from the temporal to the eternal, from the multiple to the One. Augustine's *Confessions* contains an important passage which in many ways is an archetypal description of the Christian spiritual journey. Here, the outer world is but a first step as the soul turns from external physical reality to begin an inward search for its source.

> And thus, by degrees, I was led upward from bodies to the soul which perceives them by means of the bodily senses, and from there on to the soul's inward faculty, to which the bodily senses report outward things - and this belongs even to the capacities of the beasts - and thence on up to the reasoning power, to whose judgment is referred the experience received from the bodily sense. And when this power of reason within me also found that it was changeable, it raised itself up to its own intellectual principle, and withdrew its thoughts from experience, abstracting itself from the contradictory throng of fantasms in order to seek for that light in which it was bathed. Then, without any doubting, it cried out that the unchangeable was better than the changeable. From this it follows that the mind somehow knew the unchangeable, for, unless it had known it in some fashion, it could have had no sure ground for preferring it to the changeable. And thus it was with the flash of a trembling glance, it arrived at *that which is*. And I saw thy invisibility understood by means of the things that are made.[16]

Implied in the theme of hierarchy is a particular attitude toward the earth. To transcend the mutable world is to leave the realm of the senses. "The cause is nobler than the effect," and the soul thirsts for the ultimate, most noble cause. Created symbols are valuable, but they must be left behind. Even in Bonaventure's quite positive valuing of creatures as divine vestiges, contemplation of creatures occurs at the bottom of the soul's journey to be followed by contemplation of what is within and beyond the soul.

Boyde suggests that despite his Christian faith in the goodness of creation, Dante seems to have entertained misgivings about the goodness of a universe which could not be perfect because it was neither 'simple' nor 'one'."[17] This interpretation of Dante is not surprising. The journey begins on the earth's surface which, at the place of departure, is depicted as a dark and dreary wilderness. We must leave this world if we are to find ourselves in God. Dante, in exile and disillusioned by politics and contemporary events, understandably wished to find a way out. In this, he was a Neoplatonist; a return to the Origin was the highest goal.

A Hierarchy of Knowing: Augustine distinguished at least two ways of knowing: *ratio* or reason and *sapientia* or wisdom. These are like two eyes of the soul. *Ratio* looks downward toward the mutable realm while *sapientia* looks upward toward eternal truths. In the *Commedia*, Virgil can be said to represent human reason as well as Dante's most revered poetic master. Virgil's assignment is fulfilled by the time they reach the peak of Purgatory Mountain. At this point, Beatrice becomes Dante's guide. Reason cannot guide one through the spheres of paradise. Rather it is wisdom that will lead the poet through the heavens.

Divine wisdom does not eliminate reason but incorporates lower forms of knowing. When Beatrice answers Dante's question about why there are gradations of light on the moon, her ultimate response relies heavily on the Neoplatonic notion of a hierarchy of Intelligences governing each of the celestial spheres.[18] This passage is preceded by two arguments, the first philosophical[19] and the second scientific.[20] Both are meant to refute Dante's assertion that the moon's light and dark markings are the result of differences in that orb's density.

For Dante, who was familiar with most aspects of medieval thought, philosophy and science were equally useful in making a point. An explanation of a physical phenomenon could easily weave together themes drawn from philosophy, empirical knowledge, and spiritual doctrines usually associated with Neoplatonism. However, when knowledge concerning the heavens was desired, wisdom in the form of Neoplatonic doctrine, not reason nor empirical knowledge, was the source of truth.

Celestial Influences: God creates the human soul and the angelic intelligences directly. The heavens, by means of the luminaries (the sun, moon, stars, planets), act as causes of secondary effects which include the generation of plants and animals as well as the mortal aspects of the human being. Variations among the planets and other secondary causes help explain differences among people, why some are richer or more intelligent or healthier than others, as well as differences in humankind's physical environment such as changes in weather. According to Boyde:

> All the planets and all the individual stars were . . . credited with a distinct role in the cycle of generation and corruption. . . . It satisfied the human thirst for meaning and order in that it suggested a purpose for the existence of the stars and the six other planets. . . . The path of the sun is always the same, but one summer can be hotter or dryer than the next. From time to time there occur natural disasters such as typhoons and pestilences. Metals and minerals are found in differing quantities and in differing degrees of purity. Not all copulation results in pregnancy, and not every pregnancy in a live birth. . . . All such variations could be accounted for on the hypothesis that the differences were the result of differing conjunctions of the heavens.[21]

The other great variable is the condition of the material receiving the "stamp" of the cause. Beatrice describes to Dante the series of cause of effect that starts with God and proceeds "from thing to thing to the last least potencies" until it reaches the stuff of matter, the wax that must be shaped:

> The wax of these things, and the powers that press
> and shape it, vary; thus the Ideal seal
> shines through them sometimes more and sometimes less.
>
> So trees of the same species may bring forth
> fruit that is better or worse; so men are born
> different in native talent and native worth.
> (*Par.* XIII, 68-72)

Such notions were not meant to challenge the Christian doctrine that God was the universal cause of all things, but to establish a system of causation where "the angels and the heavens are always to be conceived as workmen, using tools to realize the designs of the Supreme Architect."[22] And whatever inequality resulted from Nature's fumbling like "a painter / who knows the true art, but whose brush hand shakes" (*Par.* XIII, 77-78), the final product can also be appreciated as the hierarchy of beings which in its entirety is a unity resembling the ultimate exemplar of unity in God:

> ... "The elements
>
> of all things," [Beatrice] began, "whatever their mode,
> observe an inner order. It is this form
> that makes the universe resemble God.
>
> In this the higher creatures see the hand
> of the Eternal Worth, which is the goal
> to which these norms conduce, being so planned.
>
> All Being within this order, by the laws
> of its own nature is impelled to find
> its proper station round its Primal Cause.
> (*Par.* I, 102-111)

Notes

1. One measure of the increase is to do an online library catalogue search. For books by and about mystics like Ruusbroec and Hildegard, the median year of

publication is the early 1980s. As an example, in Boston College's library catalogue, there are as many books by and about Hildegard published before 1982 as there are after.

2. See Andrew Rawlinson, *The Book of Enlightened Masters: Western Teachers in Eastern Traditions* (Chicago: Open Court, 1997).

3. Evelyn Underhill, *Mysticism: A Study in the Nature and Development of Man's Spiritual Consciousness* (New York: E.P. Dutton, 1961), 461.

4. Unless otherwise noted, all references to Dante's *Divine Comedy* will be to the Ciardi translation; the roman numeral will refer to canto, and arabic numerals to verses. The editions used for the three major portions of the *Divine Comedy* are: Dante Alighieri, *The Inferno* (New York: Mentor Classic, New American Library, 1954); *The Purgatorio* (New York: Mentor Classic, New American Library, 1957); *The Paradiso* (New York: Mentor Book, New American Library, 1961).

5. For a classic study on the subject, see Lynn White, *Dynamo and Virgin Reconsidered: Essays in the Dynamism of Western Culture* (Cambridge: MIT Press, 1971).

6. See Ciardi's note in *The Inferno*, 212.

7. See Ciardi's diagram in *The Purgatorio*, 63.

8. Dionysius the Aeropagite, *The Divine Names*, V, 8; translation: *The Divine Names and The Mystical Theology*, trans. C.E. Rolt (London: SPCK, 1940), 140.

9. Bonaventure, *Itinerarium mentis in Deum*, II, 12; translation: *The Soul's Journey into God; The Tree of Life; The Life of St. Francis*, trans. Ewert Cousins (New York: Paulist Press, 1978), 76.

10. Bonaventure, *Collationes in Hexaemeron*, XII, 14 (V, 386); quoted in Ewert Cousins, "Introduction," in Bonaventure, *The Soul's Journey*, 26.

11. Bonaventure, *Itinerariun mentis in Deum*, II, 12; translation: *The Soul's Journey*, 76.

12. Bonaventure, *Itinerariun mentis in Deum*, I, 9; translation: *The Soul's Journey*, 63.

13. Patrick Boyde, *Dante: Philomythes and Philosopher* (Cambridge: Cambridge University Press, 1981), 223-224. The first axiom is taken from Dante himself: *Convivio* II, iv, 14; the second from Aristotle: *Metaphysics* II, 2, 994a; the third from Thomas Aquinas: *Summa Theologica* Ia, 71, ad 4.

14. Ibid., 131.

15. Arthur O. Lovejoy, *The Great Chain of Being: A Study of the History of an Idea* (Cambridge: Harvard University Press, 1936). See Lovejoy's discussion of Dante: 68-69.

16. Augustine, *Confessions*, VII, 17; translation: *Confessions and Enchiridion*, The Library of Christian Classics, v. 7, trans. Albert C. Outler (Philadelphia: Westminster Press, 1955), 151-152.

17. Boyde, 219. Boyde is referring to a passage in Dante's *Monarchia*, 1, XV, 1-3.

18. See *Par.* II, 112-149.

19. *Par.* II, 73-93.

20. *Par.* II, 94-105.
21. Boyde, 251.
22. Ibid., 265.

Chapter 2

Alpha: The Wisdom of Being

The Sages of the Perennial Tradition

To read through the *Divine Comedy* is to be immersed in arguably the most powerful and complete Christian poem ever written. Its power is grounded in the poet's mastery of language and poetic structure, its completeness in his ability to synthesize the many intellectual, historical, political, and religious themes of his time into a single visionary work. The careful reader of the poem cannot help being affected by it in some significant way, having been introduced to a poetic vision which succeeds on so many levels. For some, the fact that this is a medieval work filled with long-discarded assumptions and beliefs about the nature of the world and the universe will have become irrelevant in the face of the epic poem's capacity to engage the imagination and enlarge one's awareness of the possibilities of the spiritual journey.

Despite this capacity of the *Comedy*, some readers may continue to reflect on the applicability of Dante's presentation of earthly and spiritual reality in the modern context. Clearly, his hierarchical model of the universe, so heavily dependent on Ptolemaic astronomy and a geocentric view of the cosmos, can no longer persuade with the same absolute force that it did six hundred years ago. Or can it? A contemporary school of wisdom believes it can. It refuses to agree that the Neoplatonic metaphysics which undergirds much of Dante's cosmos in the *Comedy* has been superseded in any real way. Indeed, it believes that reality in its most profound dimensions has been obscured by intellectual developments in the West since the Middle Ages. If given a fair hearing, the spokespersons of this school can and should be appreciated as a group of extremely articulate, learned, and provocative thinkers whose arguments carry a good deal of persuasive weight. And if the sum total of their efforts resulted in a reevaluation of Dante's *Divine Comedy* as bearing a profound message for modern readers, why not give them a chance to make their case?

I have chosen to call their approach the Alpha school of spiritual wisdom for reasons which will become clear during the following discussion. The two thinkers whose work I believe serve as the best introductions to the Alpha school are Huston Smith and Seyyed Hossein Nasr. Smith's *Forgotten Truth: The Primordial Tradition* was first published by Harper & Row in 1976. A short book, it is written in Smith's highly readable and literate prose, a style which served him well in his widely read introduction to the major religious traditions, *The Religions of Man*, recently revised and retitled as *The World's Religions*.[1] Smith writes as both a scholar and a seeker, and his contacts with representatives of different religious paths have been the result of intellectual curiosity and a genuine quest for spiritual insight. Given his stature, the appearance of *Forgotten Truth* was a major breakthrough for the Alpha school because it provided a succinct statement of its general themes for the English-speaking world along with a wholehearted endorsement by a respected scholar.

Nasr's *Knowledge and the Sacred* is the book version of his Gifford Lectures for 1981. The lecture series has included a long list of distinguished scholars who since 1891 have explored the relationship between theology, philosophy, and modern science. Nasr's special distinction was to be the first Muslim, indeed the first Oriental, invited to give the lectures. Clearly, the organizers of the lecture series believed Nasr had something to say to the Western scientific and intellectual community. *Knowledge and the Sacred* shall be a second source for our exploration of the Alpha school of wisdom.

Smith and Nasr agree that if there is any problem on the part of the modern reader in accepting Dante's view of the cosmos, this is because of the rise of the empirical sciences and their success in transforming the ways in which the human mind thinks about its natural environment. The human person no longer sees the universe as a system of interconnected levels of existence. Instead of a hierarchy of being, goodness, and beauty, modern science has provided a cosmology that is essentially quantitative. Instead of a web of causal influences stretching from God through the angelic intelligences to the human realm and the natural world, physics and astronomy describe vast empty spaces within matter and the cosmos devoid of anything we normally would recognize as life.

However, the Alpha school's argument is not with science as such.

Modern science has more than proven its ability to explore the world, but the Alpha representatives would argue that it has illuminated only one level of reality, and in the grand scheme of the cosmos it is the lowest reality. The error of the modern sciences lies not in the scientific enterprise itself, but in its effort to explain higher truths which cannot be captured in the language of number and physical measurement. Within its proper domain, it is an acceptable mode of knowing the world. When it exceeds this domain, it becomes "scientism." According to Smith:

> With science itself there can be no quarrel. Scientism is another matter. Whereas science is positive, contenting itself with reporting what it discovers, scientism is negative. It goes beyond the actual findings of science to deny that the other approaches to knowledge are valid and other truths true.[2]

How does the Alpha school attempt to reinstate the reality of the Dantean cosmos? We shall look at several of its most important themes in order to see how it can assert that Dante's depiction of the spiritual journey can still be understood as a portrayal of a way to wisdom.

Being Is Knowing

For Alpha, metaphysics as ontology is the highest science because it unites the human person to his or her Origin which is the ground of all existence. In this school of wisdom, to be is to know:

> In the beginning Reality was at once being, knowledge, and bliss (the *sat*, *chit*, and *ananda* of the Hindu tradition or *qudrah*, *hikmah*, and *rahmah* which are among the names of Allah in Islam) and in that "now" which is the ever-present "in the beginning," knowledge continues to possess a profound relation with that principial and primordial Reality which is the Sacred and the source of all that is sacred.[3]

The Absolute is the source of all being and as such is beyond being. But we all have an inward capacity to know our Source, and that capacity is the intellect. The intellect is not to be confused with the mind, but it is not separate from it. More properly, it is associated with the heart which is the center of the human person and the locus of divinity, the Origin of all beings.

> The seat of the intelligence is the heart, and not the head, as affirmed by all traditional teachings. The word *heart*, *hrdaya* in Sanskrit, *Herz* in

German, *kardia* in Greek, and *cor/cordis* in Latin, have the root *hrd* or *krd* which, like the Egyptian Horus, imply the center of the world or a world. The heart is also the center of the human microcosm and therefore the "locus" of the Intellect by which all things were made.[4]

Intellect, moreover, has a natural relationship with the mind, or in other terms, *sapientia* has a relationship with *ratio*.

> This externalization of the intelligence and its projection upon the plane of the mind is, however, a necessary condition of human existence without which man would not be a man, the creature who is created as a thinking being.[5]

But whereas *ratio* is a mental activity we engage in, we *are* our intellect or *sapientia*. It is an ontological condition and the more we are our intellect, the closer we are to God.

> Knowledge remains the supreme way to gain access to the Sacred, and intelligence a ray which . . . , in its actualized state, is none other than the Divine Light itself as it is reflected in man and, in fact, in all things in different manners and modes.[6]

To know God sapientially as being is not simply to know him as an item of faith or objective fact, but to participate fully in his Reality.

Nasr's preferred label for this way of knowing is *scientia sacra*, the sacred science, although he also refers to *philosophia perennis* and *sophia perennis*, perennial philosophy or perennial wisdom. He additionally calls it metaphysics despite the variety of uses this term has received in the West which do not strictly adhere to the Alpha school's definitions. According to Nasr,

> If one were to ask what is metaphysics, the primary answer would be the science of the Real or, more specifically, the knowledge by means of which man is able to distinguish between the Real and the illusory and to know things in their essence or as they are, which means ultimately to know them *in divinis*.[7]

Levels of Being

If the science of the Real or principial knowledge (knowledge of first principles) is the core theme of Alpha, the most immediate ancillary theme of *scientia sacra* would be that of ontological hierarchy. In Nasr's words:

The knowledge of the Principle which is at once the absolute and infinite Reality is the heart of metaphysics while the distinction between levels of universal and cosmic existence, including both the macrocosm and the microcosm, are like its limbs.[8]

The perennial wisdom which, according to Alpha, is found in all the religious traditions, is part of a symbolic system which includes a perennial cosmology:

> The traditional sciences of the cosmos make use of the language of symbolism. . . . One can speak of a *cosmologia perennis* which they reflect in various languages of form and symbol, a *cosmologia perennis* which, in one sense, is the application and, in another, the complement of the *sophia perennis* which is concerned with metaphysics.[9]

Huston Smith provides a picture of the hierarchic universe, one which he characterizes as having at least four levels and which can be found in variant forms throughout traditional religious cosmologies. The first is the terrestrial plane which he also calls "the gross, the material, the sensible, the corporeal, the phenomenal."[10] It is the domain of the empirical sciences, and its major categories are space, time, energy/matter, and number.

The second level is the intermediate plane which can also be called "the subtle, the animic or the psychic plane."[11] It is the realm of phantasms, ghosts, departed souls, the higher, non-material space where shamanic dream journeys take place. If each level is dependent on the one above it, this level is the abode of Jungian archetypes which mold the psychic lives of humankind. Smith picks up on a suggestive notion in Jung's theory of the archetypes which says that the archetypes shape matter as well the human psyche.[12] This would agree with traditional teachings which believed that the upper worlds governed the lower, that the higher surpasses the lower in power and being. We have seen this theme in Dante's views of the celestial influences governing the hierarchically ordered spheres of the universe.

If space, time, matter/energy, and number are clearly definitive of the terrestrial plane, they are also present in the intermediate realm, although less so. This realm, according to Smith,

> . . . can even be the object of empirical research as in parapsychology and depth psychology, though the teeth on the rim of its wheel, so to speak, are rather flexible and barely mesh with the cogs of consensual objectivity which

even these sciences, if they are to be such, must honor as the final indices of the real.[13]

We need only to refer to our dream life to think how strangely and unpredictably we can move through space and time when no longer constrained by the limits of waking consciousness and the everyday world. We can fly through the air, go back to earlier periods of our lives, or find ourselves in vivid, often disturbing situations.

This realm is accessible to human experience via dreams, trances, visions, and the imagination. The recent increased interest in mythology in more popular forms of psychology and self-help movements can be interpreted as a resurgence of the intermediate or psychic realm in everyday consciousness. Of course, the intermediate level has never ceased to be active, but Carl Jung, James Hillman, Joseph Campbell, and others have reawakened contemporary awareness of the immediate and influential presence of archetypal realities in our psychic lives.

The third level is the celestial realm. If the intermediate plane still had traces of time, space, and matter/energy, these categories are now surpassed. The intermediate heavens of multiple gods, goddesses, angels, demons, and disincarnate spirits, where non-historical or imaginal myths can occur in mythic time/space, are transcended in this third level. Mythic archetypes are superseded by universal ones, or in Platonic terminology, forms. These are the ideas in God's mind which are the pre-existing paradigms for all that God fashions through his creative activity, either directly or through agents of intermediate realms. They are described by Dante as pages of the book which is God's mind which are then scattered as exemplars of created beings throughout the cosmos (*Par.* XXXIII, 82-87).

The terrestrial realm is the realm of everyday sense experience. Jung among others has revived the reality of the intermediate plane for the modern world. What can we make of Platonic forms? For us a thing or event is real because the senses can perceive them as being real. The senses, with or without the aid of scientific instruments, help us probe the world around us to find out the way things are and work. For example, if we look at a piece of wood carefully, we can notice its texture and composition. According to science, wood or xylem is "the principal water-conducting tissue and the chief supporting system of higher plants."[14] This tissue is composed of various kinds of cells whose structure differs according to function. Electron microscopy gives us a better idea of how wood cells develop. For the reader conditioned to view things in a certain way by empirical science, things exist in accordance with natural laws. The modern mind does not care where the laws come from, and placing them anywhere else than in the physical realm of observed objects and observing subject seems pointless.

The Neoplatonist would argue that what we have come to call natural laws are actually related to Platonic forms or divine ideas. And this point is central to the claim of the Alpha school: The modern world has separated the reality of things, the "isness" of a piece of wood, for instance, that which makes wood itself, from its Source. In place of a divine idea of wood, modern science has focused on physical data and quantitative facts. What has been lost in such a physically determined universe is the vast web of causal connections that make a seemingly physical thing part of a cosmic, moral, spiritual drama. This kind of web was made possible through the doctrine of forms, which for the Alpha school remains a revealed and sacred teaching. In the beginning was the Logos and *logoi* or ideas in God's mind from which and through which all things were made. Eckhart at several points in his sermons exhorts his listeners to see things as they really are, in their ideas which are ablaze with the light of their divine source. If such a vision is achieved, there is an extraordinary result. One sees an ordinary thing like a piece of wood in the light of intellect where it becomes as sacred as an angel:

> If someone saw a piece of wood in that light, it would become an angel and a rational being, and not merely rational; it would become pure reason in primal purity, for there is the plenitude of all purity.[15]

The pervasive success of the scientific and technological revolutions is no more apparent than in the difficulty we experience in trying to understand the doctrine of the divine paradigms. Christians have continued to believe that the world exists because God created it, but this is an act of faith, not of understanding. When the Church Fathers and the medievals wanted to *understand* what they *believed*, that the natural world was the result of an act of a Creator, many if not most adapted various forms of Platonic, Neoplatonic, and Aristotelian ontologies. When we wish to understand, we refer to modern science, hence our difficulty with the older approach to explaining what a thing *really* is.

Forms in and of themselves are impersonal. They receive the quality of relatedness from their source, God, the Trinity in the Christian tradition, most importantly the Second Person "without whom nothing was made." The forms are in God's mind and, in Dante's poetic image, bound like pages in a book by God's love. The celestial plane is the level of the personal God, the God of Abraham, Isaac, and Jacob, the Saguna Brahman or the Brahman with attributes, the deity who is the object of prayer, the soul's lover, Krishna, Shiva, Vishnu. Any anthropomorphism is perfectly valid because the human person in the depths of his or her soul needs a Thou, a divine parent or spiritual spouse with whom to speak, to confess, to live for and with.

The fourth and final level, according to Smith, is the infinite plane. For the Christian believer, this may be a level beyond traditional theism and hence suspect of heresy. But a number of Christian mystics speak of the Godhead, most notably Eckhart, Tauler, Suso, and Ruusbroec. In Bonaventure's *The Soul's Journey into God*, the fifth and sixth chapters deal with God as One and Three as well as with the mystery of the Incarnation. The seventh chapter, however, counsels a stripping away of all images and names of God in a radical turning away from all positive ways of knowing and toward an "unknowing."

> But you, my friend, concerning mystical visions, with your journey more firmly determined, leave behind your senses and intellectual activities, sensible and invisible things, all nonbeing and being; and in this state of unknowing be restored, insofar as is possible, to unity with him who is above all essence and knowledge. For transcending yourself and all things, by the immeasurable and absolute ecstasy of a pure mind, leaving behind all things and freed from all things, you will ascend to the superessential ray of the divine darkness.[16]

Thus, the Christian spiritual tradition is not without its examples of a notion of an absolute beyond a personal God.

Smith makes several points concerning the infinite level. He states that "only negative terms characterize it literally."[17] The word *infinite* denotes all that is not finite. He goes on to draw parallels from the other traditions:

> In Hinduism the Infinite is *nir*-guna (without qualities); in Buddhism it is *nir*-vana (nondrawing, as a fire whose fuel is exhausted has ceased to draw) and sunyata (emptiness, a void); in Taoism it is the Tao that cannot be spoken; in Judaism it is *'en-sof*, the not-finite.[18]

For Nasr, the Absolute is beyond being but it includes being. It is both impersonal Godhead and God and the object of *scientia sacra*, the metaphysical wisdom that is both a knowing and an unknowing.[19]

This kind of discourse which seems to confuse more than clarify matters, where unknowing can be the same as knowing, or a personal God with attributes identical with an impersonal God without attributes is particularly suitable when describing the Infinite. Smith argues for the necessity of paradoxical language. We have seen a vivid example of it in the passage from Bonaventure where the soul ascends "to the superessential ray of the divine darkness," a fusion of light imagery characteristic of kataphatic language (as we saw exemplified in Dante's version of paradise) and the darkness identified with apophatic, imageless experience of the Godhead.

Those familiar with Trinitarian and Incarnational theologies will recognize the need for paradox to describe God as One in Three Persons, or Christ who is fully human and fully divine in one person. It appears, however, that Smith reserves a special place for the Infinite, one which transcends the celestial plane, indeed transcends all of the planes. Smith uses a diagram of three concentric circles to illustrate the terrestrial, intermediate, and celestial planes. Diagrammatically, the Infinite is the space beyond the outermost circle. It permeates all the circles. It is, according to the Neoplatonic formulation, "an intelligible sphere whose center is everywhere and whose circumference is nowhere."[20] But most frequently, negatives are employed: unconditioned, ineffable, immutable, all of which is to emphasize the dual nature of the Godhead as both transcendent and immanent.

In a volume of essays published some years after *Forgotten Truth*, Smith proposes another image of the hierarchy of four levels. As one looks up from a lower level, the boundaries between planes seem like one-way mirrors. We only see reflections of what is below us. However, if one proceeds to higher levels, the levels below will be visible (the mirrors become completely transparent plate glass) while the ones above remain obscure. Thus from the mountaintop of the Infinite, all is visible below although the Infinite seems beyond everything below it.[21]

Levels of Knowing

If one accepts that a hierarchy of being exists, and that metaphysically being is knowing, then it follows that there are different levels of knowing, each specific to a particular level of being. Having explored Smith's explication of the tiered nature of outer reality, we will also examine his discussion of the four levels of the self. In his vocabulary, body, mind, soul, and spirit are levels of the self that are isomorphic with the four levels of the Real: terrestrial, intermediate, celestial, and infinite.[22] The Platonic principle, "like is known by like," applies here because each of the levels of selfhood imply a particular way of knowing.

Smith's discussion of the body touches on the body's purely physical aspects (e.g., Smith's comment on the brain: "It is the most highly organized three pounds of matter we know"[23]) and is quite brief. The reality of the second level of selfhood, that of the mind, receives a vigorous defense from Smith against some streams in contemporary science and philosophy which have reduced it completely to a function of the brain. After referring to new physiological evidence to support his position, he turns to a more philosophical argument, asserting that "from the side of insentient matter the gulf that separates it from sentience is infinite; no bridge can reach the other bank."[24]

For Smith, the mind is "stratum of the self." He believes that our experiences of mind take two major forms: waking and dreaming. In this division, he covers a wide spectrum of mental activities including sense perception, rational thought, imagination, memory, dreaming, and daydreaming. Smith argues that dreaming provides evidence for the reality of a subtle body:

> In dream the subtle body retires from the gross. The communication lines to its physical senses are disconnected, and it returns to its natural medium. For the duration of its "home leave" its pedestrian rendezvous with matter is suspended and it swims untrammeled in the psychic sphere.[25]

It is proof of the mind's isomorphic relationship to the intermediate or psychic plane.

The mind is defined by its ability to form ideas and images. Our mental world is that part of the self that is an inward reality which creates, receives, or works with different kinds of mental contents, the stuff of dreams, philosophies, arts and sciences: surreal images, metaphysical notions, musical notes, scientific hypotheses. It is like a stream that may at times slow down, at other times be a torrent, invisible to the physical senses, apparent only through conversation, artistic expression, the written word, or nonverbal communication.

The third stratum is the soul. If the mind can be likened to a stream, Smith feels the soul is like a source:

> If we equate mind with the stream of consciousness, the soul is the source of this stream; it is also its witness while never itself appearing within the stream as datum to be observed. It underlies, in fact, not only the flux of mind but all the changes through which an individual passes; it thereby provides the sense in which these changes can be considered to be *his*.[26]

Having identified the soul with a stable image, a stream's source, Smith seemingly confuses it with a contrasting comparison:

In the faint glimpses of itself that the soul affords us, it appears less as a thing as a movement; to paraphrase Nietzsche, it resembles a bridge more than a destination. Restlessness is built into it as a metaphysical principle.[27]

Much of what Smith goes on to say about the soul is similar to Tillich's discussion of faith as ultimate concern. If we accept the Protestant theologian's approach to faith, we describe the soul as that center in the human self which experiences an ultimate concern. What concerns a person ultimately differs from person to person; the range of possible concerns can be as wide as the variety of specific virtues and vices that we found in Dante's epic poem. According to Smith and Tillich, nothing less than a true absolute will fulfill the soul's driving impulse toward meaning. Augustine's declaration to God, "Our soul is restless till it rest in Thee," expresses perfectly both the fundamental kinetic nature of the soul and its need for a journey into God. Awakening to the reality of the journey can indeed be viewed as awakening to the existence of one's soul.

Some may argue that the soul is an impossible ideal and that our ultimate concern is always being distorted by our projected wants and desires; we are after all limited, finite beings. One may experience a desire without bounds, an infinite desire, and may sacrifice a great deal for a beloved because the beloved is perceived as nurturing, intelligent, beautiful, all qualities which may largely only exist in the eyes of the beholder. We see what we want to see. Smith suggests a different way of looking at the situation:

> It is not so much that he projects infinity - infinite worth - upon her as that he glimpses infinity - the Infinite - through her. She has, for the duration that his passion lasts, become for him a symbol as (for Dante) was Beatrice: she in whom Heaven's glory walked in earthly body.[28]

Smith goes on to give specific examples of love mysticism between soul and personal God and of powerful personal experiences of divine presence. Certainly the written history of Christian spirituality offers a great many moving passages which give witness to this level of the inner life.

The fourth and final level discussed by Smith is that of the spirit. In his use of the term *spirit*, Smith is attempting to indicate the reality of an inward center that goes beyond the soul at the same time including it. The soul is movement; it implies a to and from, a departure and arrival. Love mysticism which is soul mysticism is a drama of lover and beloved, or soul and Christ and the Christian tradition. It is a duality albeit a duality merging toward union in the act of mystical consummation. On the level of spirit, even this duality is overcome because spirit is isomorphic with the Infinite which admits no boundaries or limits:

> If soul is the element in man that relates to God, Spirit is the element that is identical with Him - not with his personal mode, for on the celestial plane God and soul remain distinct, but with God's mode that is infinite. Spirit is the Atman that *is* Brahman, the aspect of man that *is* the Buddha-nature, the element in man which, exceeding the soul's full panoply, is that "something in the soul that is uncreated and uncreatable" (Eckhart).[29]

The reference to Eckhart is apt. Among Christian mystics, he is the strongest representative of a mysticism that surpasses union of soul and God in its description of the oneness of God and believer in the ground of the soul. In Eckhart's words,

> The last end of being is the darkness or the unknowness of the hidden divinity.... Therefore Moses said, "He who is sent me" (Ex. 3:14), he who is without a name, who is a denial of all names and who never acquired a name; and therefore the prophet said: "Truly you are the hidden God" (Is. 45:15), in the ground of the soul, where God's ground and the soul's ground are one ground.[30]

Elsewhere, Smith describes spirit as "the bedrock of our life stream."[31] However, because it has no borders, it is not different from the stream. It simply "is" with the identical ontological supremacy as that assigned to the Infinite. There is no other. Therefore, at this level personal relationship is transcended.

In its efforts to interpret the Gospel story, the Christian tradition has taken great care to develop the notion of person as a significant term denoting divine and human realities. Much of Christian spiritual practice has focused an I-Thou relationship between human and divine persons. Although the Christian tradition may not always agree with Smith's notions of the Infinite and spirit, it has in the past had a hierarchical view of the cosmos and the self as we have seen in Dante and Augustine. My effort at this point is not to affirm all that Alpha asserts on the topic of hierarchy, but merely to point out that during a high period of Christian spirituality, a period when Dante and Eckhart created spiritual masterpieces in their respective vernaculars, the hierarchical vision was broadly accepted.

Smith goes on to argue that the isomorphism between levels of reality is more than just symmetry. The human person is meant to return to the Origin, to regain oneness with his or her Creator. The chief means of the return is through knowledge, a realization of the different levels of the self, at least a turning from *ratio* to *sapientia*, from the lower levels of mental activity to wisdom. The wounds of our sinfulness need to be healed, the fragments of our broken world remade into a whole. The inward journey toward atonement, at-one-ment, requires a map, a function served by traditional cosmologies. According to Nasr,

> The cosmos is not only the theater wherein are reflected the Divine Names and Qualities. It is also a crypt through which man must journey to reach the Reality beyond cosmic manifestation. In fact man cannot contemplate the cosmos as theophany until he has journeyed through and beyond it. That is why the traditional cosmologies are also concerned with providing man with a map which could orient him within the cosmos and finally enable him to escape beyond the cosmos through that miraculous act of deliverance with which so many myths have been concerned.[32]

But we return to our uneasiness with the Dantean cosmos. On one level, it engages our attention as much or more than any other Christian depiction of the spiritual journey. On another level, something like a nagging doubt remains. Dante's world is ours no longer. The modern reader is unable to absorb the vision in its entirety without some sense of it being an ill fit. Yet the Alpha school of wisdom is adamant about the correctness of the cosmic picture. The error is all ours. In order to elaborate its point, it has come up with its own reading of history, one which I will call the myth of the primordial tradition. It is a myth that presents a well-known mythic theme, that of a bygone golden era. I use the word *myth* not in any pejorative sense but in an effort to underscore the fact that it is Alpha's particular interpretation of the historical record. It is up to the reader, of course, to judge whether to accept the interpretation.

The Myth of the Primordial Tradition

The myth begins with the dawn of the various major religious traditions: the appearance of the Abrahamic prophets who laid the foundations for the three great traditions of the book, Judaism, Christianity, and Islam; the *rishis* or poet-sages in India who composed the oral scriptures known as the Vedas; the Taoist and Confucian sages who established the spiritual and ethical principles that defined Chinese civilization, and the Indian ascetics whose practices and teachings led to Buddhism and Jainism. This was the period of primary revelations. Scriptural traditions began and various rituals, practices, and ethical codes were established. Karl Jaspers has called this an axial period because the centuries 800-200 b.c.e. form a temporal axis, a critical turning point in history.[33]

The Alpha school argues that as a period of tremendous religious achievement, it remains unsurpassed. Various traditions have deepened their understanding of what the great axial revelations mean. That has been the role of the sacred wisdom of the Upanishads in Hinduism, Kabbalah in Judaism, Sufism in Islam, and Neoplatonism in Christianity. Buddhism and Taoism have been sapiential from their beginnings.

Nasr places a great emphasis on the term *tradition* itself, equating it with *scientia sacra* or perennial wisdom:

> Tradition as used in its technical sense in this work [*Knowledge and the Sacred*]... means truths or principles of a divine origin revealed or unveiled to mankind and, in fact, a whole cosmic sector through various figures envisaged as messengers, prophets, *avataras*, the Logos or other transmitting agencies, along with all the ramification and application of these principles in different realms including law and social structure, art, symbolism, the sciences, and embracing of course Supreme Knowledge along with the means for its attainment.... the meaning of tradition has become related more than anything else to that perennial wisdom which lies at the heart of every religion and which is none other than the Sophia whose position the sapiential perspective in the West as well as the Orient has considered as the crowning achievement of human life.[34]

Nasr devotes a whole chapter to the term and distinguishes the Tradition from the major religious traditions. *Tradition* thus understood is the essential core of spiritual wisdom found within each tradition. The Alpha school believes that the Tradition ultimately has a single metaphysics, that of the *scientia sacra*, although basic terms may be drawn from the various traditions. Nasr believes *prajna* (Buddhism), *jnana* (Hinduism), and *hokhmah* (Judaism) are equivalent words for spiritual knowledge.

Both Smith and Nasr agree that the golden age of revelation has been followed by an age of growing darkness culminating in the current period of scientism which is nearly devoid of sapiential light. The great truths and doctrines of the prophets and sages have fallen into obscurity. Nasr expands on this golden age / fall / dark age motif with more detail, borrowing from mythology as well as intellectual history:

Alpha: The Wisdom of Being   35

In paradise man had tasted of the fruit of the Tree of Life which symbolizes unitive knowledge. But this was also to taste of the Tree of Good and Evil and to come to see things as externalized, in a state of otherness and separation. The vision of duality blinded him to the primordial knowledge which lies at the heart of his intelligence. . . . Despite the layers of the dross of forgetfulness that have covered the "eye of the heart" or the seat of intelligence, as a result of man's long journey in time, which is none other than the history of forgetfulness with occasional reversals of the downward flow through divine intervention in the cosmic and historical process, human intelligence continues to be endowed with its miraculous gift of knowledge of the inward and the outward.[35]

The mythic fall of Adam, to borrow a theme from the Abrahamic traditions, led to a clouding of the intellect, but there have been other falls which occurred in history, and none are of greater concern than the descent of the West from the spiritual peaks of the medieval period into the scientific age and the consequent loss of the sapiential perspective. Smith borrows from the Hindu tradition of cycles when he identifies the current age as the *kali yuga*, the low point in the cycle of human history when civilization has become fragmented and authentic spirituality has all but disappeared.[36]

However, Nasr does believe that we are in the midst of a significant recovery of sacred wisdom:

> The overall harmony and equilibrium of the cosmos required a movement within the heart and soul of at least a number of contemporary men to rediscover the sacred at the very moment when the process of secularization seemed to be reaching its logical conclusion in removing the presence of the sacred altogether form all aspects of human life and thought.[37]

In his third chapter of *Knowledge and the Sacred*, Nasr portrays a resurgence of interest in the sacred beginning with several romantic poets and writers including Blake, Goethe, and Emerson. He also points out the revival of interest in Plotinus, particularly by Thomas Taylor. But it wasn't until this century and the appearance of the Alpha school that the *scientia sacra* as Nasr and Smith have presented it became a clearly established approach to spiritual wisdom. One of the first important figures was René Guénon (1886-1951); two others of nearly equal importance are Ananda Coomaraswamy (1877-1947) and Frithjof Schuon (b. 1907). Smith is particularly in debt to Schuon, whose works introduced him to the Alpha school and whom he has described as "a living wonder; intellectually *a propos* religion, equally in depth and breadth, the paragon of our time. I know of no living thinker who begins to rival him."[38]

It is interesting to consider the high calling Nasr is assigning to the Alpha school. "A number of contemporary men" have, as a result of "the principle of cosmic compensation" and the requirements of "the overall harmony and equilibrium of the cosmos,"[39] been given an opportunity to rekindle the flame of sacred knowledge. To some this may sound like a grandiose claim, but it is in keeping with the school's overall perspective of a perennial wisdom and the doctrine of cyclical history.

Modern Science and the Alpha School

In our discussion of the Alpha school's approach to science, we have seen its representatives accept the knowledge gained by modern science but reject it as an approach to understanding the Real in all its dimensions. Science is most appropriately pursued on the terrestrial plane. Its truths should not be extrapolated to explain the truths of higher levels of being. Nasr argues that the failure of the West to recognize the limits of science has been a major reason for the desacralization of knowledge.

An example of Alpha's stance toward modern science can be found in Nasr's critique of the Copernican revolution in astronomy. He argues that the cosmic perspective which places earth, hence the human person, at the center, has a profound symbolic meaning, that of a map for the spiritual journey through the various realms of being. To give this up entirely, as was unfortunately the case with the widespread acceptance of Copernicus' discovery, is to invite a tragic result, a serious loss in accessibility to sacred wisdom:

> If one understands what symbols mean, one cannot claim that medieval cosmologies are false as a result of the fact that if we were standing on the sun we would observe the earth moving around it. The fact remains that we are not standing on the sun and if the cosmos, from the vantage point of the earth where we were born, does possess a symbolic significance, surely it would be based on how it *appears* to us as we stand on earth. To think otherwise would be to destroy the symbolic significance of the universe.[40]

The heliocentric model which, if used spiritually, causes "a disequilibrium which cannot but result in the destruction . . . of classical physics."[41] It was a model known by people before Copernicus but they did not commit the error of *substituting* it for the geocentric one.

But Alpha's attitude toward science is a complex one. The critiques are being made by two scholars who have been well acquainted with science in their training and professional careers. Nasr was in part educated at MIT. Smith taught there for fifteen years. Nasr has taught the history of science and philosophy and written on Islamic science. But both feel that in the West a split occurred between the "laws of nature" and the "laws of God,"[42] one which had severe consequences for perennial philosophy. At the same time, both acknowledge the value of science beyond a purely material endeavor. They do this in several ways:

Science can have symbolic value. Smith quotes from a Sufi work:

> If "a symbol is something in a lower 'known and wonted' domain which the traveler considers not only for its own sake but also and above all in order to have an intuitive glimpse of the 'universal and strange' reality which corresponds to it in each of the hidden higher domains," anything, as we have noted more than once, can qualify. Even science.[43]

Smith and Nasr thus read the writings of contemporary scientists on a symbolic level. The physicist David Bohm's notions of wholeness and implicate order are interesting examples of recent theories that receive symbolic interpretations by both Smith and Nasr.[44] That leads to a second point.

Contemporary, post-Newtonian science may be closer to metaphysical truth than its predecessor, Newtonian science. The error of Newtonian science was the creation of a subject-object dualism in its empirical and analytical mode of thought and the elevation of that mode to the highest rung of the epistemological ladder. Post-Newtonian science has rejected a purely mechanistic universe while accepting qualitative categories such as symmetry, beauty, and elegance to support theories. It has also occasionally admitted the role of consciousness as part of the reality which a physicist must study, and it has described the universe as a matrix of relations between matter and energy. As a result, Alpha has come to regard it as a potentially more useful ally of the *scientia sacra*.

> The fact that a number of important physicists have shown an interest . . . in Oriental cosmological and metaphysical teachings points to a groping, even within physics, which is the heart of modern science, for the sacred and a world view not bound by the reductionism of a quantitative science imposed upon the reality of nature as such.[45]

38   *Landscapes of Wisdom*

And such "groping" points to the possibility of enlisting post-Newtonian science into the Alpha school's project of reviving sacred knowledge:

> To be sure, traditional principles cannot be proven through modern physics but this physics, to the extent that it corresponds to an aspect of reality, can be a legitimate science whose ultimate significance can be grasped only through traditional metaphysics. In fact, this science could in principle be integrated into a higher form of knowledge if only this knowledge were available in such a manner as to transform the intellectual climate of the contemporary world and if modern science were to accept the limitations inherent in its premises and assumptions.[46]

It is as if the reemergence of the primordial tradition as an "act of celestial compensation" could possibly include new developments in science, if properly interpreted. Thanks to David Bohm's notion of the implicate order, for example, we have begun to rediscover the reality of the Godhead.

Science and religion have a number of parallels. Smith enumerates six similarities between the two that go beyond the symbolic or metaphysical potential of scientific theories. The parallels include world views, methods of discernment, and ascetic discipline. More specifically, there are six parallels. I will quote Smith's formulation of each of them as well as summarize his comments:[47]

a. "Things are not what they seem." Here Smith compares the findings of modern physics with traditional religious doctrines of the world as illusory or deceptive. We now know that a table is not as solid as it seems, that there is more emptiness than matter. For Smith, the Hindu doctrine of *maya* (illusion) makes a similar point.

b. "The other-than-seeming is a 'more,' indeed a stupendous more." Whether looking at the stars or at subatomic particles, the numbers of modern science are truly "awesome." Religious traditions speak of divinity which surpasses understanding, a *"mysterium tremendum,"* tremendous mystery.

c. "In their further reaches the world's 'mores' cannot be known in ordinary ways." Neither relativity theory nor quantum mechanics are obvious to common sense. Nor are the ways of the Absolute in its essence.

d. "The 'mores' that cannot be known in ordinary ways do, however, admit of being known in ways that are exceptional." It is certainly possible for a person to learn relativity theory or study mystical doctrines, but as Smith points out, both are "exceptional" or beyond the normal ways of knowing.

e. "The distinctive ways of knowing which the exceptional regions of reality require must be cultivated." Spiritual practice requires steady and continued effort. A Christian monk or Zen disciple may contemplate with great dedication for years before spiritual insight floods his inner being. Smith's contribution here is that the same kind of commitment applies to the scientist:

> The dedication in science rivals that of saints and lovers; awakened it makes asceticism easy and natural. Was it Rutherford who, asked how he discovered the composition of the radiation emitted by radioactive substances, replied "I don't think I thought about another thing for seven years"?[48]

f. "Profound knowing requires instruments." Whether it be a telescope or canonical scripture, there has to be certain means by which insight or discovery is facilitated. To Smith's point about instruments we may add the necessity for personal intermediaries. Both scientist and spiritual aspirant require a master to show them the way to the frontier.

Smith's six parallels persuade the reader that science is more than a source of symbols or a way of reinforcing the truths of metaphysics. It can also be a powerful way of knowing and living. Smith reminds us of the original meaning of "laboratory," a place to work and pray. Both scientist and spiritual adept seek to make a leap in knowledge and are willing to make a disciplined effort outwardly and inwardly: outwardly in an attempt to re-envision the world and see it as it really is, inwardly in a concerted effort to focus one's thoughts on the problem at hand.

But when all is said and done, despite the sophisticated and complex ways that Nasr and Smith relate to modern science, their basic attitude toward it is cautious and often highly critical. For all the approval Smith gives to science, it still is the lesser discipline when compared with religion because it deals with quantities and numbers and not with qualities and meanings. Science must know its place and not attempt too much. "To be sure," writes Nasr, "traditional principles cannot be proven through modern physics."[49] We have mentioned the Alpha school's critique of the Copernican model. It exhibits an even stronger reaction against evolutionary theory, but we will examine Alpha's approach to evolution in the next section.

Time and History

Time is a dimension of the terrestrial or material plane. It also appears on the intermediate level but in a much more fluid manner. On the terrestrial plane, it can be measured as a progression of instants, each division of equal duration. This is objective time. Subjective time is another matter. Painful periods can seem interminable while a joyful event can be evanescent. The mythic realm is not subject to any rigid, irreversible temporal order; a mythic figure like Merlin can live going backward through time. Dante's earthly paradise can be in an everblooming May. When we reach the upper realms of the uncreated realities of God, the Forms, and the Infinite, we are in the dimension of the eternal; time has been transcended.

The Absolute is entirely self-sufficient, not requiring anything, perfect in itself, "the Immutable which always is but does not become."[50] "Being . . . does not become," according to Nasr.[51] He goes on to say that Ultimate Reality and the Eternal are one and the same:

> To gain an intellectual comprehension of the meaning of the Absolute is also to understand the Eternal. That same intellectual intuition which makes available through *scientia sacra* a principial knowledge of Ultimate Reality also provides a direct intuitive knowledge of the Eternal.[52]

Scientia sacra also teaches the reality of the temporal order appropriate to the lower realms. In Nasr's words:

> *Scientia sacra*, therefore, while affirming this view on its own level, seeks to provide meaning for that experience which we call time and which is also real from the point of view of change and becoming like *maya* itself, which does not exist from the "perspective" of *Atman* but whose reality cannot be denied for those living in the embrace of *maya*.[53]

We have seen Smith use the term *maya* when he noted that both religion and science claim that "things are not what they seem." *Maya* is both illusion and creativity. It is not the Absolute itself but it is the Absolute playing with possibilities, multiplying the levels of existence, creating beings because it wishes to be known:

> *Maya* is usually translated as illusion and from the nondualistic or Advaitist point of view *maya* is illusion, only *Atman*, the Supreme Self,

being real. But *maya* is also creativity and "Divine Play" (*lila*). . . . For Hinduism, . . . the creation of the world or the casting of the veil of *maya* upon the Absolute Self or *Atman* is expressed as "Divine Play," while for Islam this externalization which is none other than the activity of *maya* is envisaged as the love of God to be "known," the origin of the world being the revelation of God to Himself.[54]

Given this approach to time, it is not surprising to see Alpha accept a cyclical rather than a linear view of time and history. In Neoplatonism, the spiritual journey is a return to the Source. As each creature is a product of a flowing out of the Absolute, ultimately all return to their Origin. The exile returning home, a theme with a special meaning to Dante who was exiled from his home city of Florence, is a pervasive image of the soul's quest. In Nasr's words, "The Eternal is like the original abode of the soul which, being lost, is sought by the soul everywhere in its earthly exile."[55]

On a cosmic level, the *exitus* of the One into the many and the *reditus* of the many into the One is mirrored in the cycles of nature and human life. Both Nasr and Smith refer to the Hindu notion of *yugas* or phases of a cosmic cycle which in turn are durations within larger cycles of universal creation and annihilation: the "days and nights of the life of Brahma." Nasr refers to a related notion in Sufi thought of the world being recreated every minute. He quotes Jami:

> The universe is changed and renewed unceasingly at every moment and every breath. Every instant one universe is annihilated and another resembling it takes its place.[56]

A cyclical view of time is the traditional perspective which in turn is a continuation of what archaic religions believed. It is a doctrine which is "concerned with saving man from the withering effect of temporal process and enabling him to be saved from all-becoming."[57] There is no way out through time itself, although the three temporal moments, past, present, and future, reflect the true atemporal Reality:

> The past is a reflection of the Origin, the memory of paradise lost and the reminder of faithfulness to tradition and what has been already given by God. . . . The future is related to the ideal which is to be attained, the paradise that is to be gained. . . . As for the present which is man's most precious gift, it is the point where time and eternity meet; it symbolizes hope and joy. It is the moment of faith and the door toward the nontemporal.[58]

However, time's three moments also reflect our fallen condition. The past is what we must leave behind, the temporal dimension which we must grow beyond (which is not to say repress) if we are to mature psychologically and spiritually. Our thoughts of the future only mean we are in a state of hoping for a better life; we are not yet there. And the present moment has come to mean "living for the present," seeking immediate gratification to the exclusion of a more profound existence.

Any and all hope of salvation, therefore, lies in escaping time's treadmill and reuniting with Alpha, the Origin of all, the Eternal One. Perhaps the present now is the most precious temporal moment, because the soul's journey must be undertaken at this very instant, step by immediate step:

> Eternity then is reflected in the present now, and the now is the solar gate through which the hero must pass to reach beyond the sea of becoming and the withering effect of time whose function it is to devour all that exists in its bosom.[59]

The now moment is that temporal category most like eternity because it includes past and future and mirrors the immutable timelessness of the Absolute.

Not all traditions have, of course, accepted the cyclical view of time. The major exceptions are the Abrahamic religions which developed a linear perspective of history. But time as linear history is not accepted by Alpha as an advance in spiritual wisdom. According to Smith,

> In the primordial outlook hope is vertical, or at least transhistorical. . . . The world . . . does not itself change substantially but provides stable rungs on which the soul can climb.[60]

Nasr is quite explicit in his characterization of history as a negative dimension: "the downward flow of the river of time"; "man's long journey in time, which is none other than the history of forgetfulness."[61]

Nevertheless, he provides a couple of positive statements as well. From the perspective of the ultimate Source, nothing that issues forth from it can be considered absolutely unreal nor absent from the upper realms of being. This is true for time as well as space (and other categories of the terrestrial plane).

> Space which preserves, time which changes and transforms, . . . are

conditions of existence of not only the physical world but the worlds above reaching ultimately the Divine Empyrean.[62]

For a devout Muslim who believes in the goodness of creation, Nasr cannot erase the imprint of the Creator on the temporal process, however "withering" its effects on humankind.

Nasr offers an interesting interpretation of how those religious traditions developed which are favorable toward the linear form of history. Nasr compares the passage of human history with an hourglass. During an initial period, nothing seems to have changed. The sand, although falling steadily, seems to remain at the same level in the upper container. Primitive societies, not having an extensive past with which to compare their present condition, believed in permanence. There did not seem anything new in their lives over any given lifetime. Any change was cyclical and not in any way a real transformation of their world. However, there comes a point at which the world can't help but seem different:

> But as the sand continues its flow, the very situation of the upper compartment begins to change. It is not only the individual particles of sand that fall through the channel but the whole configuration of sand in the upper compartments begins to change and time gains a new significance.[63]

Judaism and Christianity are thus interpreted as later traditions which, having recognized the reality of linear time, invested it with religious significance. Hinduism retained a perspective more in keeping with archaic religions while Islam is described as being historical but ultimately transhistorical because "it confines the significance of man's actions in history while refusing to identify the truth with history in any way."[64] He also makes the interesting claim that "the Islamic conception of prophecy ... is based on a cyclical conception of time and not a linear one."[65]

Nasr proposes a modified model of linear history by using the image of the helix. A helical model is able to combine both the cyclical and linear aspects of time. Time initially seems to return to its starting point in a circular motion, but only in the later phases of history can it be seen that the motion has not been purely circular but helical because it included a forward movement hitherto unnoticed.[66]

More often than not, however, becoming and change are regarded negatively, especially when they emerge as major categories in Western philosophy in the writings of Hegel and Marx, which, according to Nasr,

. . . based reality upon dialectical becoming and change itself and transformed an immutable vision of things into a constantly changing one, whether this procession was taken as being spiritual or material.[67]

The way to such secular doctrines was prepared by Christianity's emphasis on salvation history, a history whose major events were creation, the fall, the incarnation, and the second coming of Christ. Once the cosmos was desacralized by the scientific revolution, secular philosophies of history could easily be developed.

But the Alpha school cannot accept any philosophy which eliminates the Transcendent in human culture and society. We are born in time and experience many earthly joys, but we also age, grow ill, and die. "Life is suffering" is the first of the Buddha's Four Noble Truths. In the person of his Son, the Christian God appeared in time but he was crucified as well. Smith's reading of Christian eschatology is that the coming, hoped-for Kingdom of God will end time. In the *Bhagavad Gita*, Krishna reveals to Arjuna his Universal Form and announces, in one translation, that "I am all-powerful Time which destroys all things."[68] Based on much of what we find within the teachings and mythology of religious traditions, the Alpha school's negative attitudes toward time have many cross-cultural parallels.

The most extensive critique by Alpha of Western views of temporal process is aimed at the theory of evolution. The members of Alpha attack it vehemently because they believe evolutionary theory has for many assumed a religious character. Smith suggests the term "prevolution":

> Phonetically the word joins *pr*ogress to *evolution*, showing the two to be faces, prospective and retrospective, of a single, Janus-like deity. In addition the word suggests the current *prev*alence of the cult of this god.[69]

Nasr is perplexed at the passionate attachment some have for the theory when, for him, it is far from being proven beyond the shadow of a doubt:

> In many ways and for profound reasons, evolution has become the substitute for religion for many people who defend it with complete intolerance while claiming to be very reasonable and tolerant beings without any strong religious beliefs.[70]

Their arguments against evolution are many. Metaphysically it is impossible because the lower comes from the higher and not the reverse. The source for all forms is the divine; evolution inverts the entire cosmological hierarchy. From the evidence of religious scriptures, "there is not one indication that higher life forms evolved from lower ones,"[71] although, according to Nasr, many religious traditions believe in great geological changes and the appearance of life forms before humankind. Logically, it is impossible to argue that consciousness could emerge from matter. Consciousness exhibits a higher order of complexity and it is absurd to think that lower orders could reorganize into higher orders or organization. In physics, energies driving living forms toward greater complexity follow the second law of dynamics which dictates decay rather than the flourishing of life.

Finally, the Alpha school dismisses conclusions drawn from the paleontological evidence itself. They side with those that argue that the fossil record indicates the sudden and dramatic appearance of new life forms, for example vertebrates, but that the record does not reveal intermediate forms which would support evolution. They are willing to admit microevolution, which is supported by the fossil record whereby species change over time in small ways but never so greatly as to become an entirely new species, e.g., flying squirrels as imitating birds, but such imitations are for Alpha more a sign of God's creative playfulness than evidence for the reality of species mutation.

We will not spend time here summarizing the case for evolutionary theory. Given the metaphysics from which Alpha develops its arguments, it is understandable that the Alpha school would prefer to see each species as a realization of an ideal archetype which preexists creation. This provides a direct link between creature and Creator, and preserves the source of creative power in the highest realm. At most, nature "matured to the point where life can be sustained" and matter can receive the form of a particular species.[72]

The figure that troubles Nasr and Smith the most on this issue is Teilhard de Chardin. Smith speaks of "Teilhard's pseudo-Christian assumptions" and goes on to quote a scathing article by a scientist, P.B. Medawar, who accuses the Jesuit paleontologist of having "alarming apocalyptic seizures."[73] Nasr is equally sharp:

> From the traditional point of view Teilhard represents an idolatry which marks the final phase of the desacralization of knowledge and being, the devouring of the Eternal by the temporal process, if such were to be possible.[74]

Smith has, since the appearance of *Forgotten Truth*, gone on to modify his criticism against Teilhard.[75] Admitting that the Medawar quotation was unduly harsh, Smith nevertheless in his first edition of

Beyond the Post-Modern Mind enumerates his problems with Teilhard's thought. First, although Teilhard states that his most important work, *The Phenomenon of Man*, should be read as a work of science, it is not scientific in the modern English sense of science. It goes far beyond the physical data in its conclusions about the presence of spirit in matter and the spiritual dimension of evolution. Second, Teilhard's whole effort is to establish a scientific foundation for theology. But science has undergone great changes, while theology has always tried to articulate immutable truths. How can one hope to capture eternal truths in a vocabulary that is doomed to obsolescence? Third, science can speak of those things which are appropriate to it, i.e., the material realm. Here Smith is appealing to his notions of a hierarchy of planes. Science cannot hope to explain what lies far above or outside its scope. Fourth, Smith reiterates his difficulty with saying that the fossil record indicates that higher life forms came out of lower forms. No problem with the claim that they came after, but nowhere has it been proven (to Smith's satisfaction) that the lower evolved into the higher. Fifth, Smith cites several scientists' view that time is relative, not ultimate, as the advocates for Teilhard's views claim.

I shall not go into the specifics of Teilhard's position here, but I do believe it is one of the foundation stones of another contemporary school of wisdom, one which I have labeled Omega. It, like all three of the wisdom schools we shall examine, is not above criticism. Smith's critique of Teilhard's assertion that *The Phenomenon of Man* must be read "purely and simply as a scientific treatise" is to the point, but we shall see if this necessarily means discarding Teilhard's entire enterprise.

Another aspect of the Alpha school's doctrines needs examination before we move on, that of its interpretation of inter-religious dialog and the relation between religions and perennial wisdom.

Tradition and Religious Traditions

Throughout the discussion of Alpha so far, it has been clear that a major tenet of this school is the universality of its teachings. Its major doctrines of sapiential knowledge can be found in all the major traditions. Different terms for wisdom have been mentioned, *prajna, jnana, hokhmah, sapientia,* but within each religious context a specific term identifies that tradition's form of sacred wisdom. Most essentially, this wisdom posits an Ultimate Reality which can be known. Wisdom reveals a path through a hierarchical universe or through levels of the soul, whether the levels be simply two, from *samsara* to *nirvana, maya* to

Atman, ratio to *sapientia,* or multiple like the seven story mountain and the ten heavenly spheres of the *Comedy* or the various *chakras* in kundalini yoga.

The Alpha school admits that the traditions have changed. They have either decayed, disappeared, or have undergone significant renewal. Indeed, each tradition is fully accepted by Alpha as an expression of ultimate truth in a particular cultural context. But this plurality of expression today is viewed by some as a problem, especially by exclusivist or triumphalist believers who consider their tradition to be the only true faith or the best of all traditions.

For Alpha, the problem is nonexistent, especially if one looks at the vastly different practices and teachings. At their most essential core, they are pointing to one truth. The multiple manifestations of the Truth were necessary, indeed an act of mercy on the part of the Absolute, because we speak different languages and live in very different socio-cultural environments. Another way of explaining the differences can be found in the mind of God. Perfection requires both unity and multiplicity. Nasr speaks of an archetype for each religion, thereby linking once again the world of plurality to the realm of the One through the metaphysics of divine forms:

> There is both Tradition and the traditions without one contradicting the other. To speak of tradition does not mean to reject the celestial origins of any of the authentic religions and traditions but to confirm the sacred in each "original" message from heaven, while remaining aware of that Primordial Tradition which is confirmed by each tradition in not only its doctrines and symbols but also through the preservation of a "presence" which is inseparable from the sacred.[76]

If a critic of Alpha accuses the school of being insensitive to the rich diversity of religious traditions, he or she will have glossed over an important fact - the considerable erudition that many of the school bring to their studies of religion. As mentioned, Huston Smith is the author of one of the most widely read books on world religions. The success of the work stems directly from Smith's ability to enter into the reality of the various traditions, to recreate them as living experiences in addition to communicating important information. His own attraction to the Alpha school was sparked by his reading of Frithjof Schuon, who has written prolifically on various religions. In particular, it was Schuon's book on Shintoism that illuminated that tradition for Smith as well as opened the door to the primordial tradition's perspective. And we have seen Nasr in

48 Landscapes of Wisdom

his *Knowledge and the Sacred* draw on a number of different religions for its examples.

Another reason for a critical stance toward Alpha is its seeming spiritual elitism. It appears to say that in order to recognize the essential, vital core of any religion requires a spiritual wisdom which is not the same as common or modern scientific ways of knowing. The latter two ways are publicly verifiable. *Scientia sacra* is the science of spiritual, inward reality which requires a developed capacity for introspection. But Nasr insists that it is this esoteric approach, one which necessitates special insight and an experience of the truth of sacred knowledge, that can truly examine religions in all of their dimensions both exoteric and esoteric:

> One might say that only serious esoterists can carry out interreligious studies on the deepest level without sacrificing either the exoterism or the certitude and "absoluteness" associated with a particular religious world.[77]

With the introduction of the terms esoteric/exoteric, I will raise my own reactions and thoughts on Alpha at this point. It is appropriate to do so now because it comes within the context of interreligious dialog and I wish to engage in a conversation with Alpha on a dialogical rather than an argumentative level. I accept the usefulness of esoteric/exoteric distinction, for I think the esoteric dimension of Christianity has been unfortunately undervalued and neglected. In saying this, I am in full agreement with the Alpha school on the foundational place of sacred knowledge in religious life. The argument arises in defining the content, indeed the very nature of sacred knowledge. I will leave off attempting alternative definitions until later.

At this point, I simply want to point out several items in Alpha's thought which I feel uneasy about. First, when reviewing my reactions to Alpha, I often feel I am thinking and speaking as a Christian who is in dialogue with Sufis and Hindus, or writers who have imbibed deeply a Sufi/Hindu perspective that is strongly Vedantist. I have raised some Christian objections to Smith's placing the impersonal Infinite above the personal God of the celestial sphere, or in his vocabulary, nondualistic spirit above dualistic soul which in Christian terms may mean personal, relational, I-Thou dualism. Nasr speaks of the Trinity and Christ as relatively absolute:

> If a Christian sees God as the Trinity or Christ as the Logos and holds on to this belief in an absolute sense, this is perfectly understandable from

the religious point of view while, metaphysically speaking, these are seen as the relatively absolute since only the Godhead in Its Infinitude and Oneness is above all relativity.[78]

For Nasr, this may seem the best way to preserve the essence of each religion's teaching of the Absolute, and explain how all the religious traditions are transcendently unified in an esoteric *scientia sacra*. But to a Christian it sounds like an elevation of the ultimate above divine plurality and above the incarnation, placing the One above the Three and the Logos who dwelt among us. This elevation would seem natural for a thinker steeped in the vedantist notions of reality and illusion, *Atman* and *maya*, but they are foreign to a Christian.

The Alpha school's reading of the development of Christian spirituality as a movement away from the Christian gnosticism or sapiential mysticism of Origen and Clement and toward love mysticism which made less use of sapiential doctrines is worth considering. This reading explains the split which occurred in Western Christian thought between the laws of God and the laws of nature. The Church became the defender of a moral code while a variety of humanist endeavors explored new ways of understanding the natural environment. With some notable exceptions (the nature mysticism of Francis of Assisi and the negative mysticism of the Rhineland mystics), Christian spirituality emphasized devotion to the person of Christ. Spirituality of the Protestant Reformation by and large focused on *fides*, faith, not the *intellectus* of Neoplatonic wisdom. In the post-medieval period, a wisdom-oriented spirituality found its greatest expressions in the writings of the Catholic cardinal Nicholas of Cusa and the Lutheran shoemaker Jacob Boehme. But in general, Western Christian spiritual theology veered away from a cosmic perspective and emphasized a more soul-centered, personal approach.

Perhaps the most interesting point made by Nasr in his discussion about religions today is his assertion that this meeting of traditions is an important event with potentially profound consequences for contemporary spirituality:

> If there is one really new and significant dimension to the religious and spiritual life of man today, it is this presence of other worlds of sacred form and meaning not as archaeological or historical facts and phenomena but as religious reality.[79]

Coming from a spokesperson of a wisdom school that is reluctant to admit to the possibility of anything significantly new under the sun, this statement is remarkable. It suggests a path of wisdom which has much to offer when it leads one into experiencing other traditions. Nasr compares it to visiting other solar systems:

> ... coming to know something of their rhythms and harmonies, thereby gaining a vision of the haunting beauty of each one as a planetary system which is *the* planetary system for those living within it.[80]

A provocative image, an intriguing point. Is Nasr proposing another kind of cosmic map, one of a multiplicity of centers in contrast to the single focus of the geocentric cosmos so adamantly defended in another chapter? And is he playing with the possibility of real historical novelty? Or is the growing availability of different religious traditions just part of the present cosmic cycle, an act of divine grace or another instance of "cosmic compensation" to help humankind out of its current spiritual crisis? Nasr's excitement at the new interreligious situation and the implications for the advancement of spiritual wisdom for humankind seems real, for he admits it is a "really new and significant dimension" for modern people, "very different from what his ancestors confronted."[81]

Conclusion

Let us return to Dante. Has our examination of the Alpha school made him more accessible? Have Nasr and Smith persuaded us that Dante's *Comedy* can still serve as a model of the path to God?

The Alpha school presents a strong case for a hierarchical model of the universe and for the value of the Great Chain of Being in spirituality and contemplation. The great Platonic and Neoplatonic contribution to the Christian tradition was to provide a metaphysics of spiritual development for the contemplative life being lived and recorded by the luminaries of the medieval religious world such as Bernard of Clairvaux, Richard of St. Victor, and Bonaventure. The Alpha views on this matter support the Benedictine scholar, Jean Leclercq, who in *The Love of Learning and the Desire for God* examined how the contemplative theology of the monasteries was eventually superseded by the scholastic, philosophical theology of the universities.[82]

Nasr believes that natural theology and divine wisdom were still wedded in Thomas' writings,[83] but the seeds of division between *sapientia* and *ratio* exist in his thought as in other great medieval scholastic *summae*:

Alpha: The Wisdom of Being   51

Yet, these syntheses, especially the Thomistic one, tended to become overrationalistic in imprisoning intuitions of a metaphysical order in syllogistic categories which were to hide, more than reveal, their properly speaking intellectual rather than purely rational character.[84]

Nasr goes on to say that Dante more than Thomas produced the great *summa* of the Christian sapiential tradition:

In fact, the purely sapiential aspect of medieval Christianity is reflected perhaps more directly in the medieval cathedrals and that central epiphany of Christian spirituality, the *Divine Comedy* of Dante, itself a literary cathedral, than in the theological syntheses which, while containing Christian Sophia, also tended to veil it.[85]

Of course, Dante was deeply influenced by Thomas, and Thomistic Aristotelianism shapes many aspects of the *Comedy*. The epic poem is a marvelous fusion of the many strands of medieval thought, but it was the Neoplatonic vision of a hierarchic cosmos that provided the major metaphysical source for the Dantean spiritual landscape.

Dante's great achievement was to have made the Christian Neoplatonic universe a living reality, a path for countless readers to follow over and over again in their imagination. One wants to agree wholeheartedly with Nasr when he criticizes the very label "Neoplatonism" as an "ideal historical tag" which could allow historians and philosophers to shelve this particular metaphysical world view as a mere chapter in the development of Western thought.[86]

If Christian theology were to reclaim the Neoplatonic tradition today, it would be that of Dante and Bonaventure which considered the Trinity and the Incarnation not as "relative absolutes" but the highest revelations of divine wisdom. These doctrines emphasized the sacredness of the notions of person and community of persons, both within divinity and between God and humankind through Christ. In the great Christian Neoplatonist texts of the Middle Ages, these teachings were experiential truths. We return to these texts today because of their witness to a sacred form of knowledge which still has the power to shape the inner person, and to provide spiritual depth to the Christian life.

Because of the quantitative approach of science, the modern version of the universe has been emptied of symbolic power, and is viewed instead as a vast continuum of matter/energy driven by impersonal natural laws. How does this fit with Christian Neoplatonism? Can we ignore the challenge posed by modern science to Christian spirituality? Our response thus far has been to leave explanations of how and what things are to scientists. When we practice a spiritual discipline, do we then bracket the scientific perspective and reconstruct a Neoplatonic universe in our imaginations?

Dante drew on scientific knowledge whenever he chose to do so, usually to explain the natural phenomena he observed on his way to God. There is an innocent, almost naive blending of science and myth in the *Comedy* that may seem strange to us today. In his use of scientific data, Dante reveals himself as a Western European living in the fourteenth century and experiencing an interest in the workings of the natural world that was but a foreshadowing of the scientific revolution in the centuries to come. Perhaps we are looking for a Dante of the post-modern age, someone to heal the rupture between science and faith and by gathering up all the major intellectual, cultural, historical, and spiritual themes of our time, create a poetic landscape that will draw us nearer to spiritual wisdom and wholeness.

I have emphasized the challenge posed by modern science to a metaphysics of spiritual wisdom. More specifically I believe the two notions of hierarchy and time to be particularly problematic. For modern Christians, the notion of hierarchy is a suspect one, suggestive of political, social, and sexual oppression. As Boyde points out:

> . . . whereas we are compelled to study a corporate body *within* our society in order to grasp the organization and *raison d'etre* of a strict hierarchy, medieval men could simply look at society at large. . . . The structure of medieval society furnished a model which tended to reinforce the likelihood that there was a hierarchy in heaven.[87]

Hierarchy, according to a modern understanding of the term, locks a person into a particular category. Therefore, to describe the universe as a hierarchy of being is to invite a negative reaction. We no longer live in the political, social, and cultural environment of the Middle Ages. Hierarchy exists in the West in business, politics, and other realms of daily life, but it no longer holds the same power to inspire the imagination attempting to chart a spiritual landscape.

On the matter of temporality, Dante offers us, I believe, an interpretation which agrees with Alpha. The essentials of Christian salvation history - creation, fall, Incarnation, redemption, second coming - are suggested throughout the poem. Moreover, the epic narrative reflects the fact that Dante was well versed in the history of the ancient and medieval worlds, or as well as he could be given his sources. Time is a factor in the sense of a succession of days and nights during the journey through hell and purgatory, but when Dante leaves the earth behind in the *Paradiso*, the diurnal cycle is also abandoned. The journey begins on Good Friday and the two poets emerge from hell on Easter, but these coincidences recall the cyclical liturgical calendar as much as historical events. In the *Comedy*, Dante moves from the world of time to the eternal spheres in Paradise. If time is a reality, it applies most to the sublunary realm and is not a major category in the spiritual journey. Space is the more prominent dimension marking his progress. Smith's quotation of Max Beckman seems appropriate here: "Time is an invention of man, but space - space is of the gods."[88]

There are, then, some basic difficulties for the modern Christian in the Alpha school's version of sacred knowledge and in Dante's poem of the soul's journey. Nevertheless, I think Nasr and Smith, as advocates for a sapiential perspective within all traditions, can teach us a great deal. Alpha can be an important influence in stimulating a renaissance of *sapientia* within Western Christianity. But we will now turn to a second contemporary wisdom school with a radically different stance toward the world and modern science.

Notes

1. Huston Smith, *The Religions of Man* (New York: Harper, 1958); *The World's Religions: Our Great Wisdom Traditions* (San Francisco: HarperSanFrancisco, 1991).
2. Huston Smith, *Forgotten Truth: The Primordial Tradition* (New York: Harper & Row, 1976), 16.
3. Seyyed Hossein Nasr, *Knowedge and the Sacred: The Gifford Lectures, 1981* (Albany: State University of New York Press, 1989), 1.
4. Ibid., 150.
5. Ibid., 151.
6. Ibid., 2.
7. Ibid., 133.
8. Ibid.
9. Ibid., 190.
10. Smith, *Forgotten Truth*, 37.
11. Ibid., 38.
12. Ibid., 40.
13. Ibid., 47.
14."Xylem," in *McGraw-Hill Encyclopedia of Science and Technology*, s.v.
15. Meister Eckhart, *The Essential Sermons, Commentaries, Treatises, and Defense*, trans. Edmund Colledge and Bernard McGinn (New York: Paulist Press,

1981), 194.

16. Bonaventure, *Itinerarium mentis in Deum*, VII, 5; translation: *The Soul's Journey*, 114-115. Bonaventure is borrowing from Dionysius the Aeropagite, *The Mystical Theology*; indeed, he quotes an entire passage from that work.

17. Smith, *Forgotten Truth*, 54.
18. Ibid., 55.
19. Nasr, 137.
20. Bonaventure, *The Soul's Journey*, 100.
21. Huston Smith, *Beyond the Post-Modern Mind* (New York: Crossroad, 1982), 53.
22. We should note that these terms are Smith's; the history of theology and philosophy has seen a wide range of terms used to identify the inward reality of human persons. Rather than comparing Smith's terminology with any number of traditional notions, we shall accept Smith's versions in order to follow his exposition of the Alpha school's doctrines.
23. Smith, *Forgotten Truth*, 63.
24. Ibid., 68.
25. Ibid., 71.
26. Ibid., 74.
27. Ibid., 75.
28. Ibid., 78-79.
29. Ibid., 87.
30. Meister Eckhart, *The Essential Sermons*, 194.
31. Smith, *Forgotten Truth*, 88.
32. Nasr, 200.
33. Karl Jaspers, *Vom Ursprung und Ziel der Geschichte* (Zurich: Artemis, 1949), 19-43.
34. Nasr, 67-68.
35. Ibid., 2, 3.
36. Smith, *Forgotten Truth*, 36.
37. Nasr, 93.
38. Smith quoted in Nasr, 107.
39. Ibid., 93.
40. Ibid., 198.
41. Ibid.
42. Ibid., 194.
43. Smith, *Forgotten Truth*, 97.
44. Ibid., 17; Nasr, 115.
45. Nasr, 116.
46. Ibid., 115.
47. Smith, *Forgotten Truth*, 98-117.
48. Ibid., 112-13.
49. Nasr, 115.
50. Ibid., 225.
51. Ibid., 223.

52. Ibid.
53. Ibid., 225.
54. Ibid., 141.
55. Ibid., 222.
56. Ibid., 233.
57. Ibid., 222.
58. Ibid., 224-25
59. Ibid., 227.
60. Smith, *Forgotten Truth*, 118.
61. Nasr, 2, 3.
62. Ibid., 135.
63. Ibid., 229.
64. Ibid., 230.
65. Ibid., 231.
66. Ibid.
67. Ibid., 43.
68. *The Bhagavad Gita*, trans. Juan Mascaro (Harmondsworth, Eng.: Penguin, 1962), 92.
69. Smith, *Forgotten Truth*, 121-122.
70. Nasr, 234.
71. Ibid., 236.
72. Smith, *Forgotten Truth*, 139.
73. Ibid., 133.
74. Nasr, 241.
75. Huston Smith, *Beyond the Post-Modern Mind*, 124-25.
76. Nasr, 74-75.
77. Ibid., 301.
78. Ibid., 294.
79. Ibid., 292.
80. Ibid.
81. Ibid.
82. Jean Leclercq, *The Love of Learning and the Desire for God: A Study of Monastic Culture* (New York: Fordham University Press, 1974).
83. Nasr, 194.
84. Ibid., 22.
85. Ibid.
86. Ibid., 44.
87. Boyde, 222, 223.
88. Quoted in Smith, *Forgotten Truth*, 65.

Chapter 3

Zero: A Journey into the Interior

The Approach

During the 1950s, American readers were introduced to a view of the world and the spiritual life that was vividly different from anything they had known. As represented in the writings of D.T. Suzuki[1] and Alan Watts,[2] Zen Buddhism seemed to offer a religious tradition at once more open to nature, humorously iconoclastic, and free of dogma than most Western religions. At its heart is an apparently simple discipline, a silent meditative practice called *zazen*, which has appealed to growing numbers of Westerners seeking inner calm amidst a rapidly changing society. But Zen has also introduced a number of arts and other disciplines including haiku poetry, flower arrangement, archery, garden landscaping, and the tea ceremony.[3] As a result, Westerners could experience Zen Buddhism not only as a practice of meditative sitting but a cultural reality whose roots stretched back to China and Japan.

As a word, *zen* is the Japanese pronunciation of *ch'an*, the Chinese version of the Sanskrit *dhyana* meaning "meditation." But it has been adopted by the West in an astonishingly broad range of contexts, and a perusal of books currently in print in the U.S. reveals how much the word *zen* has entered into common usage. *Zen and the Art of Motorcycle Maintenance* is perhaps the most well known work among those with *zen* in the title. Other examples include *Zen and Creative Management, Zen and the Art of the Internet*, and even *Zen Driving*.[4] At the same time *zen* has gained popular currency, a more intellectually sophisticated understanding of Zen Buddhism as interpreted by the Kyoto school of philosophy has become better known in Western academic circles. Before we turn to the various themes developed by two of its representatives, Keiji

Nishitani and Masao Abe, we will first experience a work by Basho as a poetic introduction to their thought.

The Haiku Master

In 1689, Matsuo Basho (1644-1694) decided to make a journey through unfamiliar territory: the northern regions of Japan's main island of Honshu. The trip, mostly on foot, would provide him with the raw material for his most famous extended work, *Oku no Hosomichi*, a travel diary composed mainly of prose and haiku. Having made revolutionary contributions to the development of haiku, Basho was a highly regarded poet, a reputation that persists to the modern day.

Observations of natural phenomena have traditionally provided the content of the short, seventeen syllable haiku form, and Basho was a master of this form. Moreover, he had immersed himself in the literary currents of his culture. Throughout his writings he quotes writers like the Chinese poets Tu Fu and Li Po, and the Japanese Buddhist poet Saigyo. His work was further enriched by an intimate knowledge of his people's customs, history, and mythology.

But Basho was not only a poet in search of aesthetic inspiration; he was also a spiritual wanderer. He had received training in Zen meditation from the priest Butcho, and he was familiar with Taoist and Buddhist classics.[5] Therefore, when Basho embarked on the journey that would lead to the composition of one of Japan's greatest literary classics, he anticipated a wide range of stimuli both within and without: places and occurrences in nature, religious shrines and temples, recollections of myths and historical events, human encounters, remembered poems, and those brief, piercing moments of insight experienced by Zen practitioners.

As a result of this variety of influences on Basho, *Oku no Hosomichi* can be studied from a variety of perspectives: literary, historical, as well as spiritual. In this respect, Basho's masterwork is comparable to Dante's. The greatness of the two poets must be attributed in part to the range of their interests. The title *Oku no Hosomichi* can be understood to have two very different meanings: one geographic and the other spiritual. Most translators agree that *hosomichi* means "narrow road."[6] *Oku*, however, can receive two interpretations. The first can refer to the furthest or northernmost regions that lay within Honshu. The second can point to a spiritual as well as geographic reality: interior, within, innermost. Thus Aitken translates the title as *The Narrow Way Within*[7] and Hamill renders it as *The Narrow Road to the Interior*.[8]

Riding the Winds of Oku

Basho begins his travel narrative with a brief meditation on time and movement. Life is movement through the years, a journey shared on the cosmic level by the daily motion of celestial bodies and on the historic level by the ancients who were constant travelers:

> The moon and sun are eternal travelers. Even the years wander on. A lifetime adrift in a boat, or in old age leading a tired horse into the years, every day is a journey, and the journey itself is home. From the earliest times there have been some who perished along the road. Still I have always been drawn by windblown clouds into dreams of a lifetime of wandering.[9]

It had only been several months since he had returned from a walking tour, but he was already beset by travel gods and an urge to return to the road. Images of faraway places began to disturb his concentration; he began to dream of the moon over the islands of Matsushima and think of the barrier gate to the northern provinces at Shirakawa.

Basho's decision to begin a new tour was not a simple one. He gave up his house, chose a limited number of possessions to take along, and departed wondering if "my hair may turn white as frost before I return from those fabled places or maybe I won't return at all."[10] Past the peak of his life and not always in good health, Basho was setting out in the face of his possible death along the way. As he climbed into a boat, Basho bade farewell to his friends. Because it was late May, the sad leave-taking found a parallel in the ending of spring. The human events are described in a haibun or short prose section; the haiku which follows it captures the mood in its natural setting:

> Departing spring!
> Birds crying;
> Tears in the eyes of fish.[11]

Basho did not travel alone; his companion Sora came with him to share the joys as well as hardships of the road. According to Basho, Sora put on Buddhist robes on the morning of their departure and changed his name to Sogo, or the Enlightened. We read later that both wore Buddhist robes,[12] a practice that may have been followed to avoid trouble in the more dangerous regions[13] or to conform to a convention among contemporary haiku poets.[14]

60   *Landscapes of Wisdom*

After visiting a shrine, the two moved on to an inn that was managed by - to Basho's delighted surprise - an honest man, indeed a model of virtue in the form of a common person:

> A merciful buddha like an ordinary man, he suddenly appeared to help a pilgrim along his way. His simplicity's a great gift, his sincerity unaffected. A model of Confucian rectitude, my host a saint.[15]

The next morning, Basho scaled Mount Nikko where he visited another shrine. There he had a deep experience that pushed him to the limits of language. The haibun mentions the shrine and its remarkable founder, but the accompanying haiku - the more intense vehicle for capturing the moment - makes no mention of temple or founder at all:

> Ah, how glorious!
> Green leaves, young leaves
> Glittering in the sunlight.[16]

Soon after, Basho arrived at a waterfall where he could pass through the plunging waters and view the falls from the other side.

> for a while I sit
> meditating by the falls -
> start of a summer retreat[17]

According to Hamill, the waterfall poem referred to Shinto and Buddhist ritual bathing.[18] Aitken explains that the last line, in Japanese *ge no hajime*, was "a seasonal reference that is generally limited to monastic vocabulary."[19] The narrative continues with descriptions of encounters with a farmer, children, friends, and visits to shrines. When taken to a mountainside temple, Unganji, he sought out the simpler one-time hermitage of his Zen teacher, Butcho. Before seeing it, Basho recollected the haiku which his teacher wrote on a nearby rock with charcoal:

> A five-foot thatched hut
> I wouldn't even put it up
> but for the falling rain[20]

When he saw it, the hermitage reminded Basho of two Chinese monks and inspired him to compose his own haiku:

> Even woodpeckers leave it alone:
> a hermitage
> in a summer grove[21]

A deep note of profound respect resounds within the apparently humorous appraisal of the hut.

After several more episodes, Basho arrived at the Shirakawa gate where he was overwhelmed by the beauty of the white unohana blossoms, and the thought of the many poets who had passed this barrier before him. Days later, he composed a haiku that reveals another moving impression received at Shirakawa gate: rural folk songs. In them, Basho recognized the roots of his art.

> The beginning of culture!
> Rice-planting songs
> In the innermost part of the country[22]

Subsequent events included visits to a chestnut tree that evoked the presence of Saigyo, the great Japanese Buddhist poet and priest, a village with a legendary stone, and a temple with tombs of two women who had fought bravely in their dead husbands' armor. At the site of the tombs, Basho admitted that he "wept bitterly."[23] While spending the night in a shabby inn, Basho suffered one of the journey's lowest points:

> A storm came upon us towards midnight, and between the noise of thunder and leaking rain and the raids of mosquitoes and fleas, I could not get a wink of sleep. Furthermore, an attack of my old complaint made me so ill that I left the inn upon the first hint of light in the morning. I suffered severely from repeated attacks while I rode on horseback bound for the town of Kori. It is indeed a terrible thing to be so ill on the road, when there still remained thousands of miles before me, but thinking that if I were to die on my way to the extreme north it would only be the fulfillment of providence, I trod the earth as firmly as possible and arrived at the barrier gate of Okido in the province of Date.[24]

The wet conditions of the roads made it impossible for Basho, still weak from his unnamed malady, to visit a particular shrine near the town of Kasashima. He wrote the following haiku:

> whereabouts is
> Kasashima? this rainy month,

this muddy road[25]

One commentator on the poem explains that Basho had constructed a poetic word-play on the name of the Kasashima, which means the kind of hat worn on a rainy day; the commentator concludes that the "association was not concocted in the poet's brain but emerged spontaneously at that time and place. The humor was spontaneous, the kind that Basho liked."[26]

Basho did get to see another hoped-for sight: a famous pine tree at Takekuma which had been appreciated by earlier poets. He describes the vicissitudes suffered by the tree, according to tradition for a thousand years, only to regain its legendary perfect shape. The belief in a thousand year duration may have been for Basho and his contemporaries a metaphor for "enduring" or "ancient." We find it being applied to a human artifact a couple episodes later - a monument which had survived the ravages of nature and preserved an engraved inscription recording the erection of a castle. This evidence of the durability of the written word aroused great emotion in the haiku poet:

> Many are the names that have been preserved for us in poetry from ancient times, but the mountains crumble and rivers disappear, new roads replace the old, stones are buried and vanish in the earth, trees grow old and give way to saplings. Time passes and the world changes. The remains of the past are shrouded in uncertainty. And yet, here, before my eyes, was a monument that none would deny had lasted a thousand years. I felt as if I were looking into the minds of the men of old. This, I thought, is one of the pleasures of travel and living to be old. I forgot the weariness of the journey and was moved to tears of joy.[27]

A moss-covered ruin becomes for Basho a vivid reminder of the greatness of the human written tradition and the source of an overwhelming happiness which helped him transcend all the distress he had been experiencing.

This meditation on the immortality of the word is followed by a visit to a grove filled with tombstones and thoughts of death's inevitability:

> There were graves everywhere among the pines, underscoring Po-Chu-I's famous lines quoted in *The Tale of Genji*, "wing and wing, branch and branch," and I thought, "yes, what we all must come to," my sadness heavy.[28]

Nowhere is Basho's ability to maintain a consistent balance between opposites - here joy and sadness - more in evidence than in these two adjacent sections.

Basho went on to the islands of Matsushima, one of the places which had lured the poet back to the road. The islands did not disappoint; Basho states that they are every bit as lovely as he had heard. His own prose reaches a crescendo of metaphor in his efforts to relate the nature of their beauty, a crescendo which must ultimately lapse into silence:

> Tall islands point to the sky and level ones prostrate themselves before the surges of water. Islands are piled above islands, and islands are joined to islands, so that they look exactly like parents caressing their children or walking with them arm in arm. The pines are of the freshest green, and their branches are curved in exquisite lines, bent by the wind constantly blowing through them. Indeed, the beauty of the entire scene can only be compared to the most divinely endowed of feminine countenances, for who else could have created such beauty but the great god of nature himself? My pen strove in vain to equal this superb creation of divine artifice.[29]

The landscape also included cottages scattered among the pines. After quoting Sora's haiku about the scene before them, Basho did not offer one of his own. He preferred to read poems about Matsushima by other poets.

Basho next takes an accidental detour into the seaside town of Ishinomaki. After getting lost on a lonely trail, he and Sora arrive at their unexpected and disagreeable destination:

> Hundreds of merchant ships were gathered in the bay. In the town the houses fought for space, and smoke rose continuously from the salt kilns. I thought to myself, "I never intended to come anywhere like this...."[30]

A greater contrast to the bay at Matsushima could not be imagined. Instead of a vision of lightly populated, pine-covered islands, we have the crowded bustle of human industry. As if to underscore the town's unpleasantness and visual unattractiveness, Basho tells us that no one offered any lodging to the two travelers.

Their next stop, the ruins of the home of a famous family in Hiraizumi, afforded the two poets an opportunity to recollect the valiant deeds of the clan's warriors and to mourn their passing. In an effort to capture the moment of his sadness, Basho composed one of his more extraordinary haiku:

> Summer grasses:
> all that remains of great soldiers'

imperial dreams [31]

Basho's commentators have shed considerable light on this piece. One says simply "here is a great deal of wordless pity." Another elaborates on the imagery: "The hokku[32] makes good use of the image of summer grass, whose leaves are scorched at their tips under the flaming sun." A third places the poem in a larger context:

> An ancient battlefield is a sacred place where mythology, history, and literature originate. It is a kind of purgatory, a place where the souls of the slain soldiers, still retaining their anger and resentment, utter war cries day and night.

A fourth captures perfectly, I think, the heart of the haiku moment: "The transitoriness of glory, the emptiness of prosperity, all are seen in the luxuriant summer grass."[33] While Basho does not refer to himself in the scene, he was fully present within its purgatorial drama, feeling the flaming sun, and - according to the preceding haibun - "seeing it all through tears."[34]

A little later in their travels, the two sojourners encountered more difficulty: a delay by suspicious guards at the Shitomae Barrier followed by a three day rainstorm. While waiting out the downpour in a guard shack, Basho found another haiku moment, or should we say the haiku found him?

> fleas, lice -
> a horse piddles
> near my pillow

With its echo of an earlier miserable night when he was attacked by bugs, the poem is not all angry outburst. It contains both a cry of indignation and a burst of laughter. Ueda explains the word translated by "piddle," *shitosuru*, refers to a child's urination. He goes on to say that "the ideograph used for *shito* is the same as *shito* in Shitomae," the place of their current misery.[35] According to another commentator,

> The humor and haikai spirit of this poem lie in the word "piddle," which compares a horse to a little child. Without that word, the image of a horse urinating near one's pillow would create a filthy impression and nothing else.[36]

Once again, Basho's spare art brilliantly reveals his inner character. Through the poem he was able to laugh at himself and his situation. Why complain about insects eating him alive when the whole rain-soaked, stinking place was as natural as horse piss, and forgivable as a child making a mess?

After the rain, the two poets reached the Mogami River and ultimately the three sacred mountains of Dewa and a Tendai temple. The temple visit prepared them spiritually for their mountain ascent because of its deep practice of *shikan*, "concentration and insight," which blessed both mountains and pilgrims with "reverence and compassion." Basho then climbed each of the three mountains; the ascent of the first, Mount Gassan or "Moon Mountain," resulted in the following concise but powerful description, perhaps the most memorable of the various ascents in his diary:

> I climbed Mount Gassan on the eighth. I tied around my neck a sacred rope made of white paper and covered my head with a hood made of bleached cotton,[37] and set off with my guide on a long march of eight miles to the top of the mountain. I walked through mists and clouds, breathing the thin air of high altitudes and stepping on slippery ice and snow, till at last through a gateway of clouds, as it seemed, to the very paths of the sun and moon, I reached the summit, completely out of breath and nearly frozen to death. Presently the sun went down and the moon rose glistening in the sky. I spread some leaves on the ground and went to sleep, resting my head on pliant bamboo branches. When, on the following morning, the sun rose again and dispersed the clouds, I went down towards Mount Yudono.[38]

After offering a meditation on a little cherry tree found on Mount Yudono, Basho - out of respect for the sacred rules governing his mountain pilgrimage - made no further comment: "To say more is sacrilege. Forbidden to speak, put down the brush, respect Shinto rites."[39]

They traveled on to Kisagata which offered more sea views of great beauty. Coming down the western coast, however, they entered another highly dangerous area. One night near the barrier gate of Ichiburi, Basho shared a roof with two prostitutes whom he overheard bemoaning their lot in life as they talked beyond his bedroom wall. The next morning, they asked for his and Sora's company as protection for their trip ahead. The two poets' priestly robes no doubt invited such a request, but Basho turned them down, feeling that he and Sora would be making too many detours to be of much use. After parting with the women, Basho could not shake off a feeling of sadness. Deeply affected by the poignancy of the situation, he composed another of the great haiku poems of the diary:

> under the same roof
> courtesans, too, are asleep -
> bush clover and the moon[40]

The *hagi* or bush clover which flowers in early autumn is a great favorite of the Japanese. The juxtaposition in the last line carries with it no condemnation of the two women, just a simple picture with intimations of compassion - the moon[41] shining over the earthly beauty of the women/flowers. Basho himself seems like the moon - "serene, unworldly"[42] - in his observation of the courtesans.

Several episodes that occurred after Ichiburi reinforce themes of sadness and loss. One day, Basho arrives in a town where he had hoped to meet Issho, a man who had gained a reputation for his devotion to poetry. Issho, however, had died during the preceding winter; instead of sharing the joys of his art with a new friend, Basho could only attend a memorial service given by Issho's brother. The following verse was Basho's lament:

> move the gravemound!
> my wailing voice,
> the autumn wind[43]

The cool autumn wind resonates throughout this final section of the diary. Four out of the next nine haikai mention the wind, and another refers to autumn coolness. It is as if the wind is driving Basho toward his journey's end. After his companion, Sora, fell ill and left Basho to stay with relatives, Basho grieved the separation. On departing, Sora wrote:

> Sick to the bone
> if I should fall
> I'll lie in fields of clover

- a poem that echoed Basho's earlier anticipation of death during the journey. Basho offered his own haiku:

> Now falling autumn dew
> obliterates my hatband's
> "We are two"[44]

Zero: A Journey into the Interior   67

The next night, Basho found lodging in a temple; with sad thoughts of Sora, he went to bed "amidst the howling of the autumn wind."[45] Later, the theme of loneliness is reinforced in Basho's description of a beach scene:

> We drank tea and hot sake, lost in a sweeping sense of isolation as dusk came on.
>
> Loneliness greater
> than Genji's Suma Beach
> the shores of autumn[46]

Basho was not alone but with a wealthy companion who had come bringing food and servants for an outing. Despite the presence of others, however, Basho still felt deeply the effects of Sora's departure.

Basho finished the journey in the town of Ogaki. With a few deft strokes, he describes his arrival as the occasion for a reunion of old friends including Sora. Basho's appearance was a cause for joy; his return seemed like a resurrection: "Everybody was overjoyed to see me as if I had returned unexpectedly from the dead."[47] But the narrative does not end there. Despite his weariness, Basho decided to go on to Ise, the site of Japan's major Shinto shrine. In a boat and launching himself on a new journey, the poet composed the final haiku of the diary:

> Clam ripped from his shell
> I move on to Futami Bay:
> passing autumn[48]

Closure is both arrival and departure. Like the turning year, Basho's wandering begins another cycle.

Zen Commentary

When I first read *Oku no Hosomichi*, it seemed like a blur of people and places, a short and shapeless work that was merely episodic, without any apparent structure. Compare Dante: The journey of the Italian poet is an approach to God. The milestones are clear: descent to the bottom of the pit, ascent to the mountaintop, and final vision of the Trinity. But Basho goes up and down mountains and has a succession of good and bad experiences with no obvious final revelation. Moreover, the meanings of the haiku are often elusive; the ability of the brief poems to evoke the reader's emotions and imagination often escape the reader.

However, I did eventually find a way into Basho's world through Zen Buddhist meditative practice. As a member of a Zen community (*sangha*), I sat for hours and days in wordless meditation. The initial breakthrough in my reading of *Oku no Hosomichi* came when I experienced the silence that permeates the narrative. At times, Basho claimed that he could not say anything more about the way a place moved him, but there is an implicit silence throughout the diary. Basho often underscored his emotions by what he left unsaid, or by an extreme economy of words.

Both Robert Aitken, an American Zen master, and D.T. Suzuki have used Basho's haiku as illustrations of the Zen viewpoint. Study of their commentaries deepened my burgeoning appreciation of Basho's poetry. In examining the second haiku of the diary,

> Departing spring!
> Birds crying;
> Tears in the eyes of fish.[49]

Aitken points out the difficulty in translating the second line as "birds weeping." The Japanese original uses a word meaning the crying of any animal. The poet's intent was to avoid using animal behavior to express human grief - the sadness of Basho's friends over his leaving. Basho is describing a more universal process of departure; his journey's beginning is but one example. The other is the end of spring. The human drama is part of the overall movement of change; the sadness is a cosmic sadness.[50]

One might insist that the two images - birds crying and fish eyes forming tears - can only be products of a human sensibility. The poet uses events in the natural world to reflect human emotions. Some might say that Basho is guilty of pathetic fallacy. Aitken takes up the argument. He turns to the gravemound haiku written after attending the memorial service for Issho, the poetry devotee. In Aitken's translation it reads:

> Shake, oh grave;
> My wailing voice
> Is the autumn wind.[51]

Indeed, Aitken roshi admits that the first two lines suggest the poetic bugaboo of pathetic fallacy. However, the last line indicates that the level of mourning transcends the merely human. Birds cry, fishes' eyes well up, graves tremble, friends weep, the poet wails, the autumn wind blows. In pathetic fallacy, birds may cry and winds may wail as metaphors or similes of human grief, but metaphors are constructs of the human mind. In metaphor, one steps back from reality. In contrast to metaphor, Aitken claims that:

> Basho's world of poetry is the world of experience, not intellectual association. The simile "as though" is supplanted by the metaphor of flowing unity. Basho disappears, and the season itself is going; the birds and fish themselves are sad. The autumn wind becomes his wailing voice. This is the nature of deepest poetry, of deepest religious insight. "Heaven and earth and I are of the same root. All things and I are one."[52]

Aitken quotes a third haiku which articulates this human-natural world unity:

> Summer grasses!
> The imprint of dreams
> Of warriors.[53]

The poem reflected Basho's reaction at the site of a historic battle at Hiraizumi. "Imprint" is Aitken's choice for translating *ato* which according to Aitken means "mark, print, impression." It is also related to idioms such as "footprint" and "toothmark." In different contexts it could mean "remains" or "ruins" as in "ruins of a temple." The grasses are the ruins of the soldiers' failed dreams of victory. As such, they are a contrast to Tu Fu's grasses and trees which flourish *despite* social decline:

> Though the nation is shattered
> Its hills and streams remain;
> It is spring [again] in the cities;
> Grasses and trees are luxuriant[54]

For Tu Fu, grasses and trees expresses an ideal of stability and regenerative power in nature that, at least for the moment, had eluded Chinese society. For Basho, the grasses are ruined dreams rooted in human tragedy. According to Aitken,

> ... for Basho, ... it is all a dream, the movement of form to form, now high drama and fierce violence, now grasses, now Basho, now you and I.[55]

If all is one, fleas may bite and make you miserable, but a horse pissing can help you regain perspective. It may take three days of being eaten up by bugs to hear the peeing intensely enough to write a haiku. R.H. Blyth offered the following comment on the "fleas, lice" haiku:

> Sometimes, not by any means always, the simple, elemental experiences of things, whether of lice or of butterflies, the pissing of horses or the flight of eagles, have a deep significance, not of something beyond themselves, but of their own essential nature. But we must lodge with these things for a night, for a day, for three days. We must be cold and hungry, flea-ridden and lonely, companion of sorrow and acquainted with grief. Basho's verse is not an expression of complaint or disgust, though he certainly felt irritation and discomfort. It is not an expression of philosophic indifference nor an impossible love of lice and dirt and sleeplessness. What is it an expression of? It is the feeling "These things too. . . ." But anyone who tries to finish this sentence does not understand what Basho meant.[56]

Insights based on direct experience of the unity of existence can also produce poems of profound compassion. For some, the lives of the two courtesans at Ichiburi had been wasted. Basho heard them bemoaning their lot in life, but he also saw something beautiful and so wrote: "bush clover and the moon." According to Suzuki,

> The prostitutes are no more fallen specimens of humanity, they are raised to the transcendentally poetic level with the lespedeza flowers in their unpretentious beauty while the moon impartially illuminates good and bad, comely and ugly.[57]

Suzuki's commentary on this haiku seems to borrow from a passage in the *Lotus Sutra* where the Buddha is described as the sun shining on the righteous and the fallen, good and evil alike.[58]

Such a perspective might be criticized as lacking an ethical dimension. Basho's poetic impulse seems to draw him beyond the realm of good and evil in a search for purely aesthetic experiences. There is some truth to this charge, but it is not the complete picture. Basho is a man deeply committed to receiving and passing on his literary and cultural traditions, traditions such as rice planting which follow the rhythms of the earth.

> The beginning of culture!
> Rice-planting songs
> In the innermost part of the country.[59]

The first line of the haiku is Aitken's translation of *furyu*. Suzuki sheds further light on the word's meaning:

Fuga (or *furyu* as some would have it) . . . means "refinement of life," but not in the modern sense of raising the standard of living. It is the chaste enjoyment of life and Nature. . . . and not the pursuit of material comfort or of sensation. A life of *fuga* starts from the identification of one's self with the creative and artistic spirit of Nature. A man of *fuga*, therefore, finds his good friends in flowers and birds, in rocks and waters, in rains and the moon.[60]

One who lives a life of *furyu* or *fuga* is a *furabo*, which in Basho's words is "a man whose life is like a windblown piece of gauzy fabric."[61] Suzuki also identifies *furyu* as following the path of *wabi* which means "solitariness," "aloneness," as well as "poverty" in the spiritual sense. Basho's letting go of his house and most of his possessions at the outset of the journey, his experiences of loneliness, and the recurring wind image can be understood as signs of an "enspirited" man - inwardly stirred by the travel gods, outwardly by the winds. Suzuki mentions the Johannine verse, "The wind blows where it will" (John 3:8), because it captures Basho's sense of spirit. One of the goals of his journey may have been to see the moon shining over Matsushima bay, but Basho was aiming for something far greater than mere aestheticism. His purpose was to practice a spirituality of intimacy with nature.

Suzuki calls Basho a nature poet.[62] Indeed, the natural world provides the essential themes for traditional haiku poetry. Basho includes literary and geographic references as well. But Western religious traditions have generally eyed nature mysticism with suspicion. The natural world is God's creation, the stage for his revelatory acts in history, and - by strict commandment - not to be confused with its divine source. To see the divine in nature invites condemnation and the label of pantheism. Much of what Aitken sees in Basho's poems, their reflection of a Zen sense of unity, could be viewed as pantheistic. But that would sell Basho and Zen short, and perhaps reveal the limited usefulness of the pantheism label.

Some Western scholars are open to a new appreciation of a spirituality of nature, for example Louis Dupré's remarks concerning nature mysticism: "To deny any resemblance between the intense, unifying experience of nature and that of a transcendent presence would be absurd."[63] But much of Western thought resists blurring the boundary between the sacred and the profane. When Basho went to visit a shrine on Mount Nikko, the shrine's spiritual power rendered the poet speechless except for a haiku:

    Ah, how glorious!
    Green leaves, young leaves

Glittering in the sunlight.[64]

For some readers, the juxtaposition of Basho's prose description of the shrine and his poetic "ah, how glorious" reaction to green leaves is an incongruity. The haibun description of a sacred space - the shrine - is followed by one of profane nature - glittering leaves. But this is Basho's nature mysticism: seeing the sacred and the profane as one. His silence reflects a deep relationship between shrine and leaves. To read the haiku as an expression of his silence before the holy is to unlock Basho's inner world.

Basho's masterwork presents us with a vivid landscape for the spiritual journey. A careful study of *Oku no Hosomichi* may lead the reader to begin viewing the earth itself as place for seeking the divine. Dante used the earth and the heavens as the stage for his *Commedia*, but in a way that we today would characterize as highly imaginative. Dante's landscape is mostly a spiritual reality; its resemblance to our physical world is slim. By contrast, the entire length of Basho's trip was within a recognizable setting. He didn't travel through the earth's core or ascend through celestial spheres but "trod the earth as firmly as possible."

The idea of nature as a place for a spiritual retreat can be found in the American literary tradition. Works by Henry David Thoreau and Annie Dillard, for example, include meditations on the natural world which have nourished many readers. But in East Asian culture, the spiritual dimension of nature is far more widely accepted. Zen Buddhism in China and Japan has long revered nature as the source of spiritual inspiration. At the same time, Zen has cultivated a spirituality of silence based on a practice of sitting meditation. In the Zen tradition, nature and meditative silence are deeply related. The central Buddhist doctrine of *sunyata* or absolute emptiness captures this relationship. Things *are* because they are *sunya*, empty. On the level of Zen practice, silence clears our minds for appreciating the world around us. The emptiness of *sunyata* permeated Basho's silence, a quiet that produced a haiku about glittering leaves.

While the Western tradition has produced important teachings in negative theology, the connection between a negative divinity - a God beyond all thoughts and concepts - and the natural world never fully developed. Nor was a spiritual discipline of silent meditation widely practiced and transmitted through generations of spiritual teachers like the zazen practice of Zen Buddhism. Zazen as it is taught and practiced today in North American and European meditation halls thus provides Westerners the opportunity to encounter *sunyata* as a lived experience. In my own

Zen practice, during its many hours of silent sitting, I slowly discovered through my very bones the rich possibilities of Buddhist emptiness and the force of Zen's insistence on the reality of the world around me. But Buddhist silence has not resulted in an absence of articulate discourse, and I am extremely grateful for the modern philosophical exponents of Zen. The next chapter will explore the metaphysical expressions of *sunyata* developed by a contemporary Buddhist school of wisdom. The members of this group I have come to call the Zero school of wisdom have carefully studied the Western intellectual tradition and have placed *sunyata* within a contemporary philosophical context. The school thus offers a metaphysical alternative to Alpha, one that is profoundly open to the spiritual significance of nature.

Notes

1. Some of Suzuki's works include: *An Introduction to Zen Buddhism*, with a forward by C.G. Jung (New York: Philosophical Library, 1949); *Essays in Zen Buddhism: First Series* (New York: Grove Press, 1949) and continued in two subsequent series with various publishers; *Studies in Zen* (New York: Dell, 1955). Suzuki's lengthy publication history actually begins in the 1920s.

2. Two early works by Watts are: *The Way of Zen* (New York: New American Library, 1957) and *The Spirit of Zen: A Way of Life, Work, and Art in the Far East* (New York: Grove Press, 1958).

3. On cultural aspects of Zen, see D.T. Suzuki, *Zen and Japanese Culture* (Princeton, N.J.: Princeton University Press, 1959), and Thomas Hoover, *Zen Culture* (New York: Random House, 1977).

4. Robert M. Pirsig, *Zen and the Art of Motorcycle Maintenance: An Inquiry into Values* (Now York: William Morrow, 1974); Albert Low, *Zen and Creative Management* (Rutland, Vt.: Charles B. Tuttle, 1993); Brendan P. Kehoe, *Zen and the Art of the Internet* (Englewood Cliffs, N.J.: 1996); K.T. Berger, *Zen Driving* (New York: Ballantine Books, 1988).

5. See Sam Hamill, "Translator's Introduction," in Matsuo Basho, *Narrow Road to the Interior* (Boston: Shambhala, 1991), p. xii; Robert Aitken, *A Zen Wave: Basho's Haiku and Zen* (New York: Weatherhill, 1978), p. 18; Basho, *The Narrow Road to the Deep North* trans. Nobuyuki Yuasa (Harmondsworth, Eng.: Penguin Books, 1966), 27.

6. So Hamill and Yuasa (see fn. 1 above); so also Donald Keene's "The Narrow Road of Oku," a commentary on Basho in Keene's *Travelers of a Hundred Ages* (New York: Henry Holt, 1989), 309-317.

7. Aitken, *Zen Wave*, 45.

8. See n. 1.

9. Hamill, 1. When quoting a translation of *Oku no Hosomichi*, I will cite the

translator - Hamill, Yuasa, Keene, Aitken, Ueda or Suzuki - and the page number. The first four authors/translators have been already cited more fully in footnotes above. The Ueda translations will be from Makoto Ueda, *Basho and His Interpreters: Selected Hokku with Commentary* (Stanford, Calif.: Stanford University Press, 1991); the Suzuki translations will be from Daisetz T. Suzuki, *Zen and Japanese Culture* (Princeton, N.J.: Princeton University Press, 1959).

10. Hamill, 5.
11. Aitken, 147.
12. Yuasa, 132.
13. Hamill, xii-xiv.
14. Aitken, 18.
15. Hamill, 7.
16. Aitken, 46.
17. Ueda, 232.
18. Hamill, note to p. 10 on p. 100.
19. Aitken, 18.
20. Hamill, 15.
21. Ibid., 16.
22. Aitken, 159.
23. Yuasa, 109.
24. Ibid., 110.
25. Ueda, 240.
26. Seisensui (1884-1976), quoted in Ueda, 240.
27. Keene, 316-317. Keene describes this passage in *Oku no Hosomichi* as the one "that moves me most."
28. Hamill, 37.
29. Ibid., 43.
30. Keene, 315.
31. Hamill, 51.
32. Earlier term for haiku.
33. The four commentators in order are: Shogatsudo (circa 1764), Nobutane (circa 1795), Yamamoto (1907-1988), and Ehara (1894-1948); quoted in Ueda, 242-243.
34. Hamill, 51.
35. Ibid.
36. Imoto (b. 1913), quoted in Ueda, 247.
37. According to Hamill's translation, the garb of a Shinto priest.
38. Yuasa, 125.
39. Hamill, 65.
40. Ueda, 261.
41. The moon has been used in Buddhist scripture as a symbol of spiritual realization; for example: "He who formerly was reckless and afterwards became sober brightens up this world, like the moon when freed from clouds." *Dhammapada*, in *World of the Buddha: A Reader*, ed. Lucien Stryk (Garden City, NY: Anchor Books, Doubleday, 1968), 58.

42. This is Ehara's opinion, quoted in Ueda, 261.
43. Ueda, 263.
44. Hamill, 84.
45. Yuasa, 137.
46. Hamill, 96.
47. Yuasa, 142.
48. Hamill, 97.
49. Aitken, 147.
50. See Aitken's discussion: 148-49.
51. Aitken, 149.
52. Ibid, 150. He is quoting the *Hekiganroku*, case 40.
53. Ibid, 151.
54. Tu Fu, "Spring - The Long View," quoted in Aitken, 151.
55. Aitken, 152.
56. R.H. Blyth, quoted in Suzuki, 237-38.
57. Suzuki, 230.
58. Ibid, 220-30; see Aitken, 97-100.
59. Aitken, 159.
60. Suzuki, 257-58.
61. Quoted in Suzuki, 259.
62. Suzuki, 230.
63. Louis Dupré, "Mysticism," in *Encyclopedia of Religion*, 10:247.
64. Aitken, 46.

Chapter 4

Zero: The Wisdom of Emptiness

The Sages of Kyoto

The representatives of the Zero perspective are members of the Kyoto school of modern Japanese philosophy founded by Nishida Kitaro (1870-1945) of Kyoto University. Two of its most prominent thinkers are Nishitani Keiji and Abe Masao.[1] Both have written widely on topics covering Western philosophy, modern science, and Buddhist philosophy. Deeply rooted in the Zen tradition, they have engaged in dialogue with Christianity and Western thought. Nishitani has produced one of the most important works on the significance of *sunyata* for the modern world: *Religion and Nothingness*.[2] Abe has been teaching at American universities and writing a series of essays that reflect the numerous dialogical encounters he has participated in with Western colleagues at various academic conferences. His significant works include *Zen and Western Thought* (a work with a two part sequel)[3] and an important essay, "Kenotic God and Dynamic *Sunyata*."[4]

The Sunyata Dialectic

For Abe and Nishitani, the concept of *sunyata* or absolute nothingness is central. To paraphrase a familiar description of Spinoza, the two Japanese thinkers are "*sunyata*-intoxicated men." In this, they are true Zen disciples, or to place them in the broader Buddhist context - fervent followers of the Mahayana, the Greater Vehicle.[5] When one reads certain Mahayana Buddhist scriptures, for example the Prajnaparamita Sutras, one can't help but be struck by the importance of the emptiness doctrine of *sunyata.*

In Christian teachings, all things receive their being from their Creator. This common source is the ground for our reverence of all things which, as we have seen in Christian Neoplatonism, reflect back on their maker as his vestiges or footprints. In Buddhist thought, all things are *sunya*, empty of being; they are not creatures fashioned and sustained by a loving creator God - they are empty, nothing in themselves. And more, there is no God at all. The Buddha may at times appear to have attained a deified status in the scriptures, but to regard him in the same way as the Judeo-Christian tradition regards the Creator would be to ignore the chasm that yawns between East and West on this point.

Abe has argued that in the West, being has been given an ontological priority over nonbeing. He quotes Tillich:

> In Volume I of his *Systematic Theology*, Paul Tillich says, "Being precedes nonbeing in ontological validity, as the word 'nonbeing' itself indicates." Elsewhere, he says "Being 'embraces' itself and nonbeing," while "Nonbeing is dependent on the being it negates. 'Dependent' points first of all to the ontological priority of being over nonbeing."[6]

This is not only Tillich's position but the majority view of Western metaphysics going back to the Greeks and developed by Christian philosophy. When God is identified with Being and is presented as the highest, most inclusive term for reality, this move subordinates all lesser notions of being and nonbeing. Because for many Christian thinkers God is Being itself, they have considered being as superior to nonbeing. Nonbeing is considered a lack or deficiency of what *is*.

In contrast, Abe argues the Buddhist view that the Absolute includes both being and nonbeing, but is neither. Using the Japanese words *u* and *mu* for being and nonbeing, he explains that the two are considered equal and reciprocal in Buddhist philosophy. The ultimate is not Being itself but *sunyata*, the Sanskrit term for *Mu* (designated by an upper case *M*), which means a formless Emptiness, and which as an absolute term is distinguished from relative *mu* (designated by a lower case *m*). *Mu* or Emptiness is transcendent and outside the *u-mu* duality, but he warns against regarding *Mu* as separate. *Mu* does not establish a second duality with respect to the first relative duality. One must not cling to Emptiness as the supreme term. Rather Emptiness must empty itself and become non-Emptiness, embracing relativity in a nondualistic whole. In Zen's dialectical mode of expressing reality, Emptiness is true Emptiness because it empties itself and becomes wondrous Being or *U*.

Zero: The Wisdom of Emptiness

Rationally this makes little sense. Abe appears to be defying logic, for example, that something can and cannot be at the same time. We have been taught (and common sense seems to indicate) that A is A because it is A and not B (or C or D, etc.). Buddhist thought is saying that A is A because it is not A: *Mu* is *Mu* because it is not *Mu*. *Mu* grounds its identity in its paradoxical ability to empty itself of its identity. For Abe, it is less important to be rational, and more important to be true to existential reality which is often irrational. The *u-mu/Mu-U* relationships express life's dynamism. Relative *u* is always becoming relative *mu* as well as sustaining itself; relative *mu* is always becoming relative *u* while sustaining itself. In Abe's words:

> Emptiness . . . is really a vast, boundless and infinite sphere which in itself is the dynamic whole of emptying activity. In this realization of true Emptiness as such an infinite dynamic sphere, the two sides of such polarities as affirmation and negation, positivity and negativity, and *u* and *mu* are paradoxically and self-contradictorily identical. Thus any point of the sphere has the same paradoxical nature.[7]

Moreover, Abe insists that the *Mu* doctrine has great salvific value. In the West, Being as ontologically prior to nonbeing is the symbol of ultimate liberation; negativity is something to be overcome by positivity. In Buddhism, positive and negative forces are equal and reciprocal. Using ethical terminology, Abe claims that

> Buddhists cannot say that good is strong enough to overcome evil. Good and evil are completely antagonistic principles, resisting each other with equal force, yet inseparably connected and displaying an existential antinomy as a whole.[8]

Liberation is not realized by good overcoming evil, but the transcendence of the entire good-evil / positive-negative tension. This transcendence, it must be remembered, does not annihilate good-evil or being-nonbeing; rather it makes such dualities more real. One is reminded of Christian saints who, despite all outward signs of perfection, become more aware of their inner struggle with sin. Buddhist enlightenment is effected by the emptying dynamic, *Mu*, which both emancipates one from the *u-mu* antinomy and embraces it in Emptiness emptying itself.

At the heart of Abe's explication of *sunyata* or *Mu* is a warning to the Western tradition: Being as the supreme ontological reality is idealistic. However, the Buddhist understanding of the inevitability of a positive-negative dialectic in human existence is not pessimistic as usually believed but "radically realistic."

> In Buddhism . . . what is essential for salvation is not to overcome evil with good and to participate in the supreme Good, but to be emancipated from the existential antinomy of good and evil and to awaken to Emptiness prior to the opposition between good and evil. In the existential awakening to Emptiness, one can be master of, rather than enslaved by, good and evil. In this sense, the realization of true Emptiness is the basis for human freedom, creative activity, and ethical life.[9]

Ethics is not abandoned but considered within a completely new perspective, that of absolute nothingness. In Zen, it is more important to *be* and thereby see things as they are - permeated with both being and nonbeing, goodness and evil - than to *be good*. Ethical action depends on judgment between good and evil; judgmental thought is inimical to Zen meditative practice which aims for a clear, empty mind. Once a clear mind is realized, ethical behavior follows spontaneously. To really see, to appreciate is to value, but not by our naming it as good. Rather, in Zen good action occurs naturally, without premeditation.

If Abe's discussion of *sunyata* is difficult to grasp, the reader should attempt an intuitive glimmer of Zen's *U-Mu* dialectic in order to envision its spiritual landscape. When Abe mentions wondrous Being, one may ask whether *sunyata* has more in common with the Western concept of Being in its most profound, transcendent, all-inclusive meaning. Maybe. But to make an immediate and complete identification of East and West on this point would be to make an unjustified and premature leap of thought. There is something about *sunyata* that is as different from Western Being as the Ryoanji Zen garden of raked gravel and stones is from Chartres cathedral. To grasp that difference requires a journey into the essence of Buddhist experience.

The Green Fields of Nothingness

Journeys imply space, and the Kyoto school has been sensitive to spatial language. Nishida described the place of *sunyata* as the "locus of absolute nothingness."[10] Nishitani refers to the "place" or "point" (*tokoro*) where things happen, the "standpoint" (*tachiba*) of a subject, and "field" (*ba*) of being or emptiness.[11] Nishida's use of "locus" may have been inspired by the notion of *topos* in Plato's *Timaeus* and the Aristotelian concept of *hypokeimenon*, but modern field theory was also influential.

According to Van Bragt, Nishida and Nishitani do not see "place" as either a simple location of "here" or "there" or as something intrinsic to the being of a thing: it is both. In Van Bragt's words:

> The place where things *are* can be envisaged at one end of the spectrum as determining things and binding them together in a purely external and superficial way; at the other, as defining their most their most intimate relationships and thus as constitutive of their very reality. The former is found in our common sense notions of place; the latter is closer to the scientific notion of "field." In the transition from the one to the other, what was originally seen as a kind of detached background becomes more immediately immanent, and the very idea of "background," usually understood as something secondary that sets the stage for things, comes to take on the richer sense of . . . the hidden, deeper reality of things normally hidden from view.[12]

Previously we spoke of Zen's paradoxical manner of identifying what makes a thing real: A is A because it is not A. It is itself because it is its opposite or its negation, and so being and nonbeing are deeply related. Now we can see how the Kyoto philosophers envisage a thing's reality in spatial terms. A bottle is a bottle because of the table (its "non-bottle" support) it stands on. The "point" or "place" of their relationship is also called the *soku*, a conjunctive which Van Bragt translates as *sive* (at times also as *qua*). Bottle is bottle because of its self-nature as bottle but also because of its "background," in particular the table. This is a physical example of what Van Bragt describes as *soku* logic, but the term is also applied to more value-laden antinomies: good *soku* evil, life *soku* death.

Nothing quite like *soku* exists in Western terminology; therefore, in translating Nishitani Van Bragt at times borrows from Christian thought and its Trinitarian notion of circumincession. While its use in Christian theology is reserved to describe the relation between the divine Persons in God, in Nishitani it indicates how things can be both one and different at the same time. Within a circumincessional relationship, the *soku* both binds opposite poles together and affirms their individual and oppositional nature. And the field of *soku* is emptiness, *sunyata*. In Nishitani's words,

> The field of sunyata is a void of infinite space, without limit or orientation. . . . Here the mode of being of things as they are in themselves, even though it arise from the sort of center where "All are One," is not reduced to a One that has had all multiplicity and differentiation extracted from it. . . . On the field of sunyata, *the center is everywhere.* Each thing in its own selfness shows the mode of being of the center of all things. Each

and every thing becomes the center of all things and, in that sense, becomes the absolute center. This is the absolute uniqueness of things, their reality.[13]

This passage reminds us of the Neoplatonic description of God as "an infinite sphere whose center is everywhere and whose circumference nowhere."[14] However, the Christian Neoplatonist focused on oneness as a divine attribute, whereas Nishitani is pointing to the oneness in nature described by Basho's glittering green leaves or "bush clover and the moon." The center is everywhere *and therefore* nowhere, not in a creator deity immanent in his creation.

Dante encountered circumincession in the final vision of the *Divine Comedy*; by using the image of circles within circles, he tried to capture the mystery of three Persons in one God with a visual metaphor. Geometric figures are abstract and colorless, but Dante gave one of the circles a fleshly hue, thereby rendering it symbolic of the second Person of Christ. Basho's circumincessional realm was the earth itself. Hence, he could paint images of his experience of the absolute with a far broader range of hues. For the haiku master, the field of *soku* is nature itself.

Abe draws a sharp contrast between Christian and Buddhist views of the relationship between humankind and nature. In Christianity, the human person alone is created in God's image. The great sweep of Christian salvation history is essentially a drama played out between divine and human persons. Mythically speaking, in Adam we sinned and in Christ we are redeemed. Abe describes Christian salvation as man-centered. In Buddhism, the fundamental problem is not human disobedience, but the hard reality of birth and death. Moreover, Buddhist concern extends beyond human mortality by embracing the birth and death experienced by all forms of life. Abe follows Buddhist teaching when he insists that not only living things but everything that exists is worthy of compassionate attention. Thus, not only the appearance and disappearance of humans, dogs, trees, and grasses, but the whole of the phenomenal world: stones, rivers, clouds - some of which appear and disappear more rapidly than others - are profound events. In Buddhism, one seeks wisdom because reality in all of its manifestations is perceived as impermanent or transitory, and therefore as deeply painful. This approach to salvation, according to Abe, is cosmic rather than human-centered:

> In Buddhism man's *samsara*, i.e., succession of births and deaths, is understood to be inescapable and irremediable unless one transcends and bases one's existence on a cosmological foundation. In other words, not

by doing away with the birth-death nature common to all living things, but only by doing away with the appearance-disappearance nature - i.e., the being-nonbeing nature common to everything - can man's birth-and-death problem be properly and completely solved. . . . The story of a monk who, looking at the fall of a withered leaf from a tree, awakened to the transiency of the total universe, including himself, bespeaks the compelling power of such a realization.[15]

And if the fundamental problem includes all of reality, then the solution likewise encompasses the entirety of the cosmos. Enlightenment embraces the human person and nature in a single movement where all things shine forth in their true nature. Thus Buddhism can declare that "mountains and rivers and the earth all disclose their *Dharmakaya* [their essential Buddhahood]."[16]

But this is not to say that Buddhism undervalues the human realm. Only the human person can perceive the reality of transitoriness, because only the human person is capable of self-consciousness. The uniqueness of the human is precisely in his or her ability to transcend the human-centered perspective; that is also the person's greatness. Abe quotes from a Buddhist verse: "Hard it is to be born into human life. / We now live it. / Difficult it is to hear the teaching of the Buddha, / We now hear it." When reciting these words, the Buddhist expresses gratitude for being born into the human realm, for one's humanity makes it possible to learn the true doctrine which leads to salvation.[17]

The teaching of the Buddha is, of course, that all things are empty, but not simply empty or impermanent when considered by themselves. Such emptiness is a relative emptiness and the source of the suffering which permeates our lives and our world. A deep experience of this relative emptiness is a part of being enlightened. Ultimate salvation, however, consists in realizing absolute emptiness, the *Mu* which grounds all relative emptiness and which was discussed above. Abe summarizes this basic position:

> What is referred to as Buddha-nature in Buddhism and is said to be inherent in everyone and everything, is simply another term for the realization of universal transitoriness, or *jinen*, in which everyone and everything discloses itself as it truly is in itself. And it is from this realization of *jinen* that the Buddhist life of wisdom and compassion begins.[18]

The Western reader may still be tempted to see nature as a stepping stone to enlightenment - the final realization of the truth of *sunyata* and the

Buddha-nature in all things. Absolute nothingness is a transcendent principle, beyond the relative being/nonbeing polarity, and so the Buddhist first recognizes the emptiness of things, and then the *Mu* which grounds all relative *mu/u*. But there is no progression of stages in Zen, although it may sometimes, for our benefit, map out the enlightenment process as a spiritual journey through phases of ever-deepening awareness. Abe is clear on this point: "There is no continuity, no ascending bridge to a higher stage from a lower stage."[19]

In order to emphasize this point, Abe refers to Dogen's version of a passage in the *Nirvana Sutra*. Dogen (1200-1253), one of the most significant figures in Japanese Zen Buddhism, was the founder of Soto Zen, and the author of important practical and philosophical Buddhist treatises.[20] The line from the *Nirvana Sutra* reads "All sentient beings without exception have the Buddha-nature;" it is interpreted by Dogen to read "All beings are the Buddha-nature."[21] Abe argues that this shift from "all sentient beings have" to "all beings are" is a "way of Dogen to express clearly and correctly what he believes to be the fundamental standpoint of Mahayana Buddhism."[22] First of all, it emphasizes a doctrine we have already encountered. The Buddha-nature pervades the whole of the cosmos ("all beings") and not just one particular dimension, that characterized by life ("all sentient beings"). Second, by replacing *have* with *are*, Dogen points to the pure actuality of *sunyata* as it is now embodied in each and every being. Buddha-nature is not a spiritual reality possessed by living beings in a way that Hindus believe in an *atman* and Western philosophers and theologians have historically believed in a soul. By identifying Buddha-nature with all aspects of an impermanent world, Dogen has succeeded in communicating its radical emptiness; Buddha-nature as emptiness (*Mu*) cannot be something that is immanent to beings nor a single immanent cause of the world because it is no-thing, entirely and absolutely insubstantial. If the verb "to have" is to be used in this context at all, then it would be truer to say that "All beings have no-Buddha-nature." Dogen is insistent on this point: any view that states we have Buddha-nature adds an unnecessary, even dangerous complexity to reality: "If (all living beings) have the Buddha-nature they must be confederates of the devil. They bring a devil to add to all living beings."[23]

When we view the landscape of the Zen journey, we see trees and mountains, nothing more nor less, not trees and mountains with the potential for revealing Buddha-nature but trees and mountains which are Buddha-nature. Another word for Buddha-nature is *mind*, as in the following passage from Dogen:

Grasses, trees, and lands are mind; being mind, they are *shujo* (living beings); being *shujo*, they have the Buddha-nature. Sun, moon, and stars are mind; being mind, they are *shujo*; being *shujo*, they have the Buddha-nature.[24]

Readers should not be confused by Dogen's phrase "have Buddha-nature;" the basic meaning here is consistent with his overall teaching - that all phenomena are Buddha-nature.

The Zero school thus presents us with a spiritual landscape that is recognizable in its naturalness. We can say with some certainty that the Kyoto sages have done us a great service in showing us a map that is familiar and promising. Wisdom is not radically other from the "real world" modernity insists must engage us. True insight is not to be gained by flight to transcendent realms but is to be found within this life and on this planet. Given this orientation, it will be no surprise that Nishitani and Abe have things to say about modern science that will differ sharply from the Alpha perspective. And as we shall see, their insights on this subject are of a piece with their wisdom doctrine.

The Deadly Sword of Science

Like Huston Smith and Seyyed Hossein Nasr, Nishitani recognizes the challenge modern science poses for traditional religion in the West. The Japanese philosopher is clear about the gravity of the situation: "The problem of religion and science is the most fundamental problem facing contemporary man."[25] Throughout much of the Western thought world, science and its support for materialistic views of the world have seriously shaken ideas and beliefs once considered cornerstones of Western culture. The notions of God and soul and ideals such as truth, goodness, and beauty have been removed from serious discourse by many. Even the last great hope for an ideal, the continual progress of science and thereby of human society, has been widely discarded. For some Western intellectuals, the only possible response has been a nihilistic existentialism. In nihilism, Nishitani has identified the ultimate target for his philosophical venture: "Indeed, the overcoming of this pessimistic nihilism represents the single greatest issue facing philosophy and religion in our times."[26]

Each of the major religions offers a particular description of the human condition. Buddhism views the human person as ignorant of the impermanence of all things and of pervasive universal suffering. As religious philosopher, Nishitani puts his own contemporary spin on the received tradition. One must speak about eternal truths in the language of the times, and therefore we may not be surprised by Nishitani's choice of focus: the problem of contemporary nihilism. A vocabulary of negation has always been essential to Buddhist discourse. But the success of his enterprise must depend on the accuracy of his analysis of the problem. I must admit that I have found him persuasive.

According to Nishitani, the root of the problem lies in the history of Western beliefs about the source and nature of the physical world. According to traditional thought, the natural world was made and organized by its Creator. Divine order lay at the foundation of both natural and human realms. The features of the traditional picture of the cosmos as Nishitani presents them are familiar to us; they are similar to the cosmic order of the Alpha school:

> The order of the natural world and the order of the human world were united in a single great cosmic order. This meant that everything in the universe existed by virtue of being assigned a specific place in the whole.[27]

Although he doesn't refer directly to it, Nishitani is describing the great chain of being where every being had its place in a hierarchical universe which had been established by divine fiat.

The universe of beings had a divine source (*arche*) who was also the ultimate goal (*telos*). But the movement of love from God to creatures and from creatures back to God involved humankind more than any other kind of being. The cosmic order, then, had an axis that was defined by the human-divine relationship. All non-human aspects of the natural world were secondary and subordinate to the primary focus:

> Man was taken as the supreme representative of all things in the world. He stood at its center.... As a consequence, the relationship between God and man became its own axis with the world pushed out on to the periphery. Whether the world was thought of positively as the creation of God or negatively as something to be cast aside made no difference. For once this axis had been set up, it was possible to establish a relationship between God and man based exclusively on human interests, and beyond that made into something exclusively "personal."[28]

Nishitani's spatial metaphors are carefully chosen, for they permit him to characterize the breakup of traditional cosmology by the rise of modern science with devastating effectiveness. Science has both rendered the natural world as an impersonal realm and established it as the locus of reality. Since the human person and his or her world now are seen as obeying the same indifferent, quantifiable laws of nature, we can neither feel at home as we once did in a divinely governed cosmos, nor can we see ourselves transcending its iron grip on the basic facts of our existence. Nishitani's analysis is to the point.

> The world cuts across the vertical God-man axis, so to speak, and sets up an independent horizontal axis all its own. . . . The total impersonality of the world came to appear as something qualitatively different from either human or divine "personality." In effect, the world cut through the personal relationship between God and man.[29]

But the contrast between Alpha and Zero positions, which up till now have been identical, soon becomes evident. Science is not criticized by Nishitani; indeed, he believes it has performed a useful function. Instead of speaking of a sacred science which needs to regain its rightful place within the West by knocking modern science off its pinnacle, the Kyoto philosopher points to the beneficial effect of the scientific endeavor on humanity:

> Science has descended upon the world of teleology like a sword-bearing angel, or rather a new demon. For the spirit which sustained most traditional religions and philosophies, the establishment of modern science, to use familiar Zen terms, spells a sort of "destruction of the house and demolition of the hearth," that is, a fatal breakup of the "nest and cave of the spirit." This turn of events has to be accepted as it is. Like it or not, it is the historical "fate" of man, or rather, in Heidegger's term, his *Geschick*. It is the sort of fate assaulting man as a "fatal" question, so that man once more gets reduced fundamentally, in his own eyes, to a question mark.[30]

Most religions have focused on "life" as the ultimate value, either in its earthly phase or in its continuation as an "afterlife". By assuming the *sunyata* standpoint, Nishitani is able to point out the need for a focus on "death" as well, for "life" is not "life" in itself but because it is also its opposite, life's negation. All Western categories which imply a purely positive existence and are considered in some sense apart from their negations - for example, "soul," "spirit," and "personality" - have usually only been thought of from the side of life. What Nishitani believes is necessary is a double vision which sees both life and death together, a double exposure which permits a perception of both aspects of reality. He quotes from T.S. Eliot's *The Wasteland* to illustrate his meaning of double vision:

> Unreal City,

88   Landscapes of Wisdom

Under the brown fog of a winter dawn,
A crowd flowed over London Bridge, so many,
I had not thought death had undone so many.[31]

Eliot saw both living and dead streaming over the bridge in an act of what Nishitani calls "double exposure"; indeed, the Japanese philosopher makes use of imagery drawn from photographic technology to make his point:

> This kind of double exposure is true vision of reality. Reality itself requires it. In it, spirit, personality, life, and matter all come together and lose their separateness. They appear like the various tomographic plates of a single subject. Each plate belongs to reality, but the basic reality is the superimposition of all the plates into a single whole that admits to being represented layer by layer.[32]

The image of superimposed tomographic plates allows him to speak of different aspects of reality without recourse to a vertically oriented hierarchical model. There is no higher or lower arrangement, simply a layering with no mention of which comes first or last among the layers. Like the hierarchical model, however, it provides Nishitani with a way of showing how no single plate defines reality by itself. Such attempts at reduction are rejected.

Life *soku* death, then, reflects what we really experience. In the West's traditional doctrine, however, God, person, and soul have been theological and philosophical terms identified with life while matter has been frequently, although far from exclusively, associated with death. God declared the goodness of his creation, but he endowed the universe with a set of natural laws which all too often seem arbitrary and cruel, far from the actions of a loving, personal deity. It is the classic problem of theodicy: If the natural order was given by God, then there must a cold impersonal side to him which permits natural disasters. If God is not responsible for natural laws, then his power is not absolute.

Alpha and Zero agree that a significant root cause of the modern spiritual dilemma lies in the rise of the physical sciences. According to Nishitani, science reduced reality to the material level. It also supported the notion that human reason could control nature. This confidence gave modern humankind a sense of freedom, of a capacity for self-determination and authority over its fate which no longer needed the structure of a divinely ordered cosmos or even God. But Nishitani takes an additional, highly significant step in his argument. Once the ground of one's existence shifts from God to rationality, the way is open for another shift -

Zero: The Wisdom of Emptiness 89

from reason to nothingness or meaninglessness. Science has made great advances in interpreting physical reality, but more often than not, it bumps up against its limits. Confronted by an often senseless universe, human rationality glimpses an abyss beyond its illuminative powers. By speaking about a "nihility" that lies beneath our very feet, Nishitani challenges us to become aware of the fragile ground we in the West are treading:

> In our times, . . . there is a sense of the meaninglessness of a purely materialistic and mechanistic world and an accompanying awareness of the nihility that lies concealed just beneath the surface of the world.[33]

An atheism which had substituted scientific progress for God was superseded by an atheism which abandoned the scientific enterprise for an entirely different foundation - the self. The scientific revolution has not brought us the hoped-for utopian society nor has it given us anything beyond a purely materialistic view of the universe. What seems most real to us is our own being. This analysis seems to be on target. It identifies the condition of modern humanity - its focus on individual freedom and its distressing inability to define values beyond self-interest. Other concerns may arise such as family and nation, but they often are secondary. The primacy of the individual as the source of value is pervasive throughout our culture. Studies such as *Habits of the Heart*[34] have made this clear. Nishitani believes that this perspective is most forcefully articulated by Nietzsche and the existentialist form of atheism. This atheism is typified by:

> . . . an awareness of a most fundamental human crisis; a suffering that is one with existence itself; and an impassioned decision to uphold resolutely the independence of human selfhood, relying on nothing outside of the self, striving to be completely oneself, and thereby to break out of the fundamental crisis of human existence.[35]

The crisis is the awakening to the nihility underfoot, a nihility that, according to Nishitani, goes beyond the *nihilum* of the Christian doctrine of *creatio ex nihilo*. Once God is no longer the supreme source of all beings, the *nihilum* of *creatio ex nihilo* is replaced by atheism's nihility. There is no subjectivity outside the human self. When this truth is fully realized, there is a radical reordering of the world. Nishitani draws from Nietzsche on this point:

> To borrow an analogy from Nietzsche, what we are dealing with here is a

catastrophic change similar to what took place in natural history when dry lands rose up out of the sea and the many animals that once lived in the sea were forced to become inhabitants of the land. . . The shift to atheism . . . represents a change so fundamental that not only the human mode of existence but even the very visible form of the world itself must undergo a radical transformation. Individual things, for example, lose their substantiality when they are grounded on nihility and come to look instead like the waves of the sea.[36]

When the human individual becomes truly aware of the extent of this sea-change in human consciousness and has a clear awareness of the insubstantiality of the world as well as the abyss beneath the very ground of his existence, "he experiences the ecstatic transcendence of his self-being."[37]

While Nietzsche may have successfully defined the new perspective of atheism, he still had to deal with the problem of the source of self-transcendence. Nishitani considers Nietzsche's proposed solution - the "will to power" - as insufficient. For the self to become itself most truly in the face of nihility, a deeper standpoint needs to be achieved. Nishitani argues that the self achieves real existence only when it experiences the ecstatic nature of its being, an *ekstasis* that acknowledges the nihility from which it arises or "stands out" from. The only standpoint on which the human person can indeed fully realize its existence must be a standpoint where God himself is in ecstasy, where divine being emerges from an absolute nothingness that is prior to the *nihilum* of *creatio ex nihilo*. Here Nishitani reveals his profound attraction to Meister Eckhart and the Dominican mystic's notion of the Godhead. It is this central theme that gives Nishitani a way of talking about God and self in terms of a *sunyata* dialectic: both God and self are themselves because they are not themselves, i.e., grounded in the deep abyss of the Godhead. Only in relation to this abyss are they truly free.

> When something that is not God but stands by itself over against God is posited, the field to which it is appointed - that is, the ground of its existence - must be a point within God where God is not God himself. In other words, it must be a point that is not the nihility of *creatio ex nihilo* but rather something like the absolute nothingness of godhead that we saw in Eckhart. Godhead is the place within God where God is not himself. When it is said that God wills a free existence that stands over against himself, the field in which that will unfolds itself must be understood as an absolute nothingness. In this way, it becomes possible for the first time to think of creatures that are free beings, who are not God but stand by themselves over against God, as nonetheless posited within God.[38]

True freedom cannot be realized if it is established by an act of divine will; human action is severely limited if defined in terms of obedience or disobedience to God. But if both divine and human wills are grounded in the nothingness of the Godhead, freedom for God and the human person will be the result of *ekstasis*. In *ekstasis*, God and human person become what they are by paradoxically standing outside what they are.

Applying this argument to the notion of person, Nishitani offers one of his most suggestive interpretations of a central theme in Western thought. He is well aware of the term's significance: "The idea of man as person is without doubt the highest conception of man yet to appear. The same may be said of the idea of God as person."[39] When we identify one another as persons, we are pointing to what makes us most real to ourselves and to others. But for the Buddhist philosopher, personhood is not without a deeply negative dimension. Nishitani reminds us that *persona* means mask, and he uses this earlier definition to describe his meaning:

> Person is an appearance with nothing at all behind it to make an appearance. That is to say, 'nothing at all' is what is behind the person; complete nothingness . . . occupies the position behind person.[40]

This nothingness again must be understood not as something in opposition to the person-as-mask; rather it is that nothingness which makes the person appear at all. One cannot understand this intellectually, but as a profound experience - a shift or sea-change in one's self-concept from someone with an abiding center - a soul, personhood - to a person grounded in emptiness.

Nishitani speaks of a need for an existential conversion. In the conversion experience, the self which usually sees "nothing at all" (i.e., nothing of itself) beyond the circle of selfhood begins to see that there is nothing within the circle. In contemporary jargon, the self begins to see emptiness "up close and personal." According to Nishitani:

> If person be regarded as the sheer mode of self-being itself, "behind" which there is nothing, this is so because the matter is being looked at from the side of the person. In this case, nothingness only goes so far as being looked at or thought about. When the "nothing at all" opens up on the near side of the personal self, however, and is seen as the sheer self itself, then nothingness really becomes actualized in the self as the true self.[41]

Having indicated how the nihility exposed by science and modern atheism has severed the personal axis of the human-God relationship, he now has introduced a new interpretation of person which absorbs nihility rather than rejects it as an abhorrent atheism or godless existentialism. A new dynamic is established between divine, human, and natural realms which includes a transcendent dimension common to all three. Human persons and natural phenomena are both appearances deeply grounded in the *sunyata* dialectic; all beings are what they "are" because they "are not" in the field of absolute nothingness. Like his creatures, God also emerges from the nothingness that is the Godhead.

Through his reading of modern history and his rethinking of traditional categories, Nishitani reaffirms the relevance of Buddhist doctrine for today. Wisdom or *prajna* is achieved by realizing the full significance of absolute nothingness in an experience of existential conversion. In place of a hierarchical universe, Nishitani has described a world of superimposed dimensions of reality. Because science has severed the ontological axis between human and divine persons, a new relationship between beings can become evident, one that is neither vertical nor horizontal. The reality of personhood can now be applied to the entire cosmos in all its manifestations, for none of us can be enlightened until all beings are enlightened, including "grasses, trees, and lands." Grasses, trees, and lands are what they are because of the same dynamic which makes us persons: we all emerge and are grounded in the field of *Mu*. To quote from a Buddhist chant:

> When I regard the true nature of the many dharmas,
> I find them all to be sacred forms
> of the Tathagata's never-failing essence.
> Each particle of matter, each moment,
> is no other that the Tathagata's inexpressible radiance.
> With this realization, our virtuous ancestors,
> with compassionate minds and hearts,
> gave tender care to beasts and birds.[42]

With Basho, then, we visit a beautiful temple. Despite all signs of erosion, that is to say the inexorable action of natural laws, this traditional expression of the sacred has lost none of its power, and we are struck with awe. But instead of praising an eternal God who transcends all impermanent phenomena, we write a brief poem to glittering green leaves, i.e., to impermanence itself. We thereby praise the emptiness behind, below, around, and within all we see, the emptiness that makes temple, erosion, leaves, and light possible. Being and nonbeing glitter in the silence before the act of writing the poem; we are so full of the presence of absolute absence that we are ready to see the sacred manifesting itself anywhere. The inherent spirituality of the landscape becomes clearly manifest in the now-moment.

The Kalpa Fires of History

If journeys imply space, they also imply time. Dante's epic took place over a period of days, but in the background of the poem one can identify signposts of Christian salvation history: creation, fall, incarnation, and final judgment. Dante also makes frequent mention of mythical and historical events. Like Dante, Basho refers to past events both real and mythical. The haiku master's tour takes place over several months, but there is no mention of any sort of salvation history. Getting a better sense of how Nishitani defines time, history, and myth will give us a clearer understanding of the Zen Buddhist notion of a spiritual journey.

Nishitani believes that the Christian view of history raises certain difficulties. He accepts a number of arguments made by Arnold Toynbee, a cultural historian who was convinced that the encounter between Buddhism and Christianity is one of the most highly significant events of this century. According to Nishitani, Christian theology has traditionally pictured world history in terms of a drama whose main driving force is the will in both its human and divine forms. The drawback to this view of history is its human-centeredness: its focus on a people or a person as chosen or saved. In Hebrew Scriptures the chosen are the people of Israel; in Christianity, similar notions have appeared such as Cyprian's "no salvation outside the Church" and the notion of the divine elect in various Protestant denominations. Nishitani understandably rejects such exclusivism but he sees it as an inevitable outcome of the Judeo-Christian version of history. The once-and-for-all historical character of the Exodus, incarnation and redemption events easily results in intolerance. In some forms of traditional Christian doctrine, only those who believe in the historically unique reality of Jesus can be saved.

Another problem identified by Nishitani is that of eschatology. The idea that there can be an end to history, a final judgment day, can no longer be accepted seriously:

> The history of Europe records any number of cases of people who, taking the eschaton literally as historical fact, went into panic thinking the end of the world to be at hand. It is no longer possible for us today to take

seriously the notion of an end to history on the dimension of historical fact taken in such a literal sense, as something immanent in history itself.[43]

To believe in final things is to regress to mythology or to an earlier mode of consciousness which also interpreted natural disasters as acts of God's will. *Regression* is Nishitani's term and it is revealing for it emphasizes his belief that mythological consciousness has been surpassed by the historical perspective of both the Judeo-Christian tradition and modern secularism.

Mythical time reflects recurrent patterns in human lives and natural processes. Human birth-maturation-death, the coming and going of seasons, and generation-extinction in nature are cyclical events. If history is repetition, then sin or defilement is disturbing the pattern. If bad times have fallen, improper performance of rituals or neglect of duties may be the cause, for such misbehavior has departed from the expected norms of mythic culture. The ability to shape one's life through a series of choices is a far less important, if not totally absent, aspect of existence. Conformity to pattern and ritual rather than freedom provides the principle for individual and social behavior. With Judeo-Christian revelation, a more profound awareness of the individual's place in history is affirmed. History is a "once-and-for-all" affair where each freely chosen act has consequences for subsequent action. Nishitani identifies the essential elements of this sort of religious historical perspective:

> When we pursue the problem of history . . . we inevitably encounter a standpoint bound up with the problem of the self-awareness of man and along with that, the problem of sin and freedom and the historicity of time.[44]

Clearly, Nishitani values the introduction of the concept of human freedom as an advance over the more restrictive mythic framework, but we must look more closely at his discussion of the Christian version of the basic themes of history.

For Nishitani, the notion of self-conscious independence emerged with the revelation of a salvation history and all that it entailed - creation, sin, fall, redemption.

> Since salvation is seen in an historic event through which this self-centered mode of being founded on original sin is conquered, and a reconciliation with God effected, religion is ultimately constituted with human freedom and historicity as its foundations and original sin as its cornerstone.[45]

History gets its forward momentum from divine and human acts of free will: God freely created the cosmos, but human beings chose not to obey his commandments. Having committed this act of original sin, humankind experienced a fall into a life of toil, suffering, and death. However, God through his Son offered a way back and reconciliation has been achieved whenever sinners have accepted God's forgiveness through Christ. The drama that is played out on the historical stage is one where the human individual becomes disconnected from his God and focused on himself; human and divine wills diverge but are reunited historically in Christ's personhood.[46]

Nishitani's interpretation of original sin finds correlates in Kant and Kierkegaard. The Japanese philosopher wants to go beyond an understanding of evil where sin is an act we commit. The roots of sinful behavior in fact exist on a much deeper level than that of the conscious self. Nishitani refers to Kant's notion of "radical evil" which is the ultimate cause of individual sinful acts:

> When Kant said that "radical evil" precedes all temporal experiences as something having its own roots in the ground of the subject, he did not mean to imply a mere chronological precedence. . . . He meant that we become aware of evil as something residing directly beneath the present time, as something that breaks through time from within the very midst of time; that we realize evil on the transtemporal ground of the subject.[47]

He also quotes Kierkegaard on evil as something one realizes in a "moment" that is "the atom of eternity within time."[48]

For the human individual, evil is a transtemporal condition that defines one's very ground of self-being; that is the meaning of "original sin" - a sin that is a fundamental dimension of our humanness. If that is the case, what hope is there to escape its clutches? What is needed is a full acceptance of evil and an experience of despair about any remedy. This in fact, according to Nishitani, is an experience of the self's nothingness in the face of one's overwhelming sinfulness. But it is a nothingness that becomes a field wherein we encounter redemption. This redemption is impossible without a sense of utter hopelessness:

> That all hope in the power of the self has revealed itself as hopeless, that no horizon of possibility opens up before the self, amounts in fact to the complete possession of the self by sin, to its identification with sin and its becoming a member of sin. But then, in twofold *realization* of sin, we see the nothingness of the self rise up to serve as a locus . . . for receiving

redeeming love.[49]

Once again, the standpoint or field of *sunyata* emerges as the basis for Nishitani's argument. A dialectical reality clearly shapes his thought on evil, but in a way that recalls some great Christian theologians. Luther's *simul iustus et peccator*, at once justified and a sinner, comes to mind; perhaps the great Reformer's use of *simul* might be fruitfully compared with the Kyoto philosopher's *soku*.

For Nishitani, then, a true appreciation of evil does not require any historical or mythical source - some primordial act of original sin. We have also seen him reject the theme of a Final Judgment as "regressive." What remains to be examined is a beginningless/endless model of history, one which may be found in modern secular thought which rejects biblical creation and eschatology as imaginative myth-making. Yet here too, Nishitani succeeds in presenting a familiar notion from the Zen standpoint, thereby offering us a new appreciation of time.

In our everyday experience, time appears to have an infinite extension, back into the past and forward into the future. Having rejected a transtemporal divinity who is the Alpha and Omega of the temporal world, the secular perspective can only regard time as having infinite openness in both directions - past and future. However, the Japanese philosopher argues that this openness is in reality nowhere else but in the present moment:

> . . . the distinguishing feature of [secular] time, the infinity (or infinite finitude) opened up in both directions, is in reality only a projection of the transtemporal infinite openness (or emptiness) opening up directly beneath the present.[50]

The image is familiar. An emptiness we thought was beyond us is immediately underfoot, in this case the now moment. Nishitani's analysis returns again and again to spatial metaphor, even in his discussion of time.

Thanks to modern science, we also have a secular notion of time with boundaries: the Big Bang which started it all at one end and a final entropic collapse of the universe at the other. On the planetary scale, the earth may be consumed by the flaring up of a dying sun. Nishitani turns to a *koan* which depicts cosmic disaster but within the context of a spiritual dialogue:

> A monk asked Da-sui: "When the kalpa fires flare up and the great cosmos is destroyed, I wonder, will 'it' perish, or will it not perish?"

Da-sui said: "It will perish."[51]

Kalpa refers to a cycle of cosmic history, a notion which Buddhism inherited from the Hindu tradition. Within the period of a *kalpa*, the universe arises, exists, and is destroyed in a great conflagration. Nishitani points to the *koan*'s mythical source but also to its validity in modern scientific terms as a description of the end of the universe according to modern astronomy and physics. The "it" of the last line refers to - in Nishitani's words - "the refreshing inner dimension of transcendence"[52] that the monk had experienced in his meditative practice. This "inner dimension" survives any physical disaster. It identifies a level of existence that goes beyond the grasp of the world of desires and fears, often described in Buddhist scripture as a "burning house." Yet Da-sui responded bluntly: "It will perish." The *koan* goes on to drive the point home:

> The monk said: "Then will it be gone with the other?"
> [The word *other* used by the monk here means the universe in the cosmic fire.]
> Da-sui said: "It will be gone with the other."[53]

Both physical universe and spiritual inwardness are negated in the final conflagration. For the Zen master, the *kalpa* fire is none other than the nothingness, the "bottomless death" that lies beneath each present moment. No enlightenment experience can be had without going through the Great Death of the ego-self, and the *kalpa* fire myth is an image expressing this necessary stage of the spiritual journey. Nishitani calls this a "Buddhist demythologization"[54] which has peeled away the mythical layer of cosmic cycles to reveal the true existential message. Ultimately the *koan* is pointing to a deeper finality: that of the Now which includes life and death, life *soku* death.

Nishitani has been drawn to this *koan* in part because of its resonance with modern scientific theories. Science, like myth, provides notions that point beyond themselves to a greater truth. In astronomy and physics, ideas of dying suns, a collapsing universe, or of the cold emptiness of space all indicate the pervasiveness of life-denying conditions beyond our planet. But, as Nishitani argues, "the essence of science is not scientific."[55] This may seem to be a cryptic remark, but Nishitani wants to show how science has a greater value than modern scientists may suspect. The physicist may conduct experiments which verify a particular theorem, but for the Zen philosopher, his work is but another illustration of the impersonal laws governing phenomena, or of the limits of life in an overwhelmingly lifeless universe. Thus, the essence of science is ultimately existential because it can orient us toward true spiritual wisdom.

The *kalpa* fire *koan* enables Nishitani to explain how myth and science can have important roles in the spiritual quest. Once their essence is grasped, they can serve to point to our true condition in the present moment:

> In the religiosity of Zen Buddhism, demythologization of the mythical and existentialization of the scientific belong to one and the same process. Religious existence in the Great Death makes possible at once the demythologizing of eschatology and the existentializing of the scientific actuality of the cosmos.[56]

Myth and science, properly interpreted, can speak to us about our true spiritual condition, that we stand on a great emptiness. At the same time, Nishitani reminds us that within this dialectical perspective, "the sword that kills is here at the same time a sword that gives life."[57] And not only life to the Zen practitioner, but to all of the universe. When seen from the other side of the all-extinguishing *kalpa* flames, i.e., the perspective beyond the Great Death, all phenomena are viewed in their utter *suchness*, as they truly are, like Basho's glittering green leaves, transient but radiant in their very impermanence.

The Journey to Nowhere

Perhaps there is a lingering thought on the part of the reader that much of what has been said is really a form of stoicism, a resignation in the face of inescapable suffering and death. Or that the *sunyata* doctrine is in fact extremely pessimistic despite its claims to the contrary.

The silence of a zendo (a Zen meditation hall) filled with meditators is a unique environment. It is a silence that, during a seven day *sesshin* or retreat, deepens to a clarity I have not felt elsewhere. Each buzzing fly, every cough, the tiniest shift of light is a felt experience. But the clearing of the senses only reflects a more inclusive emptying of the mind. This process would be impossible without the chanting of sutras, the listening to daily lectures by the Zen *roshi* or teacher, the extraordinary process of having a silent meal together, the daily assignment of cleaning the monastery, as well as the basic activity of sitting on circular black cushions and, moment-to-moment, trying to focus on one's breath, or concentrating on a Zen teaching usually expressed in a *koan*. By the end

Zero: The Wisdom of Emptiness

of the week, one is literally riding the cushion to a new level of awareness. One stands up after the final sitting and feels he or she is walking away with a gift, a new, revitalized sense of life that has emerged from all the deaths great and small that have occurred that week on the cushion. Life is indeed in dialectical relationship with death, form deeply connected with emptiness. According to the *Heart Sutra* which is chanted every day during the *sesshin*:

> Form is no other than *sunyata*,
> *Sunyata* is no other than form.
> Form is exactly *sunyata*,
> *Sunyata* is exactly form.[58]

One can't help but be grateful. The everyday world has been renewed and one knows that a spiritual path does exist in the modern world, one that is real, present, and involved with other human beings. The community one discovers has less to do with socializing and more with mutual support during an arduous spiritual discipline. Indeed, one says absolutely nothing to the persons who sit to the right and left, and yet a special kind of bond develops. Each member of the *sangha* or community has the potential to be a Bodhisattva, a compassionate savior figure, to others in the *zendo* and to the rest of the cosmos. Daily we chant:

> May we extend this mind over the whole universe
> So that we and all beings together
> May attain maturity in Buddha's Wisdom.[59]

This, of course, is the ideal, but the process has had a way of working for me, and in my experience it has had an immense drawing power for those who make a commitment to try it.

Zazen or sitting meditation can be practiced in one's home, too, of course, and the Zen tradition has made much of its teaching that enlightenment can happen anywhere. But the tradition also has plenty of examples of Zen monks retreating from cities and busy temples to mountain or forest retreats. Withdrawal has been an important part of following the path. Sitting in a *zendo* in the middle of Manhattan was my introduction to group *zazen* but *sesshins* in the monastery in the Catskills provided some of my most profound experiences.

Zen practice can help one gain a more vibrant feeling for the earth. Japan's greatest nature poet was also a Zen disciple. That the spiritual journey can follow a map deeply embedded in nature is a welcome message for those who are hungering for an ecologically sensitive religious life. On this point, the contrast between Alpha and Zero is quite sharp. Dante needed to leave the earth's surface to find the source of truth and being. Basho "trod the earth firmly" in a manner that may seem more real to the modern reader. And the earth he saw is more recognizable in its naturalness. Trees and crickets are not symbols pointing to a higher reality but are what they are on the field of emptiness.

Having said this, however, some questions remain. While Abe and Nishitani provide a way of appreciating modern science, of interpreting the powerful effect science has had on the modern mind and of appropriating science for spirituality, the Japanese philosophers do not, I think, have a full grasp of the powerful thrust of the scientific enterprise. They do not adopt the position of the Alpha school which seems to wish that modern science would disappear - or at least shrink to a more suitable size in relation to a *scientia sacra*. The Japanese philosophers assign a more important role to science. But they do not explain why it needs to exist at all. The brilliance of their teaching lies in the use they make of science to elucidate the *sunyata* doctrine. The final result, however, is one which does more justice to the timeless ground of absolute nothingness than it does to the urgent drive behind scientific research.

A second problem concerns the Kyoto views about history. The Kyoto philosophers are always careful to argue how each moment in its current fullness is, thanks to *sunyata*, truly real as a moment and not some pale reflection of eternity. Within this perspective, they offer their powerful critique of history which, by emphasizing the primacy of the now moment, reveals their predilection for a non-directional vision of time. Jan Van Bragt has described his reaction to Nishitani's analysis of history: "Our view of history seems to be systematically dismantled before our very eyes, stone by stone. . . the whole construction is reduced to so much rubble."[60] However, the Judeo-Christian tradition cannot easily dispense with salvation history, nor do I think that the modern West can reject secular forms of history. The challenge has been to see how a spiritual understanding of history and time can emerge today. Can a spiritual path be traced which is as profoundly rooted in the earth as the travel diaries of Basho, but which does not dispense with the historical perspective?

Basho's journey takes place within a Buddhist temporal framework, one of arrivals and departures of humans, seasons, the whole network of cosmic beings. In an impermanent world, things arise and fade away. People are constantly traveling through life. Like Basho we are blown about by the autumn wind. One thinks of the importance of the seasons and of traditional customs such as the singing of rice-planting songs. The ideal life is lived close to nature and its cycles. Basho's favorite scenes in *Oku no Hosomichi* include scattered cottages near the ocean. The one occasion when he encounters a more industrial town, his accidental visit to Ishinomaki, he is put off by its crowdedness, smoky kilns, and lack of hospitality. It is interesting to note that, according to scholarship, this episode has been reworked by Basho. Sora's diary reports that the two visited Ishinomaki by invitation, while Basho's narrative would have us believe that the two stumbled upon the town after having lost their way. Basho's clear preference was for isolated villages, lonely hermitages, or scenery utterly lacking in human presence. It is harder to feel the silent oneness of the earth if one is immersed in the bustle of industry and commerce. While he may have actually experienced hospitality in Ishinomaki, he evidently did not feel at home.[61]

Zen as explicated by the Kyoto school of wisdom has much to offer in our search for a spiritual landscape. Its version of a path which replaces a hierarchy of being with a blending of levels of reality (Nishitani's metaphor of tomographic plates is especially successful on this point) is compelling and may speak in important ways to a society uncomfortable with traditional hierarchical imagery. The movement of the journey is over the surface of the earth. Its practice is the silent contemplation of our place in the cosmos and our intimate relationship with all beings. Modern attitudes which have led to a growing imbalance between human consumption and natural resources can be changed by a spirituality which teaches us how to live more simply and be more sensitive toward our environment. Learning to tread more firmly may also mean, paradoxically, learning to tread more lightly. There is an emptiness beneath our feet that, if we become sensitive enough to feel it, will resound with the fullness of the wondrous being of all created beings.

But we cannot return to a golden age of isolated villages. Our contemporary spirituality will have to deal more directly with the problems of science, religion, and history. While science can be viewed as a death-dealing sword, it is also, as Nishitani reminds us, a sword of life. His meaning is, of course, a life dialectically rooted in death from the *sunyata* standpoint. But the emptiness doctrine does not illuminate how science can and should be reinterpreted and redirected into ways that will preserve the planet and improve people's lives

Some pages ago, we referred to Aitken roshi's commentary on Basho's haiku:

Summer grasses!
The imprint of dreams
Of warriors.

Grasses and social upheaval seemed part of a single reality, a oneness that was as real as the summer heat and as dream-like as Basho's imagination of the warriors' agony in defeat. Such a vision appears to require withdrawal into the kind of isolation favored by Basho in order to gain insights into the unity of existence beyond the chaos of history. Aitken once disclosed his fears of nuclear holocaust to another Zen practitioner. The latter's response was: "Well, of course the rings of Saturn must have come from a great explosion." Grasses, dying warriors, nuclear war, cosmic explosions, all form part of a whole manifesting their ground of absolute nothingness. Aitken did not disagree, but he felt a commitment to improve the situation. His comment on his friend's response was: "I acknowledge this cosmic view, as I resist the construction of the Trident nuclear submarine."[62]

A science that can develop nuclear power and a technology that can threaten the earth's ecosystems must both be radically reoriented. The Zero school's approach may be fruitful in the ways we have mentioned, but it falls short in harnessing the directionless energy unleashed by the scientific enterprise. If nature is to provide the landscape for the spiritual journey to wisdom, then any forces which threaten to disfigure that landscape must be dealt with or the landscape will disappear. And to accept this disappearance passively as part of a cycle of generation and extinction cannot - at least from a Westerner's point of view - be an element of our spirituality today.

Perhaps Nishitani's view that history is an incessant becoming, a drama being played out by an insatiable human will, is a necessary starting point for further reflection. On a more objective level, his notion of the will also seems to capture what I have termed the endless thrust of modern science to challenge itself constantly, to continue its search for the ultimate laws governing physical phenomena. The task for us, then, is to see how the will in either its humanly subjective, historic forms or its objective scientific version can have an important role in spirituality. Human will can and does lead to evil and sin, just as the scientific enterprise has resulted in the unleashing of destructive powers and the gradual erosion of natural resources. Then how may the human will and scientific pursuits be effectively integrated into a vision of wholeness?

In keeping with our principle of withholding final judgment about any particular school of wisdom, let us simply enter into the heart of the Zero approach, appreciating and expressing its most valuable insights. The images of Basho's journey must enter into our bones, perhaps as weary as his from our own journeys. The insights of the Zen tradition have shown us that wisdom's landscape can be the earth itself, and this is a great gift. If we go beyond Basho and the Kyoto school, it is because we want to incorporate history and science more profoundly into our spirituality. In order to do so, we must return to the Western world and a third school of thought.

Notes

1. I am following the Japanese custom of placing the last name first.
2. Keiji Nishitani, *Religion and Nothingness* (Berkeley: University of California Press, 1982).
3. Masao Abe, *Zen and Western Thought* (Honolulu: University of Hawaii Press, 1985). This has been followed by two additional collections: *Buddhism and Interfaith Dialogue : Part One of a Two-volume Sequel to Zen and Western Thought* (Honolulu: University of Hawaii Press, 1995) and *Zen and Comparative Studies : Part Two of a Two-volume Sequel to Zen and Western Thought* (Honolulu: University of Hawaii Press, 1997).
4. In *The Emptying God: A Buddhist-Jewish-Christian Conversation*, ed. John B. Cobb, Jr. and Christopher Ives (Maryknoll, N.Y.: Orbis Books, 1990).
5. The Lesser Vehicle being Hinayana Buddhism, the other great division within Buddhism: Hinayana is the Mahayanist name for Theravada, the way of the elders, the name preferred by followers of that segment of the Buddhist world.
6. Masao Abe, *Zen and Western Thought*, 121; he is quoting Paul Tillich, *Systematic Theology*, vol. 1 (Chicago: University of Chicago Press, 1951), 189; *The Courage to Be* (New Haven: Yale University Press, 1957), 34, 40.
7. Abe, *Zen and Western Thought*, 129.
8. Ibid., 132.
9. Ibid.
10. Nishida Kitaro, quoted in Nishitani, *Religion and Nothingness*, p. xxx.
11. See Jan Van Bragt, "Translator's Introduction," in Nishitani, *Religion and Nothingness*, xxx.
12. Ibid., xxxi.
13. Nishitani, *Religion and Nothingness*, 146.
14. Alan of Lille, *Regulae theologicae*, reg. 7.
15. Masao Abe, "Man and Nature in Christianity and Buddhism," in *The Buddha Eye: An Anthology of the Kyoto School*, ed. Frederick Franck (New York: Crossroad, 1982), 150-51.
16. Buddhist saying quoted in Abe, "Man and Nature," 151.
17. Ibid., 152.
18. Ibid., 154.

19. Abe, *Zen and Western Thought*, 15.
20. Some of the more recent translations of Dogen's works include: *Dogen's Pure Standards for the Zen Community: a Translation of the Eihei Shingi*, trans. Taigen Daniel Leighton and Shohaku Okumura; ed. Taigen Daniel Leighton (Albany, NY: State University of New York Press, 1996); *Shobogenzo, Zen Essays*, trans. Thomas Cleary (Honolulu: University of Hawaii Press, 1986); *Moon in a Dewdrop / Writings of Zen Master Dogen*, ed. Kazuaki Tanahashi ; trans. Robert Aitken, et al. (San Francisco: North Point Press, 1985).
21. Abe, *Zen and Western Thought*, 27.
22. Ibid.
23. Ibid., 44.
24. Ibid., 46.
25. Nishitani, *Religion and Nothingness*, 46.
26. Ibid., 47.
27. Ibid.
28. Ibid., 49.
29. Ibid., 50.
30. Keiji Nishitani, "Science and Zen," in *The Buddha Eye*, 118.
31. T.S. Eliot, "The Wasteland," quoted in Nishitani, *Religion and Nothingness*, 51.
32. Nishitani, *Religion and Nothingness*, 52.
33. Ibid., 54.
34. Robert N. Bellah, et al., *Habits of the Heart: Individualism and Commitment in American Life* (Berkeley: University of California Press, 1985).
35. Nishitani, *Religion and Nothingness.*, 55.
36. Ibid.
37. Ibid., 57.
38. Ibid. 67.
39. Ibid., 69.
40. Ibid., 70.
41. Ibid., 70-71.
42. "Torei Zenji: Bodhisattva's Vow," in Robert Aitken, *Encouraging Words: Zen Buddhist Teachings for Western Students* (New York: Pantheon Books, 1993), 176. "Dharmas" in this context means "phenomena"; "Tathagata" means "one who has passed over into enlightenment" and has been used as a name for Gautama Buddha.
43. Ibid., 209.
44. Ibid., 207.
45. Ibid.
46. Nishitani does not explore the ways in which elements of mythic time are retained in cultures living in historic time.
47. Ibid., 22.
48. Ibid.
49. Ibid., 25.
50. Ibid., 228.

51. Nishitani, "Science and Zen," 120.
52. Ibid.
53. Ibid., 121.
54. Ibid.
55. Ibid., 118.
56. Ibid., 123.
57. Ibid.
58. *Sutra Book* (New York: Zen Studies Society, 1978), 4.
59. Ibid., 17. From the "Bodhisattva's Vow" by Torei Enji Zenji.
60. Van Bragt, "Translator's Introduction," xxxviii-xxxix.
61. See Keene, 315, on Basho's apparent decision to change the facts of his visit. Keene describes Sora as "ever-truthful."
62. Aitken, 152.

Chapter 5

Omega: Discovering the Human Adventure

The Approach

Dante's journey took him from the dark wood of his despair to the brilliance of the Empyrean. Charting a path that had cosmic and moral dimensions, it was a poetic rendering of a medieval Christian ascent of the soul to God. But in the depths of hell we found an example of a very different kind of journey narrative, one of exploration and restless wandering: the account of Ulysses. Dante's ability to render this story so vividly owes much to his poetic skill, and one wonders if there wasn't something in Dante of the Ulyssean spirit and the desire to wander beyond the limits of the known world. But while Dante never traveled beyond known borders, his Ulysses prefigured the great explorers of the next four centuries.

Living before the age of exploration, the Florentine poet stood on the threshold of a great change in Western views about the earth and the universe. Basho was a restless wanderer, too, and we have seen how landscape and spiritual life could be deeply intertwined in the haiku poet's travels. Although parts of the journey took him through dangerous country, he was acquainting himself with a largely known geography. But when Dante's Ulysses ventured forth, he sailed into the unknown (to the West, of course), as did many Western sailors of the 15th and 16th centuries.

The Columbian era was a watershed in European intellectual history. Paralleled by startling discoveries in the sciences, the travels of the explorers greatly expanded contemporary understanding of the world. Advances in human knowledge were accompanied by new ways of learning. According to Anthony Grafton, "The world was no longer accessible only through learned books in Latin, it could be known directly."[1]

A powerful drive had been awakened in Western society to break out of the long-accepted vision of the cosmos and see the world from a completely new perspective. Of course, a variety of motives could be attributed to the explorers and their patrons for initiating the great ventures, but a fundamental result was an intellectual revolution. For example, when the Jesuit José de Acosta, an early historian of the New World, sailed across the equator, he was astonished at having an experience directly contradicting the Great Philosopher:

> What could I do then but laugh at Aristotle's *Meteorology* and his philosophy? For in that place and that season, where everything, by his rules, should have been scorched by the heat, I and my companions were cold.[2]

In this third section, we shall see that the spiritual path to wisdom I have named Omega is the depth dimension of this new Western orientation toward the earth and heavens. Instead of leaving the earth behind in a Neoplatonic ascent to God, the follower of the Omega approach accepts nature as an integral part of the journey and seeks not only to contemplate but also to experience the interrelationship of all life which is the living basis of Omega wisdom. The explorers not only redrew the physical map. They aroused an activist spirit that kept pushing the boundaries of the known. In so doing, creativity became a significant spiritual value, both the creativity of nature and of humankind. We are part of a vast, evolving cosmos, a community of beings participating in an ongoing act of creation. Like Acosta, we often find past knowledge and beliefs to be inadequate for explaining today's reality. By developing new worldviews, we increase the circle of our light further and further into the darkness of our ignorance, or at least that is our hope.

For our literary text, I have chosen Goethe's *Faust*. The philosopher George Santayana numbered Goethe as one of the three major philosophical poets of the Western world (his other two choices were Lucretius and Dante).[3] The psychologist Rollo May has characterized Goethe's *Faust* as "a poignant and powerful expression of the myth of our modern age"[4] and attributed to Goethe's writing "an element of eternity, a sense of the true use of myth."[5] Like Dante's Ulysses, Faust seeks an adventurous life beyond the boundaries of the familiar world. Unlike Dante's *Commedia* or Basho's travel diary, Goethe's drama cannot be easily linked to an established tradition of spirituality and/or metaphysics. In part, this is because Omega is just beginning to define itself. In outlining some basic notions of Omega wisdom, I will draw on the writings of the process school of thought which arose during the course of this century. Although Goethe's writings precede process thought by over 100 years and therefore cannot have been shaped by it in the same way Neoplatonism influenced Dante or Zen Buddhism influenced Basho, Goethe's vision shares some of the more significant perspectives of the process school.

As a verse play, *Faust* was a life long project. Having begun it as a young man, Goethe worked on the drama intermittently and didn't complete it until nearly sixty years later within months of his death. Its composition thus spans a remarkable life, one that embraced both the passions of the romantic movement and the cooler perspectives of neoclassicism. Goethe was a great lover of nature but also of technology and science. A model steam engine sat on his desk, and of the 143 volumes of his collected works in the Weimar edition, fourteen are devoted to essays on topics in the natural sciences.

In choosing the Faust legend for the subject of a major work, Goethe was contributing to an existing body of literature based on the exploits of a notorious magus and necromancer in early sixteenth century Germany. Rollo May believes that, as a myth, the Faust story fits "the deep psychological and spiritual needs of Europeans in the radical transition from the Middle Ages to the Renaissance and Reformation."[6] During this transitional period when new notions of individual freedom and spirituality were emerging, the Faust legend portrayed a fiercely independent figure who paid for his freedom with eternal damnation. Faust's chicanery and immoral behavior deserved damnation, but in a deeper sense, the Faust story expressed the European soul's struggle with its own sense of guilt over newly found attitudes toward church and the natural world. If Western society had discovered within itself a new urge toward activism, if it had realized a new sense of will in its desire to explore the natural world and to question traditional authority, then these developments were accompanied by an inchoate dread that holy boundaries were being transgressed and that the sacred aspects of life and society were being superseded by profane pursuits.

Goethe began his great project during the Enlightenment period and completed it in a time of great industrial and scientific progress. As we shall see, Goethe's genius produced a work that contained elements of the Faustian morality tale of damnation and the West's growing confidence in the possibilities of human achievement, but in its final form *Faust* offers a vision that transcends any simplistic understanding of either morality or progress.

"From Heaven through the World to Hell"[7]

The play's Prologue begins with the archangels portraying the world as full of activity:

> The earth's resplendence spins and ranges
> Past understanding swift in flight,
> And paradisiac lucence changes
> With awe-inspiring depths of night;
> The ocean's foaming seas runs shoreward,
> On rocky depths rebound and rear,
> And rock and ocean hurtle forward,
> Sped by the ever-hurrying sphere.
> (ll. 251-258)

In stark contrast to the cosmic grandeur of the angelic hymns, the tone of Mephistopheles' first speech is sarcastic. The object of his sneering comments is humanity, whose powers of reason don't keep it from becoming "more bestial than any beast" (l. 286). Mephistopheles is secretly proud of his access to God:

> MEPHISTOPHELES [alone]. At times I don't mind seeing the old gent,
> And try to keep relations smooth and level.
> Say what you like, it's quite a compliment:
> A swell like him so man-to-man with the Devil!
> (ll. 350-353)

while God admits to tolerating the dark spirit's presence:

> THE LORD. Then, too, enjoy free visitation;
> I never did abominate your kind.
> Of all the spirits of negation
> The rogue has been least onerous to my mind.
> (11. 337-339)

More than just being tolerant, God seems to be in a playful mood, because he makes the famous wager with the Devil. If Mephistopheles can lead Faust astray from his primal source (German: *Urquell*), then the good doctor will be forever under Mephistopheles' charge, that is to say damned to hell. In making the bet, God declares the fact of human goodness despite all evidence to the contrary: "A worthy soul through the dark urge within it / Is well aware of the right way" (ll. 328-329).[8] Goethe's humanism shines forth clearly here.

The first act opens with Faust seated in his study, described as "a narrow, high-vaulted Gothic chamber." It is nighttime, and Faust is bemoaning the uselessness of all his academic endeavors:

> I have pursued, alas, philosophy,
> Jurisprudence, and medicine,
> And, help me God, theology,
> With fervent zeal through thick and thin.
> And here, poor fool, I stand once more,
> No wiser than I was before.
> (ll. 354-359)

Clearly the glories of the past have nothing to offer Faust, and in turn he has nothing to offer anyone else as a teacher. In an effort to plumb the inner workings of the universe, he has turned away from the traditional scholarly disciplines in order to study magic. Moreover, he has invoked nature itself to clear him of the musty environment that has become his world. But it is his study of Renaissance symbolism and texts that leads Faust to a quest for new wisdom.

First, in examining a work by Nostradamus (1503-1566), Faust comes upon the sign of the Macrocosm. He perceives it as an expression of how all things are intimately related and pervaded by spiritual energies. In a few poetic lines, Goethe articulates a powerful vision of the cosmos, but it is rejected as show, a play, "ein Schauspiel nur!" (l. 454). The meaning of the macrocosmic sign is realized through contemplation of its mystery, but its vision of cosmic harmony is merely an intellectual exercise.

He then turns to the sign of the *Erdgeist* or Earth Spirit, a symbolic figure inspired perhaps by Paracelsus and/or Giordano Bruno, also both Renaissance writers.[9] The Earth Spirit represents a far from harmonious universe. When Faust summons it to reveal itself, the Spirit appears in a flame with a terrible face. Despite its horrible aspect, Faust engages it in dialogue and claims equality with its awesome reality, but the *Erdgeist* rejects him.[10] Faust is now on the verge of making a passionate commitment to the *via activa*, an active life that would be tumultuous, turbulent, and beyond good and evil like the Earth Spirit (read Nature) itself. In heeding the push of his dark urge ("dunklen Drange" - l. 328), he requires the companionship of a spirit who could help him, or so the *Erdgeist* suggests before it disappears.

Faust next has a near death and resurrection experience. Despairing at the *Erdgeist*'s rejection, he now views himself and humanity quite low on the scale of beings. Where once human imagination was expansive enough to touch the Eternal, it now was hampered by Care or Anxiety, *Sorge*, which is described by Faust as nesting secretly in the heart, causing unrest and pain in whatever life may bring. Indeed, Faust has as low an opinion of his own worth as Mephisto's views of humanity expressed in the "Prologue in Heaven":

> (FAUST.) Not like the gods am I - profoundly it is rued!
> I'm of the earthworm's dust-engendered brood,
> Which, blindly burrowing, by dust is fed,
> And crushed and buried by the wanderer's tread.
> (ll. 652-655)

Depressed by the failure of his scholarly and scientific efforts to gain wisdom and to unveil Nature's secrets, Faust impulsively decides to end his life. But in one of the most dramatic moments of the play, his suicide attempt is halted by the sound of bells and a chorus singing "Christ is arisen!" It is Easter morning, and the festive celebration outside his abode revives Faust's childhood memories of spiritual joy in prayer but also of happy times spent running through forests and meadows as a youth. The chorus continues its song, and Faust gladly welcomes its heavenly tones (Himmelstone), for in his words, it has restored him to earth ("die Erde hat mich wieder!" - l. 784).

After joining the crowds as they issue out of the city gate, Faust and Wagner, his academic assistant, walk through the countryside. Faust praises the beauties of nature and the power of spring to revive the human spirit, but in a subsequent passage, he confesses to a deep tension within himself:

> Two souls, alas, are dwelling in my breast,
> And either would be severed from its brother;
> The one holds fast with joyous earthy lust
> Onto the world of man with organs clinging;
> The other soars impassioned from the dust,
> To realms of lofty forebears winging.
> (ll. 1112-1117)

The Easter event has reconnected Faust with the transcendent spirituality of his upbringing but also with his love of the natural world. However, he cannot subordinate his earthiness to a supernatural faith. Rather, he invokes the spiritual realm to help him realize a new, more vivid life. He wishes for a magic cape (*"Zaubermantel"*) so that he might soar to new horizons. As if in response, a spirit, Mephisto, appears in the shape of a black poodle.

The play's basic pattern emerges: Faust will ask for new experience, a new life, and he will invariably get involved in a situation full of promise and hardship, joy and tragedy, in short, life itself lived to its fullest measure. Time after time, Faust will not recognize all the aspects of a situation until it has been played out, just as he only dimly suspects the poodle's true nature. In heeding the promptings of his "darkest urge" and rejecting the confines of his study, Faust goes forth to embrace life to its limits in death.

Mephisto's first appearance reveals him as a shape-shifter who transmutes through several animal forms.[11] At first a poodle, he grows into a hippopotamus, and then an elephant before manifesting himself in human form. Clearly, Faust has encountered a formidable being who is able to give him more than just a magic cape. But before Mephisto manifests himself, Faust engages in some scriptural translation. He turns to the New Testament because of a need to find some new inspiration. The joyous energy of his Easter walk has dissipated like a stream run dry. The passage he chooses is the first verse of John's Gospel. The traditional translation which reads "In the beginning was the Word" does not satisfy Faust and he struggles to retranslate Logos with Meaning (*Sinn*), then with Force (*Kraft*). He finally settles on Act or Deed (*Tat*). Immediately after uttering his preferred version of the verse, he becomes irritated by the poodle's barking, and tries to drive him out. The parallel is delicious. As Faust's reading of Logos moves from intellectual Word to volitional Act, so his intellectual preoccupations give way to life and its irritations.

In the ensuing dialogue, Mephisto declares himself to be the spirit of eternal denial whose element is evil, but whose evil activity never succeeded in prevailing over the world:

FAUST. Now I perceive your worthy role!
Unable to destroy on the scale of the whole,
You now attempt it in the little way.
MEPHISTOPHELES. It does not come to much, I'm bound to say.
What bids defiance to the Naught,
The clumsy lumber of the Aught,
Endeavor what I could against it
I never have discountenanced it . . .
                    (ll. 1359-1366)

Mephistopheles leaves but soon returns, but Faust who has woken from his dream is once again in despair. Neither the life-saving grace of the Easter morning which interrupted his suicide attempt, nor the wonderful dream-song of the spirits are enough. His days are filled with a bitterness that crushes his creative impulse. Like Dante's journey which could be described as beginning with a poetic description of a mid-life crisis, Faust's life story has reached a critical mid-point: "I am too old to be content with play,/Too young to be without desire" (ll. 1546-1547). Earlier in the play, Faust had described his agony in terms of the tension between two souls within himself, one clinging to the earth, the other soaring to heaven. This time his despair is portrayed in terms of an indwelling God whose sphere of action is severely limited:

> The Lord within my bosom bowered
> Can stir me to the inmost kernel;
> The One past all my powers empowered,
> He cannot alter anything external.
> (ll. 1566-69)

A God who sustains one's inner life but cannot enable one to realize one's dreams in reality is, for Faust, an insufficient God. Once again, Faust considers death as preferable to life: "Existence seems a burden to detest, / Death to be wished for, life a hateful jest" (ll. 1570-71).

Faust hurls a series of curses on a number of aspects of human existence which culminates in his railing at the spiritual virtues of faith, hope, and patience. Mephistopheles responds by offering to be Faust's companion and servant, someone who will enable Faust to accomplish his desires. Faust doubts the real worth of anything Mephistopheles has to offer, but the two wager on whether Faust will ever be content with anything he experiences. If Faust loses, Mephisto will claim his soul at the moment of his death. Thus, Goethe's version of the Faust story hinges not on a pact but a bet, and it's an easy bet for Faust to make, as he seems not to care about the afterlife at all:

> Beyond to me makes little matter;
> If once this earthly world you shatter,
> The next may rise when this has passed.
> It is from out this earth my pleasures spring,
> It is this sun shines on my suffering;
> (ll. 1660-1664)

The terms of the wager offer Faust a new life. It is an opportunity for Faust to live purely on the level of action, a state of heeding his deepest desires, or being true to his darkest urge. Any moment ("Augenblick") or perception of fulfillment would be his downfall. Faust would lose his soul only if he ever felt any attachment to pleasurable experiences. It seems a terrible price to pay, but Faust would accept it fully.

> If the swift moment I entreat:
> Tarry a while! You are so fair!
> Then forge the shackles to my feet,
> Then I will gladly perish there!
> (ll. 1699-1702)

By following his deepest passions, the whole range of human experience and feeling may become his own. This openness could destroy Faust as well, but he would die fully human and fulfilled.

> Henceforth my soul, for knowledge sick no more,
> Against no kind of suffering shall be cautioned,
> And what to all of mankind is apportioned
> I mean to savor in my own self's core,
> Grasp with my mind both highest and most low,
> Weigh down my spirit with their weal and woe,
> And thus my selfhood to their own distend,
> And be, as they are, shattered in the end.
> (ll. 1768-75)

The path of scholarly knowledge has proven fruitless. The possibility of a mystical experience of God does not even occur to him. His claim of equality with the Earth Spirit has been rebuffed. Nature's secrets remain shrouded in mystery. Faust's one hope for realizing his life fully is identifying with humankind. His inner path is to pursue his passions, a pursuit which on the level of outer behavior manifests itself as constant activity: "Man's active only when he's never at ease" ("Nur rastlos betätigt sich der Mann") (l. 1759). He realizes that the outcome of this path will be eventual ruin, but the way there, a life of the greatest joys and sorrows, will be its own reward. The two then begin their adventures together by flying off on Mephistopheles' mantle.

The rest of the play's first part is concerned with Faust's affair with Gretchen, an innocent young woman who is seduced by his charms (enhanced with Mephistopheles' assistance). The outcome of the affair is tragic. After Faust succeeds in winning Gretchen's love, he leaves her, unaware that he has made her pregnant. In despair over her lover's absence, Gretchen commits infanticide, and Faust kills Gretchen's brother in a sword fight (Mephisto guides the blade). The last scene in Part One takes place in the dungeon where she awaits execution. Faust appears and with Mephistopheles' help tries to rescue her, but she refuses to leave because she is overcome with the burden of her guilt and utterly without hope. She still loves Faust deeply and urges him to escape without her. Mephisto saves Faust, leaving Gretchen to die, but not before a heavenly voice proclaims her salvation. She also tells Faust that they will meet again, a prophecy of the play's final scene. Throughout the dungeon episode, Faust is in absolute agony. It is clearly the worst moment of his life. But it is a fulfillment of his wish to take on the entirety of human experience and this time it is humanity at its lowest. He wails "The woe of all mankind rends me apart" (l. 4406).

The tragedy's second part begins with Faust asleep in a wooded valley. While he sleeps, spirits undertake the task of cleansing Faust of his horrible memories, thereby personifying the restorative powers of nature. When he wakes, he responds immediately to the wondrous effect of the dawn upon the earth, clearly a parallel to his own sense of refreshment and renewal. The monologue which follows is one of the most famous of the play. It is a splendid example of Goethe's poetic gift for fusing imagery and ideas. Noting the quickening power of heavenly light (actually heaven's clarity - *Himmelsklarheit*) penetrating the shadowy depths of the landscape, he sees the forest waken and its very colors become alive. The German is almost untranslatable: "Auch Farb' an Farbe klart sich los vom Grunde" (l. 4692), literally "color upon color clears or clarifies itself from the ground" where *klaren* echoes *Himmelsklarheit,* heaven's clarity.

Faust next calls attention to the mountain peaks where the bright early morning sunlight begins its descent in successive steps down to the observer. But the light dazzles him, and he must turn away. Faust compares the experience to the highest human aspiration which, at the point of apparent attainment of its goal, reels back stunned by an overflow of fire. Instead of lighting a torch (fulfilling our loftiest dream), we are immersed in an ocean of flames. Faust wonders if it is a sea of love or hate, but because it is both extremely painful and pleasurable, it is unbearable and thus we turn back to the earth and hide ourselves in its most youthful veil: *im jugendlichsten Schleier.* Why *most* youthful? The image which follows suggests a possible explanation.

Faust has turned his gaze from the blinding sun to a waterfall which as it tumbles down seems to multiply into a growing number of streams.

His joy grows with the increase of falls within falls, and it leads to his final insight when he observes how the falling water's spray forms a rainbow, a symbol of the nature of human life in all of its creative brilliance and evanescence:

> But in what splendor from this storm evolving,
> Vaults up the shimmering arc, in variance lasting,
> Now purely limned and now in air dissolving,
> A cooling fragrance all about it casting.
> This mirrors all aspiring human action.
> On this your mind for clearer insight fasten:
> That life is ours by colorful refraction.
> (ll. 4721-4727)

Earth's "most youthful veil" here receives both natural and human examples: the evanescent spray of the waterfall and the results of human striving. Following the logic of the image, both rise out of tumult, the storm of the tumbling streams and the inescapable turmoil of human life. But the outcome is a rainbow, a moment of "lasting variance," Arndt's translation of *Wechseldauer*. Another translator renders it as "changing permanence."[12] And only when we perceive that color, i.e., the beauty of human striving in all of its newness, youthfulness, and evanescence, are we most fully alive.

Hamlin points out parallels between this passage and Dante's *Commedia*.[13] As if to invite comparison, Goethe employs *terza rima*, the meter of the Italian master's epic. Like Dante in the poem's opening canto, Faust cannot approach the sun; its brightness keeps him from even looking at it. But while Dante was lost in a threatening wilderness, Faust finds a meaningful beauty in his natural surroundings. Dante's journey will lead him to realms of the afterlife; Faust still has a great deal to learn from life on this earth.

Faust's adventures in the latter part of the tragedy take him to an emperor's court. The Emperor demands an entertainment including figures from classical mythology. Mephistopheles suggests that Faust visit the Mothers, who are described as "Goddesses [who] sit enthroned in reverend loneliness" (l. 6213). Here Faust will find a source for the mythical creations required of him, for he will be entering the realm of forms from which he could retrieve the figures of Helen and Paris. This realm is variously referred to as an emptiness (*Leere*), a desolate solitude (*Öd und Einsamkeit*), the deepest ground, and a Nothing (*Nichts*), but it is also a place of spirit-forms and of

... Formation, transformation,
Eternal Mind's eternal conversation.
Forms of all creatures floating all around;
(ll. 6287-6289; my trans.)

To penetrate this world safely, Mephistopheles gives Faust a key which glows in Faust's hand and imparts a new sense of power. It will allow Faust to keep his distance, indeed preserve his identity when approaching the awesome Mothers and the swirling spirits which, it appears, could engulf and annihilate him. Although dreading it, Faust believes that his visit to the Mothers will increase his art and power, for in this Nothing he will also find the All. The way there is described as "no way" and an ascent that is a descent. Mephistopheles characterizes Faust's journey to the Mothers as a practice of the highest art, the magic of the wise (ll. 6315-6316).

The play's audience never gets to see Faust's actual encounter with the Mothers, but in the scene just described we are given a glimpse of Goethe's fascination with the sources of human creativity. Commentators have offered interpretations of the scene's many symbols. Rollo May calls attention to Goethe's personal life, his distance from his own mother and his need for feminine companionship, which when available had favorable effects on his poetic creativity. May also suggests that the Mothers represent Goethe's belief in the ultimate source of creativity and renewal as feminine rather than masculine.[14] Altizer also characterizes the Nothing of the Mothers as "an ultimate creativity, . . . the womb of all and everything, and a boundlessness which is the final destiny of Faust."[15] Hamlin mentions the possibility of interpreting the spirits inhabiting the Mother's realm as Goethe's version of Jungian archetypes.[16] My own reading finds a number of themes similar to those which appeared in medieval German mysticism, particularly the mystical writings of Meister Eckhart. Eckhart's notion of the Godhead as a Nothing, a desert, but also a place of intense creative activity, and his use of feminine imagery to characterize this emptiness/fullness dialectic suggest possible direct or indirect influences on the German poet.[17] Though distinctions between Goethe and Eckhart may certainly be enumerated, it is clear that both German writers depict a journey to the wellsprings of creative strength as a journey to a ground of nothingness, and the parallels are intriguing.

Faust returns with spirits who will act as Helen and Paris and a play is presented before the Emperor. However, Faust is so overcome by Helen's beauty that he enters into the drama to embrace her and protect her from Paris. An explosion follows, the spirits/actors disappear, and

Faust falls unconscious on the stage. The next scene finds him again in his study. In his absence, Wagner has progressed in his academic researches enough to be able to create life in the form of Homunculus, a little man inside a test-tube. This daring creation is without any clear form but not without intellect. He advises Faust to attend a witches' Sabbath (*Klassische Walpurgisnacht*), a classical version of an event which also occurred in the tragedy's first part. Like the first *Walpurgisnacht*, the scene is filled with a variety of grotesques, mythical creatures, and erotic figures. Faust goes off in search of Helena, and a debate ensues between two philosophers about the origins of life. Anaxagoras argues for a fiery beginning, both violent and sudden, while Thales believes that life's sources were in water and that the creative process was more gradual. They have an avid listener in Homunculus, who as spirit yearns to be incarnated.

Thales' views are apparently confirmed in the subsequent pageant of Neptune. Proteus, upon learning of Homunculus' desire for physical embodiment, assumes the form of a dolphin and invites the test-tube man to mount him in order to wed Homunculus to the sea. Thales encourages this action because it will reenact the story of evolution which eventually produces the human form:

> Pursue that praiseworthy desire,
> To begin at the beginning of creation;
> Prepare for rapid effects!
> There you move by eternal norms,
> Through thousands upon thousands of eternal forms,
> And you have time enough to become human.
> (ll. 8321-8326; my trans.)

Galatea, a nymph, appears riding the sea on Aphrodite's shell and Homunculus is powerfully drawn to her. His union with the sea becomes an act of dramatic self-sacrifice. When he reaches Galatea, the test tube shatters and he dissolves in a fiery burst of light. At this climactic moment, it seems that both water and fire are fundamental elements of the creative process. The scene concludes with Sirens praising Eros as the Creator: "So may Eros reign, who began all things!" (l. 8479, my trans.).

The next act takes place in a classical setting. Faust rescues Helen from Menelaos who is bent on capturing and executing her and her followers. Faust and Helen fall in love. Their union results in the birth of Euphorion, a figure meant by Goethe to represent sacred poesy (*Heilige Poesie*, l. 9863).[18] When Euphorion attempts to fly, he falls to his death at his parents' feet. Helen, now convinced that her love could never find happiness, leaves Faust to join her son in the underworld. The Chorus which had accompanied Helen to Faust's castle are transformed into nature spirits and various natural forms.

A transitional scene follows where Faust contemplates various cloud formations, one which reminds him of Helen, and another of Gretchen (although she remains unnamed). The monologue draws on Goethe's reading of contemporary scientific research for its details about different kinds of clouds,[19] but it serves to link water imagery with feminine symbolism, and to presage Gretchen's importance to Faust as a source of redemption. Like the cloud resembling her beautiful form, Helen has faded as a character in Faust's story, but another feminine presence is discernable in the skies, one which hints at Faust's future transcendence through an act of heavenly grace.

> Like beauty of the soul, the lovely image is enhanced
> And, undissolving wafts aloft into the ether,
> Drawing away with it the best my soul contains.
> (ll. 10064-10066)

Subsequent developments in the play include a return to political activity where Faust, relying on Mephistopheles' assistance and magic, helps the Emperor gain a victory over a rival monarch. As a reward, Faust asks for and receives some land to govern. Because of his able leadership, the land is reclaimed from the sea and becomes populated with a prosperous community. In the play's last act, a successful but aged Faust complains that his pleasure in his achievements is marred by a single problem: a house on some ground he doesn't own obscures his view. When he orders Mephistopheles to have the owners, an elderly couple, moved, the result is tragic. The house is burned down and the couple is murdered. Faust's agony at this turn of events is portrayed allegorically: Care in the form of a gray woman penetrates Faust's sanctuary and blinds him, but only after Faust rails against Care's power to weaken human resolve through torment and confusion. Despite his loss of sight, Faust holds fast to his inner vision of a project for a dam to hold the sea back more securely. But while he believes Mephistopheles is complying with his order to commence the construction, his infernal assistant is actually having the workers dig Faust's grave. Faust's final speech is one that summarizes his philosophy of life, a wisdom which he thinks has resulted in the improvement in the lives of people under his care:

Yes - this I hold to with devout insistence,
Wisdom's last verdict goes on to say:
He only earns both freedom and existence
Who must reconquer them each day.
And so, ringed all about with perils, here
Youth, manhood, age will spend their strenuous year.
Such teeming would I see upon this land,
On acres free among free people stand.
                    (ll. 11573-11580)

Faust contemplates relishing this moment when it appears to him that he has made a difference in human history, a valuable contribution:

I might entreat the fleeing minute:
Oh tarry yet, thou art so fair!
My path on earth, the trace I leave within it
Eons untold cannot impair.
Foretasting such high happiness to come,
I savor now my striving's crown and sum.
                    (ll. 11581-11586)

When Faust falls dead to the ground, Mephistopheles is triumphant. He believes that Faust capitulated in his last moment and experienced satisfaction, a sense of fulfillment which he wished would last. But before he can claim Faust's soul, heavenly spirits intervene and deny him possession of Faust. He is enraged at such an apparent injustice, an anger which reminds one of his complaint early in the play when he admits that his evil activity can never prevail absolutely. However, the momentum of his argument dissipates when he is completely distracted by the angels' physical beauty and yearns to catch sight of their bare bottoms. By the time he regathers his wits, Faust and angels have disappeared. It is the play's most comic moment.

Mountain gorges form the setting for the final scene. As an agent of the Holy Mother's love, Gretchen's spirit leads Faust's soul upward to higher realms. The mountainous context is described by holy anchorites, the last earthly inhabitants of the play, and it reminds one of the beautiful and turbulent landscapes of earlier scenes. The last of the hermits, Doctor Marianus, is a devotee of the Virgin, and he addresses a hymn to her loving grace. The angels declare that Faust's redemption is the combined result of his pursuit of endless activity and of divine love:

Pure spirits' peer, from evil coil

He was vouchsafed exemption;
"Whosoever strives in ceaseless toil,
Him we may grant redemption."
And when on high, transfigured love
Has added intercession,
The blest will throng to him above
With welcoming compassion.
       (ll. 11935-11941)

Goethe, in conversation with Johann Peter Eckermann, a close friend, explained that the lines revealed his own religious views: "We can obtain heavenly bliss, not through our strength alone, but with the assistance of divine grace."[20] The play closes with a Chorus Mysticus describing heavenly perfection. What is unreachable and indescribable on earth is realized in heaven as a perpetual movement toward the Eternal Feminine:

All that is impermanent
Is a mere likeness;
The unattainable
Here becomes an event;
The indescribable,
Here it's achieved;
The Eternal Feminine
Draws us onward.
      (ll. 12104-12111; my translation)

Faust's long journey comes to a sublime end, his salvation achieved through an act of grace which in effect is the culmination of the critical role of the feminine throughout the play. The earthly Gretchen, the mythic creations of Helen and Galatea, and the heavenly forms of Gretchen and the Virgin Mary could all be interpreted as figurations of an erotic force drawing first the earthly Faust and then his redeemed soul on to further activity which, in Goethe's words, "becomes constantly higher and purer to the end."[21] Similarities with Dante's *Commedia* may be drawn, in particular Dante's ascent through the heavenly spheres and the appearance of Beatrice and Mary in the final cantos. But rather than exploring parallels between the two poets, I shall describe some of the basic themes in Faust which are fundamental to Goethe's version of spiritual wisdom. The play will serve as poetic reference point, a highly complex but vivid aesthetic stimulus to our imagination, as we explore the intellectual principles of the Omega school.

Worlds within Worlds

Beginning with the play's Prologue, Goethe depicts the cosmos as animated by contrary forces. It is a dynamic world full of beauty and ugliness, joy and anguish. Faust's goal is to pursue an active life, and in this he reflects the restlessness of the nature he loves. Like Basho, the Japanese haiku master, Faust clearly loves nature as it is in itself more than as a realm of symbols which point back to their source in the Creator. In rejecting the sign of the Macrocosmos, Faust gives a clear indication of his preference for experiencing life over contemplating symbolic or metaphysical truths.

Goethe's view of nature as a turbulent whirl of creative and destructive forces differs significantly from the morally ordered universe of Dante's grand conception. Instead of a multi-layered hierarchy of beings, dynamic movement is the principle that shapes the world. Good and evil, therefore, cannot be conveniently portrayed as occupying different cosmic levels, nor can a spiritual journey be depicted simply as proceeding from a realm of the fallen to a paradise of the saved. Faust is indeed redeemed but only after his death in the closing moments of the play. If the particular conditions of the souls in Dante's paradise, purgatory, or hell can be said to reflect the consequences of specific good or evil acts, Faust's situation at any moment is the result of following his unceasing desire for new experience. His freedom to pursue his desires sometimes results in good, but just as frequently it results in evil. And the angels make it clear at the play's end that Faust's ceaseless activity together with an act of divine grace led to his salvation.

Using theological terminology, neither faith nor good works redeem Faust. Faust is not interested in traditional faith or in ethical goodness in pursuing his passion for an adventurous life. In the Easter scene, he first recalls but then leaves behind the simple faith of his childhood. But it must also be noted that Christianity plays a critical role when the town's celebration of the resurrected God-man interrupts Faust's suicide attempt. It is an act of grace, one which reawakens Faust not to a traditionally defined spirituality but to the adventure his life could be. At the same time, Christianity had an influence on his inner life as a child. His journey is deeply grounded in a Christian upbringing which has shaped him in ways he may not always be aware of. The play's echoes of Dante seem to support this possibility. At the very least, he owes his life to the timely ringing of the Easter bells and his salvation to the mercy of the Holy Virgin.

While Faust's attraction to the natural world is evident throughout the play, he cannot claim any easy spiritual identity with the earth. *Faust* at several points portrays a deep relationship between humankind and nature, but Goethe's drama emphasizes the inescapable truth of difference, that humanity and earth are two separate realities. This is made quite clear in the scene where the *Erdgeist* rejects Faust's claim to equality with the Spirit. A return to a real or mythical golden age of oneness with nature is impossible. Yet interaction with nature is possible. The Earth Spirit sends Mephisto, who although a figure of darkness, is also a nature spirit who makes available the kind of magical power over normal life that has long eluded Faust during his extensive academic and alchemical studies. This power has both destructive and creative aspects, but significantly it provides Faust with an entry into the turbulent stream of real life. He becomes as naturally himself as any of the creatures that make up the realm of the *Erdgeist*. The truth of this naturalness, this life of continual becoming, can only be proved by the journey itself and not by mere words spoken by Faust to the Earth Spirit.

The spiritual journey, therefore, is not one of transcendence of but immersion in the world. In contrast to some versions of Neoplatonism and asceticism, Goethe is insisting that we cannot look beyond this world for our spiritual landscape. But also in contrast to much enlightenment and scientific thought, we cannot consider this world objectively. A deep relationship exists between the human and natural worlds. In the Goethean/Faustian view, the human adventure is very much in this world, but it proceeds in complex relationships with good and evil forces. Moreover, it engages the transformative power of the imagination as well as reason. The human individual can choose to reject aspects of the past, and it has established a new and freer attitude toward religious tradition. The goal of living a life of becoming is only realizable in freedom, but freedom has evil as well as beneficial consequences. Immersion in the world means undergoing the dialectic of good and evil, and evil manifests itself as a real force, not the mere absence of good as frequently defined by Neoplatonic thought. Mephisto as conceived by Goethe is a *dramatis persona*. His active, highly influential and powerful presence throughout the play contrasts strongly with Dante's Satan locked in ice.

While Faust loves nature, it remains veiled despite all his efforts to unmask its secrets. The sciences will never be able to comprehend nature fully, yet humanity and nature are both engaged in the process of becoming. Faust recognizes this shared reality during his meditation at the waterfall. Nature's seeming resistance to human understanding is described as earth's "most youthful veil," and then a light-filled rainbow of evanescent becoming and creativity. The splendor of the falls leads to Faust's insight that his life is indeed as beautiful in its evanescence as the light refracted through the foam of crashing water. Nothing is more real than perpetual becoming or *Wechseldauer*.

But nature is not the only source of insight. When, by imperial request, Faust needs to produce the figures of Helen and Paris, he is directed by Mephisto to the realm of the Mothers. He is introduced to a deeper source of creativity, one which, as I noted before, recalls the mystical doctrine of the Godhead as well as the Jungian concept of archetypes. Goethe believed that the creative imagination could draw on transcendent sources. Although we never witness Faust's visit to the Mothers and the forms swirling through a dark nothingness, and although Mephisto's description of the way Faust must take is but a few short passages, the effect on the reader/playgoer is profound. This episode more than any other seems to portray Faust encountering the source of creative power itself: "You send me to emptiness / That there my arts and powers may both increase . . . / in your Nothing may I find the All!"[22]

In the penultimate section of the play, Faust establishes a human community by reclaiming land from the sea. But even in this last phase of his earthly life, he gets enmeshed in a tragic mess of good and evil. After innocent lives are lost through his willfulness, Faust is blinded by Care, and because of Mephisto's duplicity, he mistakenly believes that the foundations for a new community of free individuals are being laid. His attempt at social action ends in failure, but at precisely this moment, he is redeemed through divine action.

It is no accident that Faust's ascent into heaven comes soon after he refuses to recognize Care's power to weaken human resolve. He remains true to "Wisdom's last verdict": "He only earns both freedom and existence / Who must reconquer them each day." Goethe thus presents us with a version of redemption that is an alternative to a good deal of Christian teaching. Faust is saved not as the result of any act of remorse, but by remaining true to his deepest self. In so doing, he is simply fulfilling the Creator's judgment of his worth stated at the outset of the play: that a good person, *ein guter Mensch*, is one who stays connected to his primal source, *Urquell*, the locus of his darkest urges. It is clear at this point that the grand scope of Faust's journey has affirmed God's understanding of human nature, its need for an active life, and its limitations in working out its salvation. Divine wisdom working through Mephisto enabled Faust to realize great joys and agonies, but it also saved him through the loving grace of Mary and Gretchen.

Having mentioned the presence of Mary and Gretchen in the final scene, it is important to appreciate the critical role played by women and the place of the feminine in the work. In the Homunculus episode, the yearning of the test-tube man for physical incarnation is followed by a deep attraction to Galatea at whose feet he is destroyed in a fiery burst of light. Erotic power which is praised as the origin of all things is portrayed as the *telos* as well. In Faust's case, the presence of Gretchen in heaven represents the importance of forgiveness and reconciliation. As an act of love, her forgiveness is all the more moving because she is someone Faust had gravely injured. And in the play's concluding line, the Eternal Feminine is hailed as an ultimate lure which will continue to draw souls upward in an endless movement of transcendence. The whole motion of the play and of Faust's journey can be seen as both a movement driven by erotic attraction (toward Gretchen, Helen, Galatea, the Eternal Feminine) and a story of reconciliation through feminine divine grace. Goethe's use of feminine language and imagery to describe the absolute, particularly in the depiction of the Mothers and the principle of the Eternal Feminine, emphasizes the critical role of the feminine in the spiritual journey.

We have noted the presence of Renaissance sources in *Faust*, in particular Nostradamus, Paracelsus and Bruno in the first scene in Faust's study. Harold Jantz, who has explored the connections between Goethe's masterwork and Renaissance thought, concludes that the tragedy of *Faust* "is the culminating expression and summation of an entire era,"[23] that is to say, the Renaissance. Jantz offers evidence of Goethe's familiarity with Renaissance works, but more important, the drama reflects many of the period's intellectual and spiritual currents.

Jantz points to important Renaissance figures including Nicholas of Cusa who in his notion of learned ignorance (*docta ignorantia*) preferred a layman's wisdom based on actual experience to a scholar's knowledge shaped by formal learning.[24] Pico della Mirandola accepted Cusa's teachings of learned ignorance, the principle of the coincidence of opposites (*coincidentia oppositorum*), and the symbolic knowledge of God. But Pico went on to emphasize the freedom of human persons to develop themselves to their fullest potential as well as the principle of correspondences between the human individual, the microcosm, and the universe, the macrocosm. By probing the self, one begins to understand the mysteries of nature, and conversely, by observing the natural world, one begins to understand one's own being. In our discussion of the Omega school, we shall have occasion to make further reference to the

Renaissance and its new modes of thought and spiritual wisdom which Jantz believes influenced Goethe

> ...not so much by ancient Neoplatonism as by the Renaissance transformation of it which gave it a new dynamism, a new relation to the activistic age of science and discovery.[25]

In his *Faust the Theologian*, Jaroslav Pelikan describes what he believes to be Faust's theological perspective. According to Pelikan, a "typological framework" for such a perspective exists in Goethe's own words in *Maxims and Reflections*: "When we do natural science, we are pantheists; when we do poetry, we are polytheists; when we moralize, we are monotheists."[26] Pelikan goes on to compare these three modes of theologizing to Kierkegaard's stages of personal development: the aesthetic, ethical, and religious. Where the Danish philosopher found these stages in fundamental opposition, Pelikan views Goethe's three "ways of thinking" as developmental "but dialectical, and therefore as interpenetrating one another."[27]

Without going further into Pelikan's discussion, I think we can appropriate this notion of interpenetrating stages as "existence-spheres" (a translation of Kierkegaard's alternate phrase for stages). In the Faustian perspective, the individual can experience divinity as immanent in nature, plural in the imagination, and transcendent in moral judgment. All three spheres shape the landscape of Faust's journey. Divine immanence is discernable throughout the drama. The natural world is alive with signs of divine presence and activity. When asked by Gretchen to describe his faith, Faust replies that he believes God to be nameless but evident in nature:

> The All-comprising
> The All sustaining
> Does he comprise, sustain not
> You, me, himself?
> Are not the vaulted heavens hung on high?
> Is earth not anchored here below?
> (ll. 3438-3444)

Within this "pantheistic" context appears the polytheistic multitude of supernatural creatures - spirits, elves, angels, the Mothers, Mephisto himself - that are intimately involved with Faust's inner life, his dreams, creative imagination, and "deepest urges." This mythical tapestry -

richest, perhaps, in the two Walpurgis Night scenes - is in turn permeated by the reality of the one God and Creator who sets the drama in motion by granting Mephisto permission to strike a wager with Faust. God's statement in the Prologue about the goodness of the human will provides a fundamental principle which resonates throughout the play, although its rightness is not always clear given the destructive consequences of many of Faust's actions. As Pelikan points out, by the end of his life Faust has developed beyond the confines of self-fulfillment to a more public vision of activity, that of establishing a community on land reclaimed from the sea.[28] A sign of his moral growth, his communal project realizes in concrete action his wish, stated early in the play, to identify with the whole breadth of human experience. He is ready for death and redemption.

If the three stages or existence-spheres describe Faust's relationship with the divine, it is important to emphasize that the journey is not linear, just as the stages are not chronological nor the spheres spatially differentiated as in the *Commedia*. So long as human striving is the dominant impulse working throughout the play, the path will be a zigzag between the extremes of joy and sorrow, good and evil. The Lord admits that human partnership with Mephistopheles and the dark forces is inevitable: "Man ever errs the while he strives" (1. 317). Whereas Dante wanders from the world through hell and purgatory to heaven, Faust's agonies do not cease until his death. He stumbles toward salvation. The worlds within worlds of turbulent but beautiful nature, destructive and creative spirits, and moral conflict between good and evil provide no clear path. The landscape of the journey is alive with possibilities. The pilgrim can only pursue what seems to be the most compelling and inviting challenge: to live a full life and become most fully human. We will now consider the Omega school and its attempt at articulating a wisdom of becoming.

Notes

1. Anthony Grafton, *New Worlds, Ancient Texts: The Power of Tradition and the Shock of Discovery* (Cambridge: Belknap Press of Harvard University Press, 1992), 5.
2. Ibid., 1.
3. George Santayana, *Three Philosophical Poets* (Cambridge: Harvard University, 1910).
4. Rollo May, *The Cry for Myth* (New York: W.W.Norton, 1991), 235.
5. Ibid., 255.
6. May, 217.

7. "Vom Himmel durch die Welt zur Hölle." This is the last line of the play's Prelude (Vorspiel). I will use the following translation of *Faust*: Johann Wolfgang von Goethe, *Faust, a Tragedy*, trans. Walter Arndt (New York: W.W. Norton, 1976). Line number references will identify the location of the quoted passage in the Arndt translation; they correspond to line numbers in standard German editions.

8. Where Arndt translates Goethe's "rechten Weges" with "appointed course," I have preferred "right way."

9. See fn. 6 in the Arndt translation of *Faust* cited above.

10. Eudo C. Mason, "The Erdgeist and Mephisto," in Johann Wolfgang von Goethe, *Faust, a Tragedy: Background and Sources, the Author on the Drama, Contemporary Reactions, Modern Criticism*, trans. Walter Arndt, ed. Cyrus Hamlin. (New York: Norton, 1976), 495.

11. Jane K. Brown has argued that Mephisto is more of a nature spirit than a personification of evil. Jane K. Brown, "Mephistopheles the Nature Spirit," *Studies in Romanticism* 24 (Winter 1985): 475-490.

12. Johann Wolfgang von Goethe, *Faust: Parts 1 and 2* (New York: Continuum, 1994). The translator is Louis MacNeice.

13. Cyrus Hamlin, "Interpretive Notes," in Johann Wolfgang von Goethe, *Faust: A Tragedy*, trans. Walter Arndt; ed. Cyrus Hamlin (New York: Norton, 1976), 324.

14. May, 242-47.

15. Thomas J.J. Altizer, *The Genesis of God* (Louisville, Ky.: Westminster / John Knox Press), 155-56.

16. Hamlin, 329.

17. These themes and images occur throughout Eckhart's writings. See especially his use of "the virgin who is a wife" portrayal of the soul in his German Sermon 2, in Meister Eckhart, *The Essential Sermons, Commentaries, Treatises, and Defense*, trans. Edmund Colledge and Bernard McGinn (New York: Paulist Press, 1981), 177-181.

18. See n. 8 on p. 244 of the Arndt translation.

19. See n. 2, p. 256, of the Arndt translation.

20. Goethe quoted by Eckermann, in the Arndt translation, p. 428.

21. Goethe to Eckermann, in Arndt, 428.

22. *Faust*, ll. 6250-6256; this is the Louis MacNeice translation, p. 167. See n. 12.

23. Harold Jantz, *Goethe's Faust as a Renaissance Man: Parallels and Prototypes* (Princeton: Princeton University Press, 1951), 9.

24. Ibid., 39.

25. Ibid., 8.

26. Quoted in Jaroslav Pelikan, *Faust the Theologian* (New Haven: Yale University, 1995), 19.

27. Pelikan, 24.

28. Ibid., 94-95.

Chapter 6

Omega: The Wisdom of Becoming

Nova Scientia, Nova Sapientia

Process thought is arguably the major metaphysical system developed in our time which provides a cosmology. The two founders of process thought, Alfred North Whitehead and Charles Hartshorne, claimed to be creating a cosmology based on contemporary developments in modern science. Whitehead was influenced by new theories in physics and by Einstein's theory of relativity in particular. Along with quantum mechanics and field theory, Einstein's theories presented reality at its most elemental level as a realm of energy, flux, and relationship. This suggested quite a different world from that of Newtonian physics where the most fundamental elements were discrete, stable objects governed by the laws of mechanics. Process thought proposed that this new perspective of the world could generate a new metaphysics and a new theology. It also raises the possibility of a new spirituality of knowing.

The age of Newton had succeeded in establishing science as the dominant mode of knowing in the West, but its worldview offered a universe of separate entities whose only interaction was external and measurable. The models of colliding billiard balls and the intricate inner working of a mechanical clock proved to be successful and influential symbols of the Newtonian universe. In contrast, the vision of the world offered by the new physics and biology relies on more difficult and complex models that are truer to the dynamic nature of the subatomic world and to the evolutionary development of organisms. Such models require new ways of understanding our world, and this is the task undertaken by Omega.

The achievements of Whitehead and Hartshorne were considerable, but my preference is to turn to thinkers who have developed the more theological themes in process thought. Two of the writers I will examine are members of the generation of process thinkers which appeared after Whitehead, Hartshorne, and their immediate disciples. John B. Cobb, Jr., was born in Kobe, Japan, and received his doctorate from the University of Chicago. He became a chaired professor at the School of Theology at Claremont, California, where he and David Ray Griffin founded the Center for Process Studies. Griffin, also a professor at the Claremont School, began a second center, the Center for a Postmodern World, which is working to develop a positive new vision of the world in a variety of disciplines. The third writer, Pierre Teilhard de Chardin (1881-1955), was a Jesuit who, after receiving a degree in geology, worked as a paleontologist in China. Because the Church forbade publication of most of Teilhard's works during his lifetime, his thought achieved its greatest recognition only after his death. While Teilhard cannot be officially numbered as one of the process school, the strong similarities of many of his themes to the process approach puts him firmly in the Omega camp. The very name I have selected for this third wisdom school in large part derives from a central theme and symbol in Teilhard's writings, and suggests the significant contribution Teilhard offers to the school.

In the following section, I will look first at *Process Theology: An Introductory Exposition*, a work collaboratively authored by Cobb and Griffin which serves as an excellent summary of process themes as they had been developed by process theologians up to the mid-1970s. In subsequent sections, other works will be referred to, such as *God and Religion in the Postmodern World* by David Ray Griffin. These will give examples of more recent developments in the process school. Because of important differences between Teilhard's thought and that of Cobb and Griffin, I will look at the Jesuit's work separately.

A Theology of Organism

The process school insists on the reality, the necessary, inescapable reality, of individual beings. Furthermore, their identity as beings is not static but constantly changing. To be *actual* is to be in process. Process thought prefers to speak of events or occasions rather than beings, entities, or things, since the latter terms are too substantive and lack the dynamism inherent in real life. Unchanging forms of things are abstractions and as such not actual. The process theme of the reality and worth of the individual provides an initial contrast to some aspects of Alpha thought which views the created realm as less real than the divine. And to equate actuality with a universe of change is radically different from the Neoplatonic emphasis on the reality of abstract, immutable forms.

Cobb and Griffin offer an alternative term for *process*, the word *enjoyment*: ". . . the statement that all units of process are characterized by enjoyment makes clear that every such unit has intrinsic value, an inner reality in and for itself."[1] Enjoyment in its process meaning has less to do with pleasure and more with opportunity to grow and develop. In Cobb and Griffin's words, "To be, to actualize oneself, to act upon others, to share in a wider community, is to enjoy being an experiencing subject quite apart from any accompanying pain or pleasure."[2]

The universe of individual subjects is essentially related. For process, to be is to be in relation. The life of each subjectivity is a stream of moments of becoming. Each moment is an opportunity for the subject to incorporate not only past experiences of its own but of other events and individuals as well. And the subject's experience can contribute to the becoming of others. In this way, relations, or in process terminology *prehensions* or *feelings*, establish a world of interacting subjectivities where each element can have a significant influence in the development of another. This is an important aspect of an individual subject, because it emphasizes its interdependence over its independence.

The universe of self-actualizing subjects is a creative community. Following Whitehead's expression for his work as a "philosophy of organism," we can say that process theology offers us a theology of organism. Each occasion of enjoyment can lead to something new and introduce novelty into the world. Thus the world is both created and creative, and for process theologians the world's creativity is one of the clearest signs of God's active and relational presence to his creation. According to Cobb and Griffin,

> If we could think at all of a world apart from God, it would be a world of repetition lapsing into lesser and lesser forms of order according to the principle of entropy. What happened in each occasion could only be the declining outgrowth of what happened before. It is God who, by confronting the world with unrealized opportunities, opens up a space for freedom and self-creativity.[3]

The world's creativity is not apart from God but deeply related to divine creativity. In Whitehead's thought, God was never understood to be an exception to the principles governing the realm of actual events, but their "chief exemplification."[4] However, God and creativity are not the same. Cobb has offered the following distinction: Creativity is the *ultimate reality* while God is the *ultimate actuality*. Both ultimates are equally primordial, because creativity does not create God nor does God create creativity. Creativity, according to Cobb, is similar to Buddhist *emptiness*, while God is the source of all aesthetic and ethical values which can be actualized. Both the human person and God exhibit creativity in an evolving cosmos, but it is God's role to lure all beings toward higher degrees of beauty and goodness.[5]

The universe is not only creative but evolving. The theory of evolution describes a developmental pattern of lesser to greater complexity, from the structural simplicity of the hydrogen atom to the complexity of organisms, from the geological aggregate of a new planet to the biological and psychological community of humanity. And in process thought, greater complexity means greater enjoyment, an increase in the *intensity* and *harmony* of experience. Intensity and harmony are aesthetic categories, but they also suggest value, and according to process theology, it is God's wish to lure the world toward ever greater realization of value and beauty. Cobb and Griffin speak of God as "the divine Eros urging the world to new heights of enjoyment."[6]

The reality of evil receives a distinctive interpretation in process theology. According to Cobb and Griffin, evil can be experienced as discord or triviality. Discord can be any mental or physical suffering, whereas triviality is unrealized potential for growth. Discord is an absolute evil, while triviality is evil to the extent it has detracted from an individual's enjoyment. Therefore it is a comparative evil. Potential for evil grows with the increase in freedom or self-creativity. When Mephisto offers his services, Faust has little idea how much greater his capacity for evil acts will become as a result of accepting the offer. It is the unavoidable price to pay for realizing his life's dreams. For process thinkers, morality is more than obedience to God the lawgiver. It is one's response to the divine aim. And God's aim is to lure us to higher levels of enjoyment or perfection of experience in harmony and intensity.

According to the process school, values exist in God but only as possibilities. Values must become actual in the created realm of finite occasions before they are most fully enjoyable. God in his Primordial Nature presents these possible ideals to creatures who can accept or reject them. Therefore, process thought proposes a notion that contradicts much of traditional theism: God needs the world in order to actualize what is only potential in the divine realm. Our experiences of the moment are transient, a perpetual perishing, while God lives "everlastingly." Cobb and Griffin have chosen *everlasting* rather than *eternal* as the term to

Omega: The Wisdom of Becoming 135

contrast divine life with human temporality because *eternal* suggests the traditional notion of God as atemporal and unaffected by human activity. But if God is lovingly responsive to his creation, then his divine life is deeply moved by all his creatures' actions, both good and evil. The two theologians offer an extensive quotation from Whitehead's *Process and Reality* which captures this divine-human dynamic:

> God "prehends every actuality for what it can be in such a perfected system - its suffering, its sorrows, its failures, its triumphs, its immediacies of joy - woven by rightness of feeling into the harmony of universal feeling, which is always immediate, always many, always one, always with novel advance, moving onwards and never perishing. The revolts of destructive evil, purely self-regarding, are dismissed into their triviality of merely individual facts; and yet the good they did achieve in individual joy, in individual sorrow, in the introduction of needed contrast, is yet saved by its relation to the completed whole. The image - and it is but an image - the image under which this operative growth of God's nature is best conceived, is that of a tender care that nothing be lost."[7]

Joys and sorrows, failures and successes contribute to God's Consequent Nature which receives and transforms our experiences, making them available for future experiences. On the one hand, the evil of Faust's behavior toward Gretchen is, in process terms, ultimately a discordant evil full of emotional and physical pain. On the other hand, Faust's deep attraction to her, their moments of transporting love, and his awful agony over her destruction are what make Faust's life a real existence. They ennoble the wretched man, reinforce his commitment to continue his constant striving, and are ultimately woven by God "into the harmony of universal feeling."

Process thought views God as adventurous. Here again we encounter a controversial theme: the limitation of God's omniscience and omnipotence. In Cobb and Griffin's words:

> ... since God's creative activity is persuasive, not controlling, it is a love that takes risks. Hence, each divine creative impulse into the world is adventurous, in that God does not know what the result will be.[8]

Moreover, what happens in the world affects the divine life, the consequence of God's relatedness to and love of the world. How the world responds to God in one moment can change the way in which God chooses to lure it to new growth in the next. The theological claim for divine changeability is a thorny issue and it needs careful nuancing, but the process school makes it in order to be consistent in its defense of the value and reality of human freedom. In any debate with defenders of more traditional doctrines of God, process thinkers will score some points in their portrayal of a dynamic and involved Creator, and their notion of God's life as a risk-taking adventure is a provocative one which may speak to modern religious seekers.

Process theology is a theology that emerges from and builds on a cosmology. This cosmology implies ways of living and knowing. The Alpha school correlated levels of being with levels of knowing, and thus could speak of a *scientia sacra*, a sacred science or wisdom which knew the highest (or deepest) spiritual reality. The Zero school based its cosmological views on the *sunyata* dialectic which is realized through meditative practice. Zen Buddhist practice leads to an intuitive experience of the real nature of the universe in all its dialectical richness and is the basis of *prajna* or wisdom. Cobb and Griffin refer frequently to reason as the mode of knowing which verifies the truth of process teachings. For example,

> The widespread modern sense of being estranged or alienated from reality is related to the dualistic view that human beings are totally different in kind from the rest of the world. . . . Whitehead, like Teilhard, holds that all actualities have an inner reality as well as an outer one. Hence, the sense of kinship with all things, which has evidently characterized human experience at most times and places, is *rationally* supported.[9]

Cobb and Griffin's understanding of rational thought is closely related to their notion of science. We will, therefore, once again turn to the role of science in the gaining of wisdom, this time as interpreted by the process school. For Griffin, the sciences must rediscover the mystery of life that permeates the world. He proposes the notion of reenchantment as a term descriptive of the new scientific worldview. The historical context for his argument suggests the presence of a reenchantment myth. Like the Myth of the Primordial Tradition, it provides a context for a particular form of wisdom. As we shall see, the Myth of Reenchantment relies less heavily on a golden age of spiritual knowing and is far more positive in its views of the scientific enterprise.

The Myth of Reenchantment

For certain authors, the term *reenchantment* refers to a particular reading of history where modern science and rationalism are believed to have disenchanted the cosmos and our natural environment. The great sociologist of religion, Max Weber, wrote: "The fate of our times is characterized by rationalization and intellectualization, and, above all, by the 'disenchantment of the world.' Precisely the ultimate and most sublime values have retreated from public life."[10] It may be that Weber was familiar with Schiller's phrase "die Entgötterung der Natur,"[11] or the "disgodding of nature" which was intended to describe a world empty of divine presence and devoid of the celestial influences that pervaded Dante's cosmos.

The transformation of an enchanted into a disenchanted world occurred some time between the medieval and modern era. According to Morris Berman,

> The view of nature which predominated in the West down to the eve of the Scientific Revolution was that of an enchanted world. Rocks, trees, rivers, and clouds were all seen as wondrous, alive, and human beings felt at home in this environment. The cosmos, in short, was a place of *belonging*. A member of this cosmos was not an alienated observer but a direct participant in its drama. His personal destiny was bound up with its destiny, and this relationship gave meaning to his life.[12]

The terms *participation* and *participate* occur frequently on the pages of scholastic thought and most often without any definition. To the writers who used them, their meanings were obvious and not matters for discussion. According to Owen Barfield, the medieval person consciously or unconsciously "did not feel himself isolated by his skin from the world outside him to quite the extent as we do" but tacitly understood himself to be thoroughly integrated within his cosmic environment.[13] Barfield also believes that "before the scientific revolution the world was more like a garment men wore about them than a stage on which they moved."[14] In medieval philosophical language, because God created and sustained things by means of his divine knowledge, the human being could likewise through knowing *be* the thing known, in other words participate in being, and ultimately in God's being.[15]

According to Griffin, the medieval worldview had three critical elements: a belief in a personal Creator, a sense of the human person as made in God's image and the crown of his creation, and faith in an afterlife. All three elements, however, have been eventually discarded in the modern worldview which relies on the physical sciences for its understanding of reality. Neo-Darwinism has replaced a belief in divine creativity with impersonal forces ("chance and necessity"). Human beings are no longer seen as privileged or as made in God's image. The qualities of human existence such as emotion, virtue, and aesthetic judgment are no longer considered the primary values of reality, having been replaced by the quantitative measurements of size, shape, and mass. Even the qualities of color, sound, taste, and so forth now have a secondary importance to measurable data "because they are thought to refer to nothing really 'out there' in the objective world, apart from human subjectivity."[16] To be really real, from a scientific perspective, is to be in some sense quantifiable and observable in the physical realm. This perspective has the effect of depersonalizing the world and relegating "human beings with their distinctively personal qualities to an insignificant status."[17] It is no surprise that scientific materialism eventually led many to deny the reality of the afterlife because its reality does not depend on any physical, measurable signs for proof.

Griffin proposes the notion that the modern worldview has gone through two stages. During the first stage, thinkers like Robert Boyle, Isaac Newton, and René Descartes did not challenge belief in a personal God, the special significance and uniqueness of the human person, and the reality of life after death. God was accepted as the absolute Creator, which meant that the natural world had no creativity of its own. The human soul was made in God's image, but as such it was of a completely different level of reality and no longer part of the great chain of being which structures the cosmos. This initial stage of modernism is characterized by dualisms of God and world, soul and body, mind and matter, supernatural and natural. Beyond the initial act of creation, God's relationship to the world was limited to special acts of supernatural intervention. By itself, the world followed natural laws which were discoverable by the newly developing physical sciences. In defining the increasingly dominant paradigm of knowing, these sciences depended on the reality of the detached observer whose mind was qualitatively different from the objective world being observed. None of the defining features of human consciousness could be found in nature. The universe was composed of matter which lacked any feeling or creative power of its own.

Emerging at the end of the eighteenth century, the second stage of the modern worldview developed easily from the first. If nature followed invariable, mechanistic laws, there was little reason to believe in a supernatural, transcendent God. Apart from scripture, no evidence could be discerned for divine intervention, at least through scientific methods. Moreover, if God were so transcendent and powerful, the problem of evil became increasingly difficult to resolve. A mechanistic cosmos set in motion by its Creator should be working flawlessly, but clearly it did not. It also became more difficult to understand how the human mind could interact with the physical world because of the absolute difference between them. The mind, therefore, came to be considered as an epiphenomenon, "an alien ghost in a machine,"[18] which had no power over its own body. When eventually it became equated with the brain, a number of scientific approaches developed which believed that the mind could be studied like any other physical thing.

Characterizing the modern worldview in its latter phase as atheistic and materialistic, Griffin argues that it is not without its flaws, nor is it the only worldview which can incorporate the physical sciences.[19] Despite its position of dominance in the intellectual world, it is open to criticism and challenge:

> The materialistic-atheistic view did not win out in intellectual circles because it is free from problems; it is not. . . . Rather, it won out partly because it fit the spirit of the times and partly because it could easily point out the problems in dualistic supernaturalism, which it presumed to be the only serious alternative. Once we realize this, we become more free to challenge the reigning orthodoxy by presenting a third alternative.[20]

Much of what Griffin describes as a third alternative, in his words "a postmodern worldview," has already been summarized above under the heading "A Theology of Organism". However, in using the term postmodernism, he makes an important clarification. Griffin distinguishes the process version of postmodernism from a more nihilistic one rooted in Nietzsche and the German philosopher's claim for the "death of God." Griffin argues that this negative postmodernism is opposed to all worldviews which claim absolute status. They are far from absolute, having been formed by a variety of linguistic structures and social influences. A worldview gains acceptance because of the claims it makes for ultimate importance, but the postmodernist method of deconstruction claims to reveal the forces which shaped it, thereby eliminating its apparent ultimacy. This nihilistic version of postmodernism, therefore, is not concerned with proposing a metaphysics or recovering the reality of the soul in the face of modern materialism. It is not about proposing anything, and for process thinkers, therein lies its weakness. According to Cobb:

> The deconstructive model [of postmodernism] is something like peeling an onion. As one sees through the meanings by which we have been conditioned to live at one level, one finds another, and another, level of meaning. But if one could see through them all, peel them all away, there would be nothing left. Some hold that "nothing" to be salvation, somewhat as the Buddhists do, although this Western "nothing" is not identical with that of the Buddhists.[21]

Griffin argues that its roots are in the very modernism it attempts to deconstruct. Deconstructionists like Derrida and Foucault are simply completing the job begun by modernists of dismantling the traditional thought world and its foundations in ultimate values and beliefs.

Process thought proposes a constructive rather than a deconstructive postmodern worldview, which, unlike the nihilistic view, accepts some of the insights of the premodern thought world (e.g., some features of the enchanted cosmos of the medieval period). However, Griffin's constructive postmodernism rejects a complete reclamation of premodernism, a step taken by fundamentalists and others calling for a renewed religious orthodoxy, or by advocates of a "perennial philosophy." Here Griffin is referring specifically to Huston Smith.[22]

In the postmodern vision that Griffin is proposing, the human self is once again an integral member of the cosmic community. It also is "the chief exemplification . . . of the qualities that all creatures embody."[23] Constructive postmodernism promotes the Einsteinian insight that things in the universe are not composed of dead matter but matter which embodies energy. The energy and mass of a thing are simply two convertible aspects of its existence. Griffin follows Whitehead in preferring creativity to energy as the fundamental term and extends it beyond the atomic world to refer to living cells and minds. This permits him to argue against any dualism between mind and body or spirit and matter because all occasions in the cosmos have creativity.

Calling this universal capacity for creativity *panenergism*, Griffin complements it with the notion of *panexperientialism*. All occasions, whether an atom or a human, are composed of experiences. The universality of experience allows for soul and matter to interact and for mind and body to share the same reality. Griffin's position, therefore, offers a more fruitful approach for exploring the mind/brain relationship:

The cells comprising the brain are different only in degree from the mind - *greatly* different in degree, to be sure, but different only in degree nonetheless. These cells themselves, considered from within, have experiences, or *are* experiences. The mutual influence of brain and mind is therefore not unintelligible: Brain cells and the mind share feelings with each other.[24]

Qualities of experience and human consciousness which had been downgraded in importance by the modern worldview now regain their significance. Beauty becomes an extremely important value. Our experiences can, through God's saving grace, contribute to the beauty of the world. The theme of God as active and creative presence in the world is recovered as central to metaphysics, but it receives a different interpretation from premodern or early modern notions of divine presence. Instead of a God who created the universe out of nothing and therefore absolutely transcends it, the constructive postmodern vision proposes a God who creates by bringing order out of chaotic energy. He does not miraculously intervene in history nor control his creatures through omnipotence but lures them to new levels of creativity and beauty. All created beings have the power to resist the divine lure, but they also share a potential for fulfilling the divine aim and adding to God's everlasting life. This potential opens the door for a new understanding of the afterlife, because our lives can find an ultimate significance in God and therefore transcend death. This is not a hope limited to individual or human salvation but expansive enough to envision the salvation of all beings. In the constructive postmodern worldview, the universe is composed of experiences, filled with feeling and creativity, and intimately related to God's continuing, active presence. It is "reenchanted." The word *participation* regains its ability to describe the relationship of the human person with his or her environment. I quote from Cobb and Griffin:

> Insofar as we influence one another, we participate in one another, and through all sorts of complex patterns all of us influence one another. This is a part of our preflective knowledge that comes to expression from time to time in spite of our normal conscious adherence to a conceptuality that denies it. John Donne reminds us that 'no man is an island' and that every man's death diminishes us. . . . Process theology calls for still further extension of the sense of participation. The whole of nature participates in us and we in it.[25]

For Griffin, the philosophical theologian, a worldview implies a

142   Landscapes of Wisdom

metaphysics, and the constructive postmodern worldview he is describing is an expression of process metaphysics. For the process school, metaphysics and cosmology are not purely speculative disciplines but deeply related to the physical sciences. However, these are not the sciences of the modern worldview. Because science plays such an important role in the Omega school of wisdom, much more than in Alpha or Zero, we need to now turn to Griffin's discussion of a postmodern science.

The Reenchantment of Science

For Griffin, the word *science* refers largely to the activities and disciplines developed since the "scientific revolution" of the 16th and 17th centuries for studying natural phenomena. However, it is important to note that his idea of science goes beyond the traditional definition. According to Griffin, the history of science parallels what I have called the "myth of reenchantment." The rise of the modern worldview meant disenchantment of the cosmos, but also of the scientific enterprise. Griffin disagrees with those who list science as a reason for the development of a soulless nature. Science itself became disenchanted, bereft of the possibilities still open to it in its earliest phase.

In agreement with new insights offered by historians and sociologists reexamining the origins of modern science, Griffin argues that many of the greatest scientists of the sixteenth and seventeenth centuries did not subscribe to a mechanistic view of nature. Newton, frequently cited as the chief architect of the modern scientific worldview, was drawn to ideas about nature that we might today call "magical." Such notions were widely accepted among alchemists and Hermeticists, also scientists in their fashion, who did not presuppose a dramatic split between matter and spirit but saw an intimate relationship between the two. Some of the greatest thinkers of the Renaissance period such as Pico della Mirandola who were familiar with Hermetic and Cabalistic writings supported the newly emerging sciences by arguing that humanity was capable not only of passive contemplation but also of active operation within nature.[26] Yet the magical, hermetic version of science, a science that devoted itself to the study of an enchanted world, eventually disappeared. Certainly, the great successes of the mechanistic sciences had a role to play in the demise of this particular scientific approach, but Griffin attributes several extrascientific factors.

Soul-body, God-world, and spirit-matter dualisms supported certain philosophical and theological positions. For example, God's existence could be argued from motion in terms of causality (Thomas Aquinas' first argument) and argued more forcibly. If the world is entirely without self-movement, it is thus dependent on a First Mover. The doctrine of the immortality of the soul could be defended on similar grounds. The body needs the soul, a non-physical reality capable of causing motion, because on its own it is powerless. In death, the soul leaves the body and attains its other-worldy immortal status. The testimony of saints' lives and scriptural accounts of God's miraculous activity in the world seemed more acceptable when supernatural and natural realms were understood to be distinct and separate. Such arguments, of course, drew from commonly held notions of a hierarchical universe similar to the ones we encountered in the chapter on Alpha. However, the intimate relationships between levels of being which characterized the Dantean cosmos were radically de-emphasized in favor of a more rigidly stratified universe.

Reasons for promoting a dualistic worldview went beyond theology and philosophy. A cosmological hierarchy, as we also saw in the Alpha discussion, had parallels in the human social and political spheres. The more rigid the differences between levels of being, the more stable the hierarchy. Stability became the goal of the established religious and secular authorities who were eager to preserve their power over the populace:

> These motives for mechanism were not simply theological but were equally sociological, in that they defended the Church's authority and thereby the State at a time when they were under attack. The Church's authority depended importantly upon the idea of rewards and especially punishments after death, which was thought to require a supernatural God and an immortal soul. This idea was considered essential for the preservation of the sociopolitical order against those who were seeking a wider distribution of material goods and political enfranchisement.[27]

Griffin draws from recent feminist thought when he characterizes the science of the Hermeticists and alchemists as "feminine" or "hermaphrodite" and mechanistic science as "masculine." The eventual victory of mechanistic science meant its approach toward nature supplied the dominant method and goal of the scientific enterprise. In its view, nature, devoid of spirit and feeling, was an object to be studied. Its external, observable features defined its reality. Because the physical senses, often enhanced by instruments such as the microscope, gathered the data, there was no scientific justification for relying on other human modes of interaction with the world such as feelings and intuitions. The ultimate purpose of science was to control rather than cooperate with nature. Such notions, basic to the "masculine" version of science, were more the result of what Griffin calls sociological or psychodynamic influences than any principles inherent in science itself.[28]

For Griffin, a "postmodern science" will, in part, revive some of the notions of Renaissance science. It will recognize that all things and beings have a "within," an interior life of feelings. Individuals are capable of spontaneous action, their interiority making it difficult to predict future behavior. Predictability, an important ideal for modern science, can only apply to aggregates (Griffin offers rocks, planets, and computers as examples[29]) or large numbers of individuals where the law of averages frequently predicts the course of future activity. But all individuals have some power of self-determination, higher-level beings enjoying more than those on lower-levels.

Science assumes a fundamental level of reality, currently a subatomic realm of particles and energy. By contrast, a postmodern science recognizes a plurality of levels, where each stratum has the capacity to affect others. Science has also assumed that simpler levels of being effect changes in the more complex, for example mental disorders having chemical or neurological causes. The philosophical term here would be upward causation. Griffin raises the possibility of downward as well as upward causation. To use the previous example, the mind can have an effect on as well as be affected by an internal physical condition. Postmodern science, therefore, will look for evidence of downward causation where more complex individuals have influenced the activity and nature of simpler levels of being. It follows that the new science will not be "scientistic," excluding insights and beliefs offered by "nonscientific" sources such as religion. Rather, science in its postmodern phase will be able to accept a God who, as final cause, attracts individuals to new and higher levels of being.

Griffin sees in evolutionary theory an opportunity for a postmodern theism and a postmodern science to complement one another:

> Postmodern theism suggests that God, as the appetitive soul of the universe, lures the creatures to actualize values that will result in greater richness of experience. . . . Whether the creatures' appetites are whetted is partly up to them. Whether they actualize the new possibilities once their appetites are whetted is fully up to them. Once they have actualized them, their outer demeanor is different, and the question of

their viability in the environment is raised. However, the environment in question may be only that of an animal's physiological system; the internal change may not yet have produced a change in the animal's external demeanor upon which the external environment would pass judgment.[30]

In postmodern science, neo-Darwinist notions of "chance and necessity," the mechanisms whereby the "viability" of changes in a creature's physiology or behavior are tested, are not rejected but regarded from a much broader perspective. The traditional scientific focus on a creature's "external demeanor" has been enriched with a new understanding of its inner life and an appreciation of the role of the divine lure in influencing its growth and development.

According to Griffin, modern and postmodern science agree on two basic principles. For Griffin, science must seek truth while remaining untainted by any ideology or politics. It must also include demonstrations which can be replicated in order to confirm or deny any conclusions. Griffin points out that these two shared concerns are free of any "limitations (1) to any particular domain, (2) any particular type of repeatability and demonstration, or (3) any particular contingent beliefs."[31] Being free of "any particular domain" means that science need not restrict itself to the physical realm or to efficient causation as the only kind of causation. Nor should it ignore data unavailable to the senses or scientific instruments. Animal and human behaviors are affected by external stimuli but also by internal causes such as purpose and experience. Science, therefore, must be open to the subjective as well as the objective dimension of existence.

Traditional science has understood its project to include discovering the "laws of nature." In this, it has proven to be quite successful, having uncovered numerous "laws," defining them with mathematical precision, and often applying them in technological advances. However, the notion of "laws of nature" has a limiting affect, apparently precluding efforts to explore their origin. "Laws" qua "laws" seem to need no justification for their existence, but a postmodern science which is not restricted to the physical realm or to efficient causation, both essential to the effort of discovering "laws," is free to consider the question why "laws" exist at all. Here Griffin suggests that we speak of "orders" instead of "laws" where one can observe phenomena within an "order" exhibiting "habits" rather than invariable obedience to "laws." This sort of terminology is vulnerable to critique by advocates of traditional science who see it as the vocabulary of a "soft" science which has abandoned more rigorous standards. Proponents of the "softer" sciences, however, reply that scientific rigor has too often depended on an assumption that "nature is dead and 'obedient' rather than generative and resourceful."[32]

Science requires a way of proving its theories, but the laboratory experiment need not be the only or most desirable method of demonstration. Field studies and historical records (e.g., reports of comets) also offer ways of verifying conclusions. At times, purely aesthetic or qualitative criteria seem to be the only justification for a theory, such as the beauty, simplicity, or elegance of its claim. However, by insisting on the laboratory as the preferred venue for scientific investigation and emphasizing predictability as the criterion for successful experimental design, representatives of traditional science are working on

> . . . the materialistic, nonecological assumption that things are essentially independent of their environments, so that the scientist abstracts from nothing essential in (say) removing cells from the human body or animals from a jungle to study them in a laboratory; . . . [and] the reductionistic assumption that all complex things are really no more self-determining than the elementary parts in isolation, so that they should be subject to the same kind of strong laboratory repeatability.[33]

Assumptions are based on beliefs, and Griffin argues that "the scientific pursuit of truth is not tied to any set of contingent beliefs" and "not limited to any particular type of explanation."[34] However, postmodern science does have some beliefs, even though it may not be "permanently wedded" to them.[35] Griffin cautions against considering them to be universally acceptable, although at the same time he hopes that they "would transcend perspectivalism."[36] But by rejecting any close relationship between beliefs about nature and the scientific enterprise, and then proposing a set of beliefs as significant scientific presuppositions, his position seems vulnerable to charges of inconsistency.

His argument succeeds only if we accept his characterization of the difference in attitude toward scientific beliefs. Beliefs of traditional science were apparently regarded beyond question - that things in nature lack feeling, that the laws of nature are unchanging, that causation occurs upwardly, and so forth. Postmodern beliefs, however, are "proposals to be subjected to ongoing public discussion among those with diverse worldviews."[37] They are not axiomatic principles but necessary only insofar as science requires a set of beliefs in order to proceed. But why this set of beliefs and not some other? Griffin claims that the postmodern vision, which is the source of the beliefs influencing postmodern science, "must be self-supporting"[38] and not based on supernatural revelation. The ideas emerging from this vision "must be based upon their intrinsic convincingness: they must pass the usual tests of self-consistency and adequacy to all the facts of experience."[39]

Griffin's argument appears to be circular. Science can verify ideas, but ideas (as contingent beliefs or presuppositions) are necessary for science to proceed. His argument also raises questions concerning his definition of experience, as he names experience as the source of "the facts" to which all beliefs and ideas must be adequate and self-consistent. Experiences often prove to be contradictory, irrational and therefore unpromising material for self-consistent beliefs. I ask these questions because they are obvious ones to raise at this point. Indeed, a reexamination of the process notions of reason and experience may yield what I believe would be a "deeper" interpretation of knowing. But first let us complete the summary of Griffin's discussion of postmodern scientific beliefs.

Griffin proposes five beliefs or principles for postmodern science as important presuppositions for postmodern science. The first three deal with causality. The first states that "every event is causally influenced by other events." Consistency dictates that the *creatio ex nihilo* doctrine must be rejected because, according to this principle, something must always arise from something, including the universe itself. The second principle states that humans and other beings are capable of self-determination and are not limited to the external environment for stimuli. The third principle stipulates that effect must follow cause in time. Time is a significant and real dimension of reality and it is unidirectional like an arrow arcing toward the future.

The last two principles are science's criteria for truth. The fourth deals with truth as a correspondence between statements and objective facts. Griffin recognizes the validity of contemporary critiques of the correspondence principle. Language can never fully capture reality because words about experience are not the experience itself. However, he parts company with those critics who deny the capacity for language to express nonverbal reality meaningfully and who prefer to characterize language as a closed circle. In Griffin's view, postmodern organicism has a more open position:

While language as such does not correspond to anything other than language, it expresses and evokes modes of apprehending nonlinguistic reality that can more or less accurately correspond to features of that reality. Hence, science can lead to ways of thinking about the world that can increasingly approximate to patterns and structures genuinely characteristic of nature.[40]

Human thought has the capacity, therefore, to interpret nature through language, and to test intellectual understanding through scientific trial and error. Results of scientific exploration in turn revise human thought. Griffin clearly believes science can gradually narrow the distance between inward mental activity and outward natural processes: "science can lead to ways of thinking about the world that can increasingly approximate to patterns . . . of nature."

The final principle, also concerned with scientific truth, is the principle of noncontradiction. He agrees with those who argue that certain claims can be made for opposite truths yet seem equally truthful. However, Griffin argues that these claims, if more closely examined for multiple levels of meaning, possibilities of vague language, or other sources of misunderstanding, can ultimately be shown to agree. The principle of noncontradiction is essential for meeting the requirement of coherence among scientific propositions, a requirement Griffin extends to human thought and practice.

In summarizing the major themes of postmodern science, Griffin identifies its ability to "allow us again to *feel* at home in the universe."[41] Scientific progress can now be understood in terms of reintegrating humanity and nature and reenchanting the world. The volume edited by Griffin, *The Reenchantment of Science*, serves as an introduction to postmodern scientific themes. Charles Birch, a biologist, speaks of self-determination on the molecular level and "an alternative to Cartesian mechanistic biology."[42] Rupert Sheldrake, a biochemist and cell biologist, proposes the existence of morphogenetic fields which act as organizing and structuring influences outside the immediate cause-and-effect chain.[43] The physicist David Bohm explains how his notion of unbroken wholeness describes the most fundamental dimension of reality more successfully than the mechanistic view of discrete objects.[44] Brian Swimme, another physicist, argues that postmodern science has revived the possibility of telling a cosmic creation story that communicates value and meaning.[45]

In order to pursue such promising ideas, science assumes certain beliefs called "principles" (to use Griffin's term). Although Griffin's five principles appear to have the authority of basic standards or laws, he and Cobb agree that constructive postmodern beliefs, even when presented as principles, can and should be material for discussion. Cobb suggests that the notion of truth is perhaps unhelpful, especially when it is applied to defining reality in all of its complexity and immensity. In place of truth, he prefers the notions of insight and understanding because they capture the provisional character of any particular act of knowing. In his words,

> An insight need not be absolutely and unambiguously true in order to direct thought and action into new and effective channels. Understanding is a matter of degree, and again, it does not entail the ability to give an unambiguous and exact account. . . . New insights will open up awareness of other aspects of [the] causal matrix without basically invalidating my previous understanding. The challenge will be to understand myself better through creative integration of the new insight and the old understanding.[46]

Postmodern science, then, can and should function within the wider scope of the postmodern vision. Science must admit it proceeds not by truths but by insights and understandings which can change over time. In the process school, if becoming describes how things *are* in the universe, it seems also to describe how we *know*. We have seen that knowing is being in Alpha and nothingness or not-knowing in Zero. I am proposing that in process theology and (as we shall see) the Omega school of wisdom, knowing is becoming. Since we become in time, the temporal is an essential dimension of our existence. The implication is that time has ontological significance. How this plays out in process teachings must be our next subject.

Time's Arrow and the Kingdom of Heaven

The process school develops its notion of time in three important areas of thought: physics, evolutionary theory, and theology. Whether considering the sub-atomic realm, the evolution of the cosmos, or Judeo-Christian scripture, process writers consistently represent time as a fundamental reality. Because physics concerns itself with what many consider to be the most basic elements of being, its understanding of time is critical for contemporary intellectual inquiry. It should come as no surprise that Griffin edited and contributed to a volume titled *Physics and the Ultimate Significance of Time*.

In his introduction to the book, Griffin describes time as having three characteristics which are drawn from human experience: "(1) a one-way direction that is in principle irreversible, (2) categorical differences between past, present, and future, and (3) constant becoming."[47] By focusing on human awareness of time, Griffin can offer an alternative to physics which traditionally views it as sequence of reversible events, graphically represented as the t-coordinate. For the process school, time is composed of distinct phases - past, present, and future. Griffin also uses the phrase "constant becoming" to express the dynamic nature of the now moment which is never still and always changing. From the perspective of the "moving now," the past is always different because each new event enters into the past and alters its content. According to Griffin, this understanding of the temporal distinguishes it from time in physics, at least in its classical, mechanistic version.

> More precisely, [in process thought] the present "now" never divides the same sets of events into past and future. In each new "now" there are events in the past that were not there before and that previously had been at most anticipated as possible, or perhaps probable, events. This is the feature of time that has been asserted by many writers to be most totally absent from physics.[48]

Griffin groups recent Western theories about time into three categories. The first view follows traditional physics in refusing to define it beyond the "laws of nature" discovered by science. The consequence of this restriction is that time has little reality. Indeed, for some it is illusory. The second view claims time emerged at more complex levels of being with the appearance of life or the development of mind. While this interpretation attributes a greater level of actuality to time than the first view, it considers the temporal as a contingent dimension, secondary in reality to the "facts" of the physical realm. This division between temporal and atemporal realms can lead to a metaphysical dualism.

The third view, that of the process school, accepts time as a metaphysical principle. As such, it cannot be defined by the theories or conclusions of specific sciences. It is both real and foundational, an ever-present aspect of existence which did not simply emerge at a later stage of cosmic evolution. Time itself does not refer to any concrete occasion, but rather to the relation between occasions. More accurately, it is "a relation of conformity to and inclusion of the past."[49] Griffin argues that in its treatment of time, traditional science has committed an error identified by Whitehead as the "fallacy of misplaced concreteness" when it applies its conclusions beyond the realm of its activity. What is unreal within the boundaries of classical physics is claimed to be unreal in nature.

Despite the intellectual nature of the claim being made for time as a metaphysical principle, Griffin insists that the proof for time's reality is in human experience. The final criterion for accepting this claim should be "hard core common sense" and the test of practice in everyday life. Griffin distinguishes "hard core" from "soft core common sense" by defining the latter as pertaining to local, "provincial" ideas and the former to "those notions that all people in fact presuppose in practice" and which "cannot be consistently and meaningfully denied since the very attempt to refute them would presuppose them."[50] To accept time's actuality, as people easily and often unconsciously do, is to recognize that important elements of our lives are not available to the senses. Rather, our nonsensory experiences of anticipation and memory verify that time does play a role in life, and an extremely important one at that.

Griffin's goal in critiquing physics' traditional understanding of time is, in part, to invite greater dialogue between that science and other sciences which have given time greater recognition. As we have already seen, evolutionary theory in particular has provided the process school with data and ideas which support a metaphysics of becoming. According to theory and corroborating geological and biological data, evolution has occurred through the development of more complex occasions out of simpler ones over great periods of time. According to process thought, this development is in part the result of the divine lure drawing created beings to higher levels of enjoyment. Complexity and enjoyment are directly related because intensity and harmony, potentially greater in more complex creatures, determine the quality of enjoyed experience. The more complex the creature, the greater its capacity for intensity and harmony, and hence for enjoyment.

Long periods of time were necessary because God acts through persuasion rather than control. The divine lure can only provide possibilities for actualization, which each being can select or refuse. The creative process requires a back-and-forth between Creator and creation, and true freedom must allow for error as well as perfection. Also, each new order of complexity requires a period of stabilization before new developments can appear, and developments usually occur in limited increments. Transmutations which are too dramatic usually do not survive and contribute to future events. Time, therefore, is an inevitable dimension in evolution, and like time in human experience, it has its defining categories of past, present, and future:

> Each stage of the evolutionary process represents an increase in the divinely-given possibilities for value which are actualized. The present builds upon the past, but advances beyond it to the degree to which it

responds to the divine impulses. This advance is experienced as intrinsically good, and it also provides the condition for an even richer enjoyment of existence in the future.[51]

Non-living entities such as atoms and molecules tend to preserve the given order. They do not introduce anything new into their level of existence. Living beings, however, are capable of novelty which increases the variety and intensity of their experience. By merging scientific data (evidence of increasingly complex organisms appearing over time) and experiential categories (creatures' increasing capacity for enjoyment), Cobb and Griffin can claim that "the evolutionary development of our world propounded by modern science can be interpreted in harmony with the character and purpose of God."[52]

For process thinkers who are also Christian theologians, the single most important public expression of God's purpose is scripture because it provides a record of God's action in history. Griffin argues that specific divine actions need not be interpreted as supernatural acts of intervention or interruptions of the natural order. When an event conforms more closely than usual to God's ideal aim of increasing value in the world, the result may be identified as an act of God. At times, an individual or community may choose to exercise an extraordinary degree of freedom over and above the limits of traditional behavior. Such moments can be understood to be occasions of effective divine influence. The specialness of the events, reflected upon by subsequent generations, can be emphasized by focusing on God's role in the event, but Griffin believes that such a focus need not eliminate the creature's capacity for self-determination. The notions of "revelation" and "acts of God," therefore, can find new meaning within a process context and biblical theology can be understood "as the discipline that attempts to carry out the task that the biblical historian who as a (process) theist could in principle attempt, i.e., of reconstructing the development of the biblical tradition employing 'divine influence' as one of the categories."[53]

As a record of God's activity, scripture is a source of historical hope. God's commitment to love and guide the world is clear throughout the biblical narratives. Cobb believes that historical hope has three basic prerequisites. The first, the openness of the future, reflects the opportunity for the human individual or community to make choices and shape events. The second is the widening of one's perspective to include others, "for a purely private hope is not historical."[54] The third is the potential for participating in a larger process of beneficial development. All three elements are present in Jesus' teaching of the Kingdom of Heaven which called people to act, to serve in the community, and to enter into the Kingdom's immediate and future reality as a new world. Historical hope, therefore, if vigorously upheld, could effectively oppose fatalism or lack of faith in the possibility of changing the status quo, defend its idealism through compassionate service to others, and reject negativistic worldviews of universal decay or the primacy of brute force.

However, history can and often does undermine our feelings of hope. The devastating effects of intermittent global and regional wars, the pervasive structures of racial, sexual, and economic oppression, the increase in disparity between rich and poor, and a variety of growing ecological crises seem to diminish the efforts of individuals and groups working to heal the human community. Science and technology seem to promise solutions, but have only alienated humanity from its natural environment.

If we turn to history for reasons to be hopeful, the best we can say is that the historical evidence is ambiguous. Even when something valuable is achieved, it cannot and perhaps should not last. What seems like a good and useful course of action can become limiting and even destructive if pursued too long. We seem doomed to a perpetual struggle. (Recall that Faust actually *chose* struggle as a way of life, a point we must return to later.) For some, time itself is the culprit because, in Whitehead's phrase, it is a perpetual perishing. But Jesus offered an alternative to historical ambiguity: the doctrine of the Kingdom. When the Kingdom of Heaven was accepted as a transformative reality, one's actions became grounded in a new realm and a new age:

> To witness to the Kingdom by word or by the cup of water to the thirsty neighbor might lead to suffering for oneself and even for others, but it was not thereby rendered questionable in its value. All such acts belonged to the Kingdom already and would be fulfilled in it.[55]

The Kingdom therefore validated worthy effort in the face of ambiguity and all its power to shatter hope.

A challenge remains: how to translate a doctrine expressed in premodern biblical terms into a belief that has contemporary meaning? The New Testament message of the imminent coming of a new age no longer has the same power to sustain hope. In Cobb's terms, "our relation to this rhetoric ... is broken." A "new conceptuality" is required but one that is "homologous" with the Gospels. Jesus' teaching of the Kingdom succeeded in establishing a basis for hope. It affirmed the possibility of virtuous action in history without identifying history itself with goodness, which would be idolatrous. Any contemporary effort at creating a new rhetoric would need to communicate similar values, and Cobb believes that Whitehead's version of the Kingdom of Heaven provides a viable option.

In Whitehead's thought, Christ as Logos is God in his Primordial Nature. The Logos is both transcendent to creatures and immanent within them, timeless in his capacity to offer ideal possibilities and incarnate in creatures' lives as a force for growth and development. According to Cobb, Whitehead identified the Logos as "the principle of concretion, the principle of limitation, the organ of novelty, the lure for feeling, the eternal urge of desire, the divine Eros."[56] The Logos, then, provides both the ideal forms of beauty toward which we strive and the fundamental impulse toward their actualization.

However, we often fail to realize the ideal. We refuse to recognize God's aim for us, or our historical context limits and distorts our efforts. Even if we succeed in actualizing an ideal, the passage of time dissolves our achievements. But failures, defeats, and time itself do not deprive our lives of ultimate meaning. God in his Consequent Nature, which Whitehead called the Kingdom of Heaven, has the power to gather up all that is valuable in our lives and reshape them into a new whole. God's responsive love is profoundly receptive to our activities, accepting a far greater range of good and evil than we can accept among ourselves. In Whitehead's thought, therefore, the Kingdom exemplifies the qualities of permanence in its everlasting love and fluency in its openness to novelty. Far from being a realm of changeless perfection, the Kingdom is a perpetually changing state of redeemed experiences contributing to its everlasting and growing harmony.

In a manner similar to Jesus' teachings on the subject, Whitehead's version of the Kingdom of Heaven recognized the ambiguities of the world and the reality of human freedom to make decisions. While all human actions are gathered up into the Consequent Nature of God, not all actions are equally good. How one acts in a given moment can affect the Kingdom as well as shape the kinds of possibilities available for future events. Human beings have the capacity to choose to be creative, to assist their fellow human beings, and to enrich their environment. They may, of course, opt for destructive behavior, but belief in the Kingdom and the ultimacy of a healing love in God makes historical hope possible. The Kingdom affirms the value of our efforts; it thereby affirms the value of history itself.

The close relationship between philosophy and theology can be seen

Omega: The Wisdom of Becoming 155

in Whitehead's writings, who despite his clearly philosophical focus occasionally adopted Christian terms such as the Kingdom of Heaven. Cobb, a process thinker who is also a Christian theologian, believes there is enough evidence of a religious nature in Whitehead's work "to claim him . . . as a servant of Christ."[57] Quoting Whitehead, Cobb compares the twentieth century thinker's vision with that of Jesus which "dwells upon the tender elements of the world, which slowly and in quietness operate by love; and it finds purpose in the immediacy of a kingdom not of this world."[58]

But Whitehead believed his project to be primarily a contribution to Western philosophy which in turn would be transformed and displaced by newer philosophical perspectives. This emphasis by the founder of the process movement on philosophy, particularly in its traditional mode of rational discourse, has had its effect on process theologians and continues to shape their perspective. For example, Cobb and Griffin follow Whitehead in describing the emergence of the great religious traditions during the first millennium b.c.e. as the rise of "rational religion."[59] Both place great significance on adequacy and coherence as criteria for a postmodern worldview. Griffin has written that a "formal point to make about a postmodern vision is that it must be self-supporting; that is, its claim to truth cannot be based on some alleged revelation."[60] But if not on revelation or some supra-rational mode of entering the divine mystery, then on what can truth in its deepest, most profound aspects be based? This returns us to the question central to this book: How can we talk about wisdom in contemporary terms? I am deeply persuaded by both Alpha and Zero (and my own experience) that there is a form of knowledge that is spiritual and that the "postmodern vision" can be grounded on something greater than reason (but not excluding it). We must now ask: Does process thought offer wisdom as a way of knowing?

Notes

1. John B. Cobb, Jr. and David Ray Griffin, *Process Theology: An Introductory Exposition* (Belfast: Christian Journals, 1976), 16.
2. Ibid., 17.
3. Ibid., 29.
4. Alfred North Whitehead, quoted in David Ray Griffin, *God and Religion in the Postmodern World: Essays in Postmodern Theology* (Albany: State University of New York Press, 1989), 41.
5. The process claim for *two* ultimates presents a metaphysical problem. The

very definition of *ultimate* excludes plurality. Further work needs to be done, perhaps along the lines of John Macquarrie's proposal that trinitarian thought be a way of pulling several process themes together, namely Creativity, and the Primordial and Consequent Natures of God. See John Maquarrie, *In Search of Deity: An Essay in Dialectical Theism* (New York: Crossroad, 1987), 151. See also Lewis Ford, "Process Trinitarianism," *Journal of the American Academy of Religion* 43 (1975): 207; Joseph Bracken, *The Triune Symbol: Persons, Process and Comment* (Lanham, MD: University Press of America, 1985); and *Trinity in Process: A Relational Theology of God*, ed. Joseph Bracken and Marjorie Hewitt Sochocki (New York: Continuum, 1996).

6. Ibid., 26.

7. Cobb and Griffin, 123. They are quoting from Alfred North Whitehead, *Process and Reality* (New York: Macmillan, 1928), 525.

8. Ibid., 57.

9. Ibid., 18.

10. Max Weber, "Science as Vocation." Quoted in Anthony J. Cascardi, *The Subject of Modernity* (Cambridge: Cambridge University Press, 1992), 16.

11. Cascardi, 16, n. 1.

12. Morris Berman, *The Reenchantment of the World* (Ithaca, N.Y.: Cornell University Press, 1981), 16.

13. Owen Barfield, *Saving the Appearances: A Study in Idolatry* (New York: Harcourt Brace Jovanovich, 1965), 78.

14. Ibid., 94.

15. Ibid., 89.

16. David Ray Griffin, *God and Religion*, 16.

17. Ibid.

18. Ibid., 22.

19. I am describing the modernist viewpoint in the present tense because it still characterizes the outlook of much of contemporary culture and society. It thus coexists with the postmodern perspectives I am about to summarize.

20. Ibid., 22-23.

21. John B. Cobb, "Two Types of Postmodernism: Deconstruction and Process," *Theology Today* 47 (1990): 149-64.

22. Griffin, *God and Religion.*, 20 and n. 11, p. 149.

23. Ibid., 23.

24. Ibid., 24.

25. Cobb and Griffin, 155-56.

26. Griffin refers to the scholarship of Frances Yates, in particular *Giordano Bruno and the Hermetic Tradition* (Chicago: University of Chicago Press, 1964), 155-56, 161.

27. David Ray Griffin, "Introduction," in *The Reenchantment of Science*, 11.

28. For these points, Griffin credits two feminist thinkers: Carolyn Merchant, *The Death of Nature: Women, Ecology and the Scientific Revolution* (San Francisco: Harper & Row, 1980) and Evelyn Fox Keller, *Reflections on Gender and Science* (New Haven, CT: Yale University Press, 1985).

29. Griffin, *God and Religion*, 79.
30. Ibid., 81.
31. Griffin, "Introduction," 26.
32. Ibid., 27. For the notion of "orders," Griffin credits David Bohm and Evelyn Fox Keller, and cites Keller's *Reflections on Gender and Science*, 131-136.
33. Ibid.
34. Ibid., 28.
35. Ibid.
36. Ibid.
37. Ibid.
38. Griffin, *God and Religion*, 23.
39. Ibid.
40. Griffin, "Introduction," 29.
41. Ibid., 31.
42. Charles Birch, "The Postmodern Challenge to Biology," in *The Reenchantment of Science*, 76.
43. Rupert Sheldrake, "The Laws of Nature as Habits: A Postmodern Basis for Science," in *The Reenchantment of Science*, 81 ff.
44. David Bohm, "Postmodern Science and a Postmodern World," in *The Reenchantment of Science*, 65-66.
45. Brian Swimme, "The Cosmic Creation Story, " in *The Reenchantment of Science*, 47-56. See also Brian Swimme and Thomas Berry, *The Universe Story: From the Primordial Flaring Forth to the Ecozoic Era - A Celebration of the Unfolding of the Cosmos* (San Francisco: HarperSanFrancisco, 1992).
46. Cobb, "Two Types," 157.
47. David Ray Griffin, "Introduction: Time and the Fallacy of Misplaced Concreteness," in *Physics and the Ultimate Significance of Time*, ed. David Ray Griffin (Albany: State University of New York Press, 1986), 1.
48. Ibid., 2.
49. Ibid., 6.
50. Griffin, "Introduction: Time . . . ,", 8.
51. Cobb and Griffin, 67.
52. Ibid., 69.
53. David R. Griffin, "Relativism, Divine Causation, and Biblical Theology," in *God's Activity in the World: The Contemporary Problem*, ed. Owen C. Thomas (Chico, Calif.: Scholars Press, 1983), 135.
54. John B. Cobb, Jr., *Christ in a Pluralistic Age* (Philadelphia: Westminster Press, 1975), 221.
55. Ibid., 225.
56. Ibid., 71.
57. Ibid., 229.
58. Whitehead quoted in Cobb, *Christ in a Pluralistic Age*, 229.
59. Cobb and Griffin, *Process Theology*, 90.
60. Griffin, *God and Religion*, 23.

Chapter 7

Omega: The Becoming of Wisdom

Visions and Intuitions

Cobb and Griffin view human experience as the source of insight and they rely on reason to supply the appropriate means of understanding and interpreting experience. In *Process Theology*, they claim that the notion of the kinship of all things is "rationally supported" by process arguments.[1] In *God and Religion in the Postmodern World*, Griffin states that postmodern theology (i.e., process theology in its more recent phase) is really philosophy in the sense that "it argues for its positions in terms of strictly philosophical criteria, making no appeal to special revelation to support its truth-claims."[2] We have also seen that for Griffin, the final criterion for accepting truth-claims should be "hard core common sense" derived from experiences of everyday life. But he also admits that "without a direct experience of God, which is at the heart of mysticism, the roots of the ethical side of spirituality will shrivel up."[3] Cobb and Griffin suggest that Buddhist meditation may have something to offer to the Christian tradition,[4] but without exploring the ways in which such meditation or mystical experience may introduce alternative modes of knowing. It often seems that while the two process thinkers place an overwhelming emphasis on reason, they are just one step shy of enlarging their epistemological framework. Consider, for example, Griffin's statement that postmodern theology's positions must be established "solely in terms of the criteria used in scientific and philosophical reasoning at its best, that is, self-consistency, adequacy to the relevant facts, and illuminating power."[5] The first two criteria, self-consistency and adequacy, are familiar rational principles, but what are we to make of "illuminating power"? For some readers, it may suggest a quite different epistemic territory despite its appearance in a pitch for rationality.

An opportunity for examining this and other issues arose during a dialogue between David Ray Griffin and Huston Smith.[6] Given what we know about both schools of thought, it comes as no surprise that the two differ sharply over a number of key themes and ideas. Smith prefers to speak of God as impersonal and the world as perfect and included in God's existence.[7] Griffin emphasizes God as personal and the world as "very good on the whole" but not perfect because of the presence of genuine evil.[8] Smith's overall metaphysical movement is toward an ontological unity where existence is most real in the Absolute. Griffin seeks to preserve the irreducible plurality of the universe and the freedom available to finite beings. On the subject of temporality, Griffin presents time as always having been, while for Smith it is causally (not temporally) derived from the timeless infinite.[9] The primordial traditionalist sees no reason for elevating time to a metaphysical principle operating on the level of the Godhead.

When the conversation turns to epistemological issues, their debate raises questions about the process school's reliance on reason. Smith argues that reason and common sense are insufficient for establishing a worldview. His preference is for another noetic faculty, intellect, which proceeds by immediate intuition rather than the more deliberative approach of reason. To Smith, Griffin seems more like a Western philosopher aiming for a "cookie cutter" clarity of ideas, while religion and theology recognize the need for a certain vagueness in their foundational beliefs, a vagueness that at times expresses itself paradoxically or in ways quite mad to the rational mind. Smith believes process thought to be too much of this world:

> Herein lies my focal dis-ease with theology that is process based: it accommodates theology to philosophy, religion to the world, the deepest wisdom of the ages to styles of thought that secularization has influenced profoundly. "Spiritual wisdom, from a worldly point of view, is a kind of madness," I chance to read in the course of revising this page. Process theology proposes to critique that madness from the world's perspective.[10]

Elsewhere, Smith writes: "Religion must, to be sure, be intelligible in certain ways, but to try to make it *rationally* intelligible, fully so, is to sound its death knell."[11] While Smith and Griffin are critical of modernism,[12] Smith believes Griffin has retained the modernist emphasis on reason.[13]

Both Griffin and Smith insist on the importance of experience and the need for data in constructing a worldview. Indeed, Smith argues that the disagreement is not about coherence but about data. According to Smith, the facts derived from everyday life are acceptable up to a point. Common sense ideas resulting from those facts are at times contradicted by the insights of mystics and sages who frequently express their wisdom in paradox. For Smith, the notion of paradox is an important one and central to the process of religious insight.

> Paradoxes should not be entered into lightly, but only soberly and advisedly, which is to say: not until ineluctable evidence forces us into them. Whereupon, if one comes to sense the reasons that require them, the frustration they initially provoked gives way to delight - the "ahas" of the eureka response; so *that* was why their two sides seemed at odds: they were being viewed from different angles or planes.[14]

The realization of paradox is an aspect of the religious worldview which through "the eyes of faith" perceives reality in tension. The everyday world can for the most part seem uniform and predictable, but the "finely honed" sensibility of the mystic can see it as a world alive with tensions between perfect and imperfect, good and evil, life and death. The intellect far more than reason can recognize this deeper level of reality.[15]

By arguing that scientific method includes subjective (i.e., aesthetic and ethical) values, Griffin defines science more broadly than has traditionally been the case. Smith points out that the medieval curriculum numbered sciences among the liberal arts, but he believes Griffin wants to subsume the arts under science. Smith is doubtful whether Griffin's version of a postmodern science will ever persuade the National Science Foundation enough to win its financial support.[16] He accuses Griffin of being unrealistic because the sort of science that has been heretofore successful has been the kind that Griffin attacks, a science intent on discovering ways of gaining control over nature, of being effective in the world. By "science," therefore, Smith means classical science, the discipline which aims to produce effective knowledge. He cannot believe that Griffin's version will be equally effective.

Smith does point to a pair of terms in Griffin's vocabulary which suggest other noetic possibilities, in particular *prehension* and *vision*. But in the final summation of their differences and agreements, both agree that Smith's *intellect*, "an intuitive way of knowing," is closer to *prehension* which Griffin characterizes also as "an intuitive way of knowing." For Griffin, *vision* is broader in meaning than any epistemic category:

What I mean by "vision," by contrast, is a preconceptual, prepropositional way of seeing reality which is largely inherited from one's culture - even in the case of visionaries who modify it significantly. It is not in itself a way of knowing; it is - even though most people do not have the self-transcendence to think of it this way - more on the order of a hypothesis about reality. A particular *vision* of reality, such as the biblical vision of the world as creation, or the Buddhist vision of all things as empty, proves itself to be true, to the extent that it does, by giving birth to a *conceptualization* of a reality that is more coherent, more adequate, and more illuminating than rival visions.[17]

Cobb and Griffin, however, do not employ this particular definition of *vision* throughout their writings. For example, Griffin speaks of "an *acceptable* postmodern vision" which "must be self-consistent and must be adequate to the facts of science as well as to the moral, aesthetic, and religious dimensions of our experience."[18] Cobb describes the postmodern project as an effort "to *develop* an alternative vision of nature and society, of the way the world is and human life could be."[19] They are clearly attracted to the term and use *vision* on occasion to express something available to a wide range of people to "accept" and "develop." It appears that the term *visionaries* can be applied more widely than to founders of religions and acknowledged spiritual masters. Moreover, there is nothing in their usage of *vision* which eliminates *knowing* as a possible meaning unless one were to limit *knowing* to *reason*.

At the same time, we need to note the rich possibilities in the process notion of *prehension*. Whitehead used the term to talk about a variety of experiential data including "perception, causation, memory, time, space, enduring individuality (or substantiality), the mind-body relation, the subject-object relation in general, and the God-world relation."[20] Given its importance, it would useful to quote in full Cobb and Griffin's description of *prehension*:

> ... a momentary experience is essentially related to previous experiences. In fact, it begins as a multiplicity of relations, and achieves its individuality through its reaction to and unification of these relations. It is not first something in itself, which only secondarily enters into relations with others. The relations are primary. Whitehead's technical terms for these relations are 'prehension' and 'feeling'. The present occasion 'prehends' or 'feels' the previous occasions. The present occasion is nothing but its process of unifying the particular prehension with which it began.[21]

If we grant noetic status to *prehension*, we could rephrase the final sentence to say every being (present occasion) is defined by its becoming (process) through knowing (prehending or feeling). In process philosophy, becoming is knowing, or conversely, knowing is becoming.

By speaking of "feelings" and "visions" as forms of "knowing," I am suggesting that process thought includes modes of knowledge other than reason. Griffin admits that reason alone cannot create a worldview, but must base itself on religious vision which is nonrational. He states that "any worldview presupposes a nonrational (that is, prerational) vision of reality."[22] Such a view is basic to Eastern philosophy which assigns a far greater role to intuition than do philosophers of the West. We have seen how the Kyoto philosophers, drawing from Buddhist tradition and meditative experience, can write dialectically about the meaning of the *sunyata* doctrine. Emptiness is empty because it is fullness, life is life because it is death. E.A. Burtt has pointed out this ability of Eastern philosophers to base their systems on contradictory statements. By and large, the West has followed Aristotle's "laws of thought," and these laws include the law of non-contradiction adhered to by Griffin. Thinkers in Hindu and Buddhist philosophy, however, have believed "it would be fatal to allow ourselves to be enslaved by these principles."[23]

In Eastern thought, philosophical statements are not strictly independent, objective facts, but claims made by human individuals deeply concerned about gaining spiritual knowledge and freedom. And one of the gravest dangers to true freedom is "the dogmatic tendency of people to assume that there is only one way to the saving truth."[24] In other words, we must admit the reality of contradictory experiences, truths, principles, and beliefs. Spiritual wisdom must rely on intuition more fundamentally than reason. Burtt is quite clear in claiming an elevated, spiritually sophisticated meaning for intuitive knowledge. It is far more than "mere hunches or snap judgments" but a deep insight into one's inner nature.

> Full self-knowledge involves an awareness of all the turbulent desires and passions stirring the soul, which are the source of inner conflict and which block the path toward the achievement of an integrated personality. Moreover, this is a practical and not just a theoretical awareness; it is such an understanding of these passions as illumines the way to release from them and the realization of the spiritual perfection that lies potentially within us. To achieve this apprehension is a long and arduous process; it is a matter of increasing intellectual insight. In this context, understanding and knowledge are no mere affairs of reason and logic as they are for the West - they involve much more than the gaining of information about formal structures or matters of fact. They are the intellectual aspect of an inclusive process of growth toward the maturing

of one's whole personality, in which respect for logic and for fact in the Western sense plays a significant but fractional part.[25]

Over the years, Masao Abe and John Cobb have engaged in a number of dialogues where the nature of God and *sunyata*, good and evil, freedom of the will, time, and history were central issues. In his essay, "Kenotic God and Dynamic Sunyata," Abe considers the place of reason in Buddhist thought. Identifying reason as "a mental ability to think, to measure and discriminate objects," Buddhists have viewed it as an obstacle to the gaining of wisdom or *jnana*.[26] Recognizing that the place of reason has been quite different in the West, Abe admits that Buddhism's devaluation of reason has made it impossible for pure science and theoretical philosophy to develop within his tradition. At the same time, nondiscriminating wisdom is not an absence of thinking, because that would be a dualism between thinking and not-thinking, and Buddhism rejects dualisms. Rather, wisdom is non-thinking thinking, a "primordial thinking prior to the distinction and opposition between thinking and not-thinking." By being primordial, it includes both.

> (Primordial thinking) can include rational, discursive thinking and even pure theoretical reason. This is, however, only *potentially* so, for historically Buddhism has been hasty to go beyond human reason to arrive at the nondiscriminating wisdom because of the stance that human reason is merely discriminative. Thus Buddhism has not known the creative possibility of human reason developed in the modern West in terms of science.[27]

In his response to Abe, Cobb calls for Buddhism to follow its non-thinking wisdom and realize a "primordial discrimination prior to the opposition between subject and object."[28] But he does not explore this intriguing suggestion any further to see if it has any implications for process thought.

Smith and Abe are in agreement, then, about the reality of a mode of knowing different from rationality. For Smith, the *intellectus* can be sharply distinguished from the *ratio*, a distinction in Christian thought that goes back at least as far as Augustine.[29] Abe presents wisdom in terms similar to the *sunyata* dialectic of being/not-being. Both believe that spiritual wisdom and empirical science have developed along separate tracks. For a wisdom more appropriately expressive of the process *vision* of the world, we must look beyond the process thinkers who have based their work on Whitehead. We must, I believe, turn to Teilhard de Chardin. He has been recognized by many as a process thinker who is also a mystic.

We will begin by briefly examining his credentials as a process theologian and then look more closely at his contribution as a spiritual writer.

Teilhard's Process Thought

In the texts we have used to examine the process school's themes, Cobb and Griffin number Teilhard among process-oriented thinkers and quote him on occasion.[30] However, they do not devote space to a more deliberate exploration of the Jesuit's writings. For such an exploration, we must look elsewhere. Ewert Cousins, the editor of an anthology of process theologians, argues that "Teilhard can be considered a process thinker both in terms of the content and the context of his thought,"[31] and therefore includes excerpts from Teilhard's works in the anthology. The collection also offers an essay by Ian Barbour comparing Teilhard's thought with Whitehead's. This essay will serve a two-fold function for us: as an introduction to Teilhard's speculative work and as a way of affirming his place in the process school.

Barbour believes that Teilhard's writings can be variously interpreted: "as evolutionary science, as poetry and mysticism, as natural theology, and as Christian theology."[32] Barbour's goal is to point out those aspects of Teilhard's thought which make him a process theologian. His method is to compare him with Whitehead on seven major themes while bracketing certain elements in his life and work, "including the profound spirituality and mysticism which were his most impressive characteristics."[33] However, as we shall see, mention of Teilhard's mystical experience cannot be easily excluded from even a short summary of his thought.

Both Whitehead and Teilhard view the world as composed of events and processes rather than static substances. Time cannot be regarded as an aspect separate from things, because "duration permeates the essence of every being."[34] Not only are all things in the process of becoming, but they are constantly interacting as well. Things are, in fact, made up of their relationships. In Teilhard's words, "However narrowly the 'heart' of an atom is circumscribed, its realm is coextensive at least potentially with that of every other atom."[35] This is similar to Whitehead's notion of reality as a society, and his critique of the traditional scientific idea of "Simple Location" which regards objects as independent and separable from their relations to other objects. Despite this emphasis on re-lationality, both thinkers are pluralistic insofar as they recognize each being's capacity for self-creation and freedom. Barbour argues, however, that Whitehead is more thoroughly pluralistic, seeing time's flow as "an interconnected series of discrete events,"[36] which is a contrast to Teilhard's "temporal threads running back to infinity."[37] Teilhard speaks of the "convergence" and "centration" of the cosmos and thus presents a universe with a greater tendency towards oneness. Barbour suggests that Teilhard's descriptions of cosmic evolution can make it seem rather like "a single Whiteheadian concrescence,"[38] but this holistic perspective of history may reflect the influence of mystical experience and biblical eschatology on the Jesuit's thought.

The second common theme Barbour examines is the presence of subjectivity throughout the created world. A frequent Teilhardian term for subjectivity is the *within*, but he also uses other words synonymously, among them *interiority*, *psychic life*, *mentality*, and *consciousness*. For Teilhard, the *within* can be found at all levels of existence, from the atomic to the human. Although molecules can be said to have a degree of consciousness, they have it infinitesimally, while in humans it is present to a much higher degree. Teilhard believes consciousness to be directly correlated with the complexity of an entity. In higher organisms this complexity occurs in increasingly more intricate nervous systems. Similarly, Whitehead describes the "subjective pole" of an entity but he applies it selectively. It is absent in stones, barely perceptible in cells, and fully present in animal life. In the Whiteheadian schema, psychism and awareness are evident only in higher, more evolved beings. A stone maintains its being through the sheer cohesion of its elements and thus is a "corpuscular society" without any "subjective pole." This contrasts with Teilhard's notion of a greater continuity of consciousness or the *within* across all levels of existence.[39]

Whitehead and Teilhard find subjectivity in the world around them because both thinkers have accepted the notion that human experience provides the basic categories for understanding nature. Barbour believes their reasons for accepting this idea are similar. First, both see a unity of the human realm with its natural environment. Teilhard states that "the roots of our being are in the first cell."[40] Neither writer can accept the notion that consciousness is an epiphenomena reality separate from physical nature. Second, both see history and evolution as a continuous process. What occurs now is deeply rooted in what occurred in the past. Third, the terms we use to interpret the world should be coherent. Human experience offers a vocabulary upon which to build a consistent metaphysics of the whole of reality. Although Teilhard did not identify his work as metaphysics, Barbour believes that "a similar concern for intellectual coherence seems to have been one of Teilhard's motives."[41] Fourth, both thinkers were concerned with overcoming the mind-body (and for Teilhard, the matter-spirit) dualism that has characterized the Western intellectual tradition since Descartes. Mind-body or matter-spirit are not separate realities or levels of existence but closely related aspects of one process. One difference between Whitehead and Teilhard occurs in their understanding of the relationship between the "within" and the "without," or the subjective and objective aspects of existence. Whitehead believed subjectivity and objectivity described two successive phases of an event, while Teilhard saw each entity as a unity of its subjective and objective dimensions.

The third common theme Barbour discusses is the relationship between freedom and determination. Based on his scientific studies, Teilhard argues that our world "exhausts *only a part of what might have been*,"[42] and each event in cosmic history is unique and unrepeatable. He thus speaks of "blind chance," "random mutations" and "trial and error," ideas that apparently favor a view of evolution free of determinative natural laws or divine fiat. But Barbour also points out those passages in Teilhard's writings which use a more deterministic vocabulary. Here Teilhard describes evolutionary stages as "inevitable," "inexorable," or "necessary." The process of global socialization and the convergence of humankind upon itself is "irresistible," following the path of "sure ascent." Barbour lists three ways in which Teilhard attempts to reconcile this apparent clash between freedom and determination. First, he makes use of the law of high numbers and applies its principle of statistical predictability to evolutionary chance and human activity. The outcome of an individual coin toss is unpredictable, but the results of many tosses follow a more predictable pattern. Similarly, individual human actions may be free and indeterminate. Hence, they can be successful or failed contributions to history, but "by a sort of 'infallibility of large numbers,' Mankind, the present crest of the evolutionary wave, cannot fail."[43] Second, Teilhard can at times characterize the universe as having its own sense of purpose and power that can override the interests of the individual: " . . . nothing, as it seems, can prevent the Universe from succeeding - nothing, not even our human liberties."[44] Third, God's omnipotence assures the Christian believer that an Omega will be reached, that the world will converge and achieve a spiritual transformation. Teilhard's references to a "strong" version of God's activity in the world strike a contrast with the process school's gentler notions of the divine lure, and Barbour mentions the inevitable theological problem Teilhard's position raises. How can he reconcile individual freedom with divine omnipotence? According to Barbour, Teilhard "throws little new light" on the issue. For his part, Whitehead refuses to accept the notion of a divine plan. While God has "unchanging purposes," his goals for any specific event can change in response to the choices made by his creatures. Individual freedom is thereby preserved. To show that Teilhard is far from being a pantheist, Barbour quotes those passages where the Jesuit insists that an individual's personal identity is fulfilled rather than annihilated by mystical union. According to Teilhard, "union differentiates,"[45] and thus his form of mysticism includes "the expectation of perfect unity, steeped in which each element will reach its consummation at the same time as the universe."[46]

As the fourth theme, both thinkers believe in God's ongoing and active presence in the world. Divine creativity does not refer to a one-time event but to an immanent reality at work within the processes of evolution and history. According to Barbour, both Whitehead and Teilhard diverge from the classical Christian teaching of *creatio ex nihilo*, but "both men share the *motives* which led the church fathers to the formulation of the traditional doctrine."[47] These include a desire to emphasize the goodness of matter and divine sovereignty. While Teilhard and Whitehead appear to restrict this sovereignty, they do not do so absolutely and therefore avoid a dualism of God and cosmos. Teilhard, however, seems less clear than Whitehead in describing the ways in which God interacts with the world, at times seeming to portray God's role as the provider of the natural laws of evolution and at other times suggesting a more intimate presence in the internal life of his creatures. As we have seen in our examination of Cobb and Griffin, the Whiteheadian system depicts in detail God's specific functions in the various stages of an event. The process school's analysis of an entity's becoming, including the roles played by past events and divine ideals, provides "a set of categories which allow for lawfulness, spontaneity, and divine influence in the 'continuous creation' of the world."[48] This kind of analytical specificity is lacking in Teilhard.

The fifth shared theme is the reality of change in the divine life. As Teilhard and Whitehead contend that such change does occur, they diverge from the traditional doctrine of God's immutability. According to Barbour, Teilhard's defenders claim that he is simply building on equally traditional notions of God's absolute freedom: God freely chose to limit himself in wanting the world to complete him. Moreover, human activity, in cooperation with the divine purpose, is helping to build up Christ's Body in the world, which is simply another way of saying that the human community has the capacity to "complete" God.[49] This capacity is a gift from God. Whitehead's Primordial Nature of God is similar to Teilhard's Alpha. Each represents the envisagement of the divine purpose. Teilhard's Omega is similar to Whitehead's Consequent Nature because both express that aspect of the divine life which is affected by the world.

Both deal with the problem of evil, Barbour's sixth theme, in comparable ways. For Teilhard, evil is an unavoidable outcome in an evolving cosmos. It arises from the clash of incompatible alternatives presented by the world. According to this perspective, we suffer not because of sin, but because we are in the process of growing and developing.

> Physical and moral evil originate from a process of becoming; everything which evolves experiences suffering and moral failure. . . . The Cross is a symbol of the pain and toil of evolution, rather than the symbol of expiation.[50]

If God has created creatures who are truly free, evil, sin, and suffering necessarily follow. Failures as well as successes contribute to the Omega. The origins of original sin are therefore embedded in the very nature of creation rather than the result of a human act: "Evil appears with the first atom."[51] We have seen how, for Whitehedians like Cobb and Griffin, evil is the consequence of incompatible possibilities but also of triviality. In the case of triviality, the individual chooses something less valuable than the occasion calls for. In both Teilhard and Whitehead we find a God who receives both evil and good contributions and transforms them into a new harmony. In Whitehead's words, God "loses nothing that can be saved."[52] But here too, according to Barbour, the process philosopher appears to present a more limited God in order to maintain the freedom of the individual and his or her capacity to affect the divine life: "Even more than in Teilhard's writing, the future actualization of the divine ideal is understood to be dependent on the world's activity."[53]

The seventh and last theme is the world's future. For Teilhard, humankind's convergence upon itself is clear when one examines the evidence of the past and the fact of increasing complexity and consciousness. The earth has developed through significant stages from geosphere to biosphere to noosphere, or in other terms, from earth to life to human civilization, each subsequent stage emerging from and incorporating the previous one. Over long periods of evolutionary time, physiological and neurological complexity has increased. Because of the earth's curvature, the noosphere, the most recent layer around the earth formed by human culture and thought, is undergoing a process of "planetary compression." For Teilhard, this process reveals the unitary nature of the world's evolution, while Whitehead stresses the continued and irreducible plurality of the universe. For the process philosopher, each event is the result of a convergence of multiple possibilities, and it in turn becomes available for contributing to a new event. In Whitehead's memorable phrase, "the many become one, and are increased by one."[54]

Teilhard's christology plays a crucial role here. His faith in the "cosmic Christ" as the ultimate center toward which all things are converging allows him to see evolution as a personalizing and "Christification" of matter. Redemption is the perfection of the entire cosmos through evolution and not simply a saving of individual human souls. The Eucharist celebrates this process and represents God's incarnational participation in the cosmic story. The biblical eschaton need not be a cataclysmic event but rather a culmination of a long collaborative work by God, humankind, and nature. Whitehead also believed in evolution and the appearance of significantly new orders of existence, but without any notion of a final convergence and consummation. He preferred to speak about a series of "cosmic epochs," none of which represented a completed transformation of the universe. We might say he preferred multiple eschatons.

Barbour's comparison of the two thinkers, therefore, makes it clear that Teilhard tended toward a unifying vision while Whitehead was more pluralistic. While Barbour attempts to bracket Teilhard's mysticism, he keeps referring to it as an influence on Teilhard's version of process thought. And indeed, such references were inevitable because the intellectual and the spiritual are two deeply related aspects of the Jesuit's thought world. We will now turn our attention to the story of Teilhard's intellectual journey and see how his spiritual development led to his particular worldview.

A Spiritual Autobiography

While we consider Teilhard as a spiritual writer and mystic, it is important to keep in mind that much of his life was devoted to scientific work. As a paleontologist, he contributed to geological and fossil research in Asia and helped to discover a skull of Peking man in 1929. A number of Teilhard's theories and findings are still considered valid and important purely on a scientific level.[55] But throughout his life, developments in his understanding of the physical world were deeply influenced by his spiritual growth. As a result, his scientific writings were complemented by a number of more controversial spiritual works, but the publication of the latter was forbidden by his order until after his death. Born and educated in France, he traveled widely, frequently to China for his paleontological research, and he spent his last years in the United States. He died in New York City in 1955.

In 1950, Teilhard had returned to the Auvergne, a province in central France where as a child he had enjoyed its rough landscape of volcanic hills and forests. Here he composed most of the text of *The Heart of Matter*, a work regarded by Ursula King as "his autobiographical masterpiece."[56] The setting was important because it provided the environment, both natural and psychological, wherein he could, according to N.M. Wildiers, create the essay that "exposes the very foundations from which arose the whole structure of his work."[57] Teilhard described his project in a letter to friends:

> Facing the Puys mountains, far from every railway and in the midst of oak trees, . . . I am jotting down a first outline (definitive?) of an essay about which I have been thinking for a long time: "Le coeur de la matière" (not at all in the sense of Graham Greene!). It is an essay on the reconstruction of the psychological genesis which historically has brought me (since my childhood) to pass from a vague and general cosmic sense to what I now call "the Christic sense."[58]

The Heart of Matter, therefore, can be read as a key work, an introduction to Teilhard's other, perhaps better known works such as *The Phenomenon of Man* and *The Divine Milieu*. Because of its intensely personal nature, it offers a vivid picture of how the man developed inwardly, and, as I hope to show, provides important clues about the kind of wisdom that is Omega's version of spiritual knowing.

Teilhard begins his essay by enumerating three "universal components" which have shaped his life: "the Cosmic, the Human, and the Christic." These three are distinct but convergent within a process of mutual transformation. The depth of Teilhard's belief in the reality of this process at times intensifies his prose into poetry. In the following passage, Cosmic, Human, and Christic are called Matter, Spirit, and Person.

> Crimson gleams of Matter, gliding imperceptibly into the Gold of Spirit, ultimately to become transformed into the incandescence of a Universe that is Person - and through all this there blows, animating it and spreading over it a fragrant balm, a zephyr of Union - and of the Feminine.[59]

Although not listed among the three components, "Union and the Feminine" are also important elements of his vision introduced later in the text. *The Heart of Matter*'s three main sections cover each of the "three components" more or less in chronological order. In other words, Teilhard's spiritual autobiography begins with his intense interest in and attraction to the realm of Matter, moves on to describe his subsequent recognition of the significance of the Human, and concludes with his experience of the Christic. The first section, "The Cosmic, or the Evolutive," includes a reflection on what Teilhard considers to be a universal phenomenon: the need for a sure foundation for one's existence, a "Unique all-sufficing and necessary reality" which Teilhard calls the "Sense of Plenitude." This need pervades his own story and thus acts as "a clue to lead the reader through these pages, . . . an axis that will give continuity to the whole."[60] This "Pleromic Sense" is "biologically guided," at work beneath all the activity of his "psychological substratum." From the very first, we can see how Teilhard believes that the motions of Spirit are rooted in the "Stuff of Things," in this case the stuff of his physical being.

Teilhard describes his early attraction to Matter (the capitalization is his) when, as a child of six or seven, he began to collect objects made of iron. The lock-pin of a plow, a metal bolt, bullet shells from a firing-range provided bits of "the Absolute in the form of the Tangible," pieces of the "Iron God" who is incorruptible.[61] When the boy found his hidden metal treasure to be susceptible to scratches and rust, he turned to other minerals such as quartz and amethyst crystals. It was the beginning of an ever-widening process to identify Plenitude within the material world, a search for Consistence that eventually led him to a more universal "stuff," the "Stuff of Things," away from specific things like metal objects or minerals to "an Elemental permeating all things." Although Teilhard's journey was to take him into a more traditionally spiritual territory, he confesses he "was never to feel at home unless immersed in an Ocean of Matter."[62]

In the years of his youth and young manhood, between the ages of ten and thirty, he became increasingly more interested in the vegetal and animal realms. From the perfections of the Solid and Incorruptible, he turned to the New and the Rare and began collecting zoological and botanical specimens. His more formal education introduced him to physics and its world of electrons, nuclei, waves, and "the vast cosmic realities" of energy, mass, permeability, radiation, curvatures, and so forth which later served Teilhard as "archetypes" for describing "the Christic."[63]

But this expansion of perspective brought with it a hunger for something yet more basic, a desire to know "a common substratum of the Tangible" by an experience of self-surrender to the All behind manifest reality. He recognized this as an attraction to the monistic mysticism of the Hindu tradition which would have diverted him from his scientific studies if he had not encountered the theory of Evolution.

In particular, Henri Bergson's *Creative Evolution* started Teilhard on an important new intellectual path. Bergson's ideas gave him a way of comprehending the universe as a synthesis of Matter, Life, and Energy, the three "cults" which had captivated Teilhard thus far in his attempts to gain an enduring Sense of Plenitude. In place of a static cosmos, Teilhard began to conceive of a more dynamically organic universe evolving through the process of Cosmogenesis. Moreover, he questioned religious and secular teachings which presented matter and spirit or body and soul as two separate substances. Within an evolving universe, they could be seen as "two states or two aspects of one and the same cosmic Stuff."[64] Although many questions remained to be answered, Teilhard had achieved a fundamental insight. Matter was becoming progressively spiritualized and the process was irreversible. His work in paleontology provided him with sufficient proof that "by its gravitational nature, the Universe, I saw, was falling - falling forwards - in the direction of Spirit as upon its stable form."[65]

But this insight led Teilhard to another problem. The evolutionary model meant that Plenitude was not the "extremely simple" but "an extreme organic complexity," and complexity meant mutability or corruptibility. He identified the problem as a paradox: "How could what was most corruptible become, as a result of synthesis, the supremely Indestructible?"[66] Or was there something else which would help him understand how Life and Thought, though fragile and mutable compared to the mineral world, were indeed higher evolutionary stages? The resolution of the paradox could be found in the human community.

In the essay's second section, "The Human, or the Convergent," Teilhard describes the two major prejudices which hindered him from recognizing the significance of the human in the world. The first was based on the instability of the human body, the second on the sheer diversity of the human world. Although it was inconceivable how humanity could contribute to the world's transformation in any enduring and unifying way, Teilhard eventually came to see how central the role of the human was. He identifies three stages in the development of his views on the issue, and they appeared between his thirtieth and fiftieth years.

The first stage was his recognition of the reality of an envelope or layer of thought which he came to label the Noosphere. This reality presented itself to him in the trenches of the First World War where he experienced not only the dreadful consequences of combat but also the exhilarating sense of the size and intensity of humanity: "The 'Human-Million,' with its psychic temperature and its internal energy, became for me a magnitude as evolutively, and therefore as biologically, real as a giant molecule of protein." If life as the Biosphere formed a "living membrane" over the earth's surface, then

> . . . around this sentient protoplasmic layer, an ultimate envelope was beginning to become apparent to me, taking on its own individuality and gradually detaching itself like a luminous *aura*. This envelope was not only conscious but thinking, and from the time when I first became aware of it, it was always there that I found concentrated, in an ever more dazzling and consistent form, the essence or rather the very Soul of the Earth.[67]

His ability to see this Soul was not often shared by his friends, which astonished him and led him to think that it required a "gift or faculty of *perceiving*, without actually *seeing*, the reality and organicity of collective magnitudes [that] is still comparatively rare."[68]

Having realized this capacity to perceive the Noosphere, Teilhard then began to discern the details of the process by which this "ultimate envelope" had emerged. Matter follows both a "concentration-curve" whereby it forms larger and larger molecules, and an "arrangement-curve" which leads it to greater complexity. Teilhard also speaks of matter's tendency toward self-involution and interiorization which, in its activity of self-arrangement, results in greater consciousness and "a rise in psychic temperature." Heat and fire as metaphors help Teilhard describe the emergence of life and thought out of matter as if through a chemical reaction. The reaction takes place within the "planetary crucible,"[69] another metaphor involving fire that appears elsewhere in his writings.[70] The chief ingredient of the reaction is the crucible itself, i.e., Matter, and the product is Spirit: "Matter is the matrix of Spirit. Spirit is the higher state of Matter."[71]

Having realized that a Noosphere (or Soul of the World) exists, and that it emerges from Matter, Teilhard concluded that this layer, like the physical layers before it, followed an evolutionary course which he called Noogenesis. The earth's evolution has advanced to the level of "a rapidly rising *collective Reflection*," a development so obvious "that we cannot but recognize the objective, experiential reality of a directionally controlled transformation of the Noosphere as a whole."[72] The hominization and personalization of the planet is still underway, following an irresistible process of convergence toward a "final critical point." This goal of Noogenesis is the Omega:

> The "piece of iron" of my first days has long been forgotten. In its place it is the Consistence of the Universe, in the form of the Omega Point, that I now hold, concentrated (whether above me or, rather, in the depths of my being, I cannot say) into one single indestructible centre, WHICH I CAN LOVE.[73]

Although the Omega is the focal point of a converging humanity, it is difficult to explain why Teilhard would consider it as an object worthy of love. It seems impersonal and too much like an abstract ideal. Even Teilhard admits that the unbeliever might come to recognize the existence of the Omega through "close rational study." The explanation lay in Teilhard's next stage of development, his rediscovery of an experiential Christianity and its role in interpreting cosmic evolution.

The essay's third major section, "The Christic, or the Centric," describes how Teilhard's childhood yearnings for a "Sense of Plenitude" in nature were accompanied by a more "'supernatural' Sense of the Divine" received from his mother who practiced a devotion to the Heart of Jesus. As a spirituality, this devotion seemed to Teilhard to be "oddly limited" in its obsession with human sinfulness and its use of "curiously anatomical realism." Nevertheless, Teilhard was eventually drawn to the heart symbolism because of its capacity to represent incarnate divine reality beyond a particular historical being, "a Christic beyond Christ."[74] The speculative interest of Teilhard in the Omega as Cosmic Center was transformed into a flame of love for the Omega as Person. Teilhard struggled to achieve a synthesis of the Above with the Ahead, of the traditional transcendent God with the emerging Spirit of an evolving universe. The way to that synthesis led from "a patch of crimson in the center of Jesus" to "a glowing core of fire, whose splendor embraced every contour - first those of the God-Man - and then those of all things that lay within his ambience."[75] But the path to a unified vision was far from smooth.

Teilhard was trained in traditional forms of Christian ascesis during his years in school and the novitiate, but his training did not diminish his fascination for the natural world. A conflict arose between his ascetic training which emphasized detachment from the material realm and his budding love of the earth, and it became a "trial" for the young Jesuit. He eventually believed that a new type of spirituality was needed, one which merged detachment and attachment, renunciation and development, a practice which allowed "the ascensional faith in God and the forward-driving Faith in the Ultra-Human to react freely upon one another in the depth of (one's) being."[76] Teilhard admitted this kind of inner discipline could and would evoke terror in the individual, not only because of its novelty but also because of the "paradoxical potentialities of attitudes" it involves. The paradox lay in the very aim of the person's spiritual efforts: "to attain Heaven by bringing Earth to fulfillment" and "to Christify Matter."[77]

Mystical experiences played a critical role in shaping Teilhard's new spirituality. One occurred during the battle of Verdun while the Jesuit was sitting in a church preoccupied with a problem "half philosophic and half aesthetic": what would Christ look like if he were incarnated before Teilhard's eyes? An important aspect of the problem was Teilhard's inability to envision a Christ in a world whose multitudes could pass by him and remain unaffected. The question found its pictorial representation in a portrait of Christ hanging on the church wall. The very particularity of Christ's features as they appeared in the painting disturbed Teilhard:

> I could not see how it could be possible for an artist to represent the sacred Humanity of Jesus without giving him this over-exact physical definition, which seemed to cut him off from all other men: without giving him a face whose expression was too individual - a beautiful face, no doubt, but beautiful in a particular way which excluded all other types of beauty.[78]

At some point in his reflection, the painting began to dissolve into a vision. The halo around Christ's head expanded from the usual symbolic ring into a radiance "in which could be seen a continuing pulsing surge which reached out to the furthest spheres of Matter." Teilhard perceived the whole universe to be vibrating in a movement emanating from Christ's heart. Turning to Christ's garment, Teilhard saw that it had changed from a robe of ordinary cloth to "a florescence of Matter" which "had spontaneously woven itself, working with the most intimate essence of its substance." Over Christ's face appeared an iridescent play of light and color, an incessant movement of beauties beneath which "the incommunicable Beauty of Christ" remained hidden. But it was in Christ's eyes that Teilhard found "a fathomless complexity" of human emotions: the sweetness and tenderness of Teilhard's mother, the passion and imperious-

Omega: The Becoming of Wisdom 177

ness of a noblewoman, the courage and virile strength of a man. A series of facial expressions culminated in a final glance "which dominated and summed up all that had gone before." Its powerful intensity allowed no easy interpretation: "I could not say whether it evidenced an unspeakable agony or, on the contrary, an excess of triumphant joy. All I know is that, since that occasion, I believe I have seen a hint of it once, and that was in the eyes of a dying soldier." The vision had moved him to tears, but it had also helped him realize that Christ could be found in "the full stream of man's work," and that God is "the Heart of All."[79] By the end of the visionary experience, Teilhard had an answer to the question that had troubled him: Christ and the human were indeed deeply related, and the individuality of Christ's incarnate person was no different from the individuality of each human being in the fullness of his or her life's activity.

Teilhard's struggle with the "paradoxical potentialities" of a new spirituality ultimately resulted in a "'pan-Christic' mysticism" which had its formative experiences "in the two great atmospheres of Asia and the War."[80] His mysticism must be viewed within the great Christian mystical tradition, but it also made a significant new contribution. Like his predecessors, Teilhard wrote mystical texts that were records of inward experiences but also descriptions of encounters with a divine reality. According to Louis Bouyer,

> . . . mysticism was never reduced by the Fathers to the level of a psychological experience, considered merely, or primarily, in its subjectivity. It is always the experience of an invisible objective world: the world whose coming the Scriptures reveal to us in Jesus Christ, the world into which we enter, ontologically, through the liturgy, through the same Jesus Christ ever present in the Church.[81]

Teilhard valued scripture and liturgy as sources of spiritual nourishment, but the experiences these sources nourished were not only of "an invisible objective world" but also of a visible one, and this is Teilhard's bold new development of the tradition.[82]

In "The Mass on the World," a luminous text showing Teilhard's spiritual life as both earth-oriented and liturgically inspired, Teilhard expands the traditional parameters of the eucharistic ritual to include the earth itself. Without the usual sacramental materials, he turns to the elements of the surrounding environment (the Gobi desert) to celebrate the world itself as the substance of consecration. I shall quote the opening paragraphs:

178   *Landscapes of Wisdom*

> Since once again, Lord - though this time not in the forests of the Aisne but in the steppes of Asia - I have neither bread, nor wine, nor altar, I will raise myself beyond these symbols, up to the pure majesty of the real itself; I, your priest, will make the whole earth my altar and on it will offer you all the labors and sufferings of the world.
> Over there, on the horizon, the sun has just touched with light the outermost fringe of the eastern sky. Once again, beneath this moving sheet of fire, the living surface of the earth wakes and trembles, and once again begins its fearful travail. I will place on my paten, O God, the harvest to be won by this renewal of labor. Into my chalice I shall pour all the sap which is to be pressed out this day from the earth's fruits.
> My paten and my chalice are the depths of a soul laid widely open to all the forces which in a moment will rise from every corner of the earth and converge upon the Spirit. Grant me the remembrance and the mystic presence of all those whom the light is now awakening to the new day.[83]

The source for Teilhard's planetary eucharist is the traditional mass and its symbolic use of earthly materials, but the ritual enacted in the Asian desert employs the elements of Teilhard's immediate outer and inner worlds. And this is what makes it something new.

Another theme, evolution as the completion of God, is perhaps more controversial. Its basis is Teilhard's intuition that the world can no longer be regarded as merely the product of creative Origin but must be viewed as contributing to the life of its Creator. In *The Heart of Matter*, he states that "God is in the process of 'changing,' as a result of his magnetic power and our Thought."[84] As God receives the results of our creative labors, he "transforms himself,"[85] a phrase which indicates both the unambiguous power of divinity (God transforms *himself*) and the essential role of the world in that transformation. Both God and universe are "necessarily 'Christified' in Omega, at the upper limits of Cosmogenesis."[86] This theme can be said to provide the essay with its climactic moment of insight:

> When all is said and done, I can see this: I managed to climb up to the point where the Universe became apparent to me as a great rising surge, in which all the work that goes into serious enquiry, all the will to create, all the acceptance of suffering, converge ahead into a single dazzling spear-head - now, at the end of my life, I can stand on the peak I have scaled and continue to look ever more closely into the future, and there, with ever more assurance, see the ascent of God.[87]

God, World, and Humankind are "surging" and "ascending" toward the Centric where all will be personalized and where "the manifold oppositions which constitute the unhappiness and anxieties of our life begin to disappear."[88] For Teilhard, the evidence of a lifetime revealed God's capacity for "completion and fulfillment" by an evolving creation.[89] The certainty of his vision whereby he sees the divine ascent ("with ever more assurance") suggests the certainty of a new kind of knowledge, one which perceives not only the spiritual "within" of Matter and the Human Soul of the World but the Absolute Being as creator and fellow traveler, 'evolver' and 'evolving.'

The passage just quoted is not the essay's conclusion. In the final section devoted to "The Feminine, or the Unitive," Teilhard pays homage to the women "whose warmth and charm have been absorbed, drop by drop, into the life blood of my most cherished ideas."[90] No names are mentioned, but we have seen the critical role his mother played in his early formation, and there were other women as well. A cousin, Marguerite Teilhard-Chambon, knew him from childhood, and as a writer herself, she was able to appreciate Teilhard's intellectual interests. But the woman who may have come closest to Teilhard's heart was Lucile Swan, an American artist who fell in love with Teilhard and proved to be a supportive and thoughtful critic of the Jesuit's work.[91]

Teilhard's experience with women led him to realize the spiritual significance of the emotions in general, and love in particular. An intellectual in his scientific and theological interests, Teilhard experienced love of the opposite sex as an essential stage in the movement toward spiritual convergence. For Teilhard, this did not necessarily mean physical love (although it did for Lucile) but rather the sublimation of sexual attraction into a higher form of relationship. On its highest levels, interpersonal attraction leads to "the Breakthrough into Amorization." By the act of loving someone, a human individual, the "reflective monad," is transformed into the "affective dyad" which in turn moves toward completion in the Pan-Christic. Human love as experienced in interpersonal attraction completes the person who then "explodes into flame." On the cosmic level, love, evocatively called the Universal Feminine by Teilhard, permeates and helps realize the very process of convergence:

... the gradual and majestic development of a Neo-cosmic, of an Ultra-human, and of a Pan-Christic ...
All three not only illuminated in their very roots by Intelligence, but also impregnated throughout their entire mass,
as though bonded by a unifying cement,

by the Universal Feminine.[92]

These are the essay's closing words. It is tempting to comment on their resemblance to the final verses in *Faust*, but we must at this point summarize what we have gleaned from Teilhard's work. Teilhard's quest for an integrated knowledge which combined his fascination with the earth, his recognition of the greatness of the human, and his Christocentric spirituality resulted in a new kind of wisdom. It was a wisdom growing out of the struggles experienced by an inquiring mind, a spiritual form of knowing that couldn't be rationally achieved but had developed through the discipline of religious training, the horrors of war, the rigors of desert life, the demands of scientific research, and the fires of human love. And it was a wisdom that transformed the traditional cosmos structurally defined by a distinction between Spirit and Matter into a dynamic cosmos shaped by relationships and a universal desire to form a loving union of persons.

Creating Wisdom

We can now attempt to summarize the main themes of Omega wisdom. In all three of the sources we have examined - *Faust*, process theology, and Teilhard - nature is filled with spirit and energy. Moreover, all three describe the spiritual journey as an active life within the world. Faust spurns the life of scholarly withdrawal and interprets the Prologue to John's Gospel as proclaiming the Logos as Deed (*Tat*), not intellectual Word. Neither the process theologians nor Teilhard regard nature allegorically and both process and Teilhard see the natural world as evolving toward higher levels of complexity (or intensity and harmony). And in the Omega perspective, all levels of reality - natural, human, divine - are intimately related. The natural world, human beings (especially Gretchen), the spirit realm (especially Mephisto), and God through his acts of grace - all have a role to play in Faust's journey toward redemption. In process thought, an individual's becoming is shaped by past events in the natural and human worlds as well as divine ideas offered by God in his Primordial Nature. For Teilhard, the Cosmic, the Human, and the Christic are converging toward the Centric or Omega, and each of the three is changed and transformed by the others.

Each of the three sources in some way is deeply grounded in tradition. Process thought as a philosophy looks back to Heraclitus and more recently to Hegel and the romantic literature of the nineteenth century. As a theology it claims to offer a more accurate reading of Christian scripture and to support a theology of a God who acts in history. Teilhard is clearly shaped by his training as a Catholic priest whose spirituality is scriptural and liturgical. Faust's debt to the Christian tradition is symbolically represented by the ringing of the Easter bells which interrupt his suicide attempt. Moreover, Goethe's great drama has echoes of Dante's epic throughout.

But Omega wisdom is a wisdom that also goes beyond tradition. Both Teilhard and the process thinkers incorporate nature and the cosmos far more profoundly than Christian theologians of the past. Their notion of a God who develops along with his evolving creation, who at times seems to *need* his creation in order to be fulfilled, is a challenge to traditional theology. Faust no longer finds the inspiration he needs from the Christian world of his childhood. Moreover, he considers his theological studies as an unfortunate exercise ("und leider auch Theologie / Durchaus studiert" - ll. 356-357). To the extent that traditional theology has been identified with dogma and intellectualism, Faust's option for lived experience over theological formalism is a departure from tradition. Indeed, it seems quite contemporary.

A fundamental teaching of Omega wisdom is the significance of time. The notion of the spiritual journey is based on our repeated experience that we as human beings grow through stages. Temporality is a metaphysical principle in process philosophy and theology. Faust realizes early in the play that he can only be fulfilled by living life, not contemplating it. The symbol of the Macrocosm which Faust encounters before the *Erdgeist's* appearance represents some profoundly important truths about reality, but Faust rejects it as a representation and not the real thing. The real thing is life itself, and the challenge to live it isn't felt until after his suicide attempt on Easter morning.

We have seen that, for Teilhard, time is also an extremely important element, given the central role evolution plays in his thought. We may agree with Huston Smith and the primordial traditionalists that evolutionary theory is only a theory, and therefore open to disproof or displacement by another, more adequate theory. But the Omega school would add "what a theory!" It clearly gave Teilhard a new lease on his own spiritual and intellectual life. It functioned not only as an intellectual symbol of the nature of reality in the manner of the Macrocosm in *Faust*, but additionally as a way of connecting the various strands of Teilhard's deepest concerns. Inner struggle and outer vision merge in Teilhard's interpretation of evolutionary theory as an expression of divine presence in creation. Time was necessary for Teilhard not only as the principle behind cosmogenesis but as the measure of his own spiritual development as well. His particular process of maturation as a person and thinker required that he experience in successive stages the worlds of Matter, the Human, and the Christic as powerful realities. For Teilhard, science, autobiography, and cosmic history were not separate realms but deeply related by the temporal dimension. World, self, and God are moving in time toward union.

We have seen how process thought presents its basic themes as principles but also as provisional beliefs. Both Cobb and Griffin declare themselves open to dialogue with other schools of thought and prove their openness by engaging in conversations with representatives of the Alpha and Zero schools. Teilhard was prepared to understand the relationship between matter and spirit, science and religion, from a completely new perspective. In going beyond tradition, Omega exemplifies an openness to novelty not only in the world around us, but also in the ways we think and believe. However, this kind of intellectual and spiritual openness often will require a surrender of traditional modes of understanding and belief. Teilhard admitted that an individual might experience terror when realizing the difficulty and enormity of trying to combine worldly activity with other-worldly spirituality. This openness can seem like a nothingness, an abyss that opens up beneath our feet much like the Buddhist emptiness of *sunyata* underlying and pervading all things. Faust experienced terror at the prospect of visiting the realm of the Mothers, the Nothing that is the All, but he recognized it as a resource for creativity.

Although willing to explore the unfamiliar, the Omega thinkers we have considered have not always gone beyond certain limits in their thought. In his dialogue with Huston Smith, Griffin rejected non-rational modes of knowing as unsuitable for interpreting the data of experience. In so doing, he minimizes the role of intuitive modes of knowing and the human capacity to envision reality apart from an ability to think about it rationally. While open to the contributions of science, Teilhard did not engage in any fruitful give-and-take with members of other religious traditions.[93] Yet his vision might have been much richer if he had recognized parallels to his own thought in other faiths. For example, the writings of Sri Aurobindo in Hinduism and Rabbi Abraham Isaac Kook in Judaism offer the possibility of fruitful dialogue.[94]

Omega wisdom uses reason, and we have seen this most clearly in process thought. But it also transcends reason. It recognizes that once a person expresses an insight in rational, understandable terms, he or she risks misrepresenting life which often cannot be explained in clear and distinct ideas. Wisdom thus often hovers between silence and word, preferring stories, koans, poems, and paradoxical sayings to clear statements. In process thought, a person grows and matures through a series of choices between possibilities presented by past events and divine ideas. The notion of choice suggests rational behavior, a weighing of options. But how we shape our lives is a complex process which involves emotional and other psychological dynamics we cannot always be aware of. Haas has pointed out that while Teilhard's intellectual influences (e.g., Bergson and Hegel) have been thoroughly examined, "it is astonishing how rarely the significance of visions for Teilhard's worldview has been pointed out."[95] The importance of the unconscious has been admitted by Griffin and Cobb who have dialogued with representatives of the Jungian branch of psychology, but this path has yet to be more fully developed by the process school.[96] One possible avenue of discussion between the process and psychological approaches may be the correlation between Whitehead's divine ideas and Jungian archetypes. We may also recall that Huston Smith speaks of the intermediate realm, equating it with the realm of Jungian archetypes and mythological figures, and its isomorphic equivalent in the human mind which can dream and have visions as well as pursue rational thought. Further conversations between process thinkers and Jungians may examine how the dynamics of choice can have both a dimension of psychological depth explored by analytical psychology and the temporal dimension described by process philosophy. According to John Cobb, "If we all moved freely back and forth between images of depth and images of the temporal past, the power of our imagination would be enhanced."[97]

In Zero, we encountered a circumincessional reality where beings are both themselves and every other being. There is also a deeply circumincessional quality to the Omega vision of the cosmos. Faust's adventures took place in a multi-dimensional world which we characterized as worlds within worlds, an overlay of natural, mythical, and ethical dimensions which made for a complex but poetically rich environment for his journey. Teilhard's presentation of the three basic components of Matter, Human, and Christic emphasizes the mutually developmental relationship between them, Humanity evolving out of Matter, Spirit evolving out of both Humanity and Matter and becoming the Christic. The three have circumincessional qualities: Consciousness is inherent in matter, Christ works in and through Matter and the Human in their mutual transformation, and in the transformative process, God is fulfilled through the contributions of his creation.

The reality of the three in one, one in three dynamic suggests that none of the three is possible without the other two. According to Omega wisdom, the human bears within it the natural and divine realities. I would argue that this sort of humanism pervades Goethe's drama. Faust never behaves as a traditionally pious believer, but he displays an ability to reach beyond himself in striving for new experiences. This is the quality which Goethe depicts as receiving divine approval: the capacity for continuing the daily struggle and never settling for any particular achievement. In Hindu terms, it is the practice of *bhakti yoga*, acting without attachment to the fruits of one's actions. But in Goethe, it is practiced without any recognizable spiritual devotion. Omega wisdom, therefore, recognizes the contribution of human effort which is often expended without reference to divine presence or influence. At the same time, it believes in the genuineness of human freedom.

The profundity of the humanist vision is quite clear in *Faust*. We have also seen Teilhard's strong sense of the Human as the Soul of the World. His understanding of humanity was in part based on an experience which embraced the extremes of destructiveness and courage. The experience occurred in the midst of war where he perceived the opposing armies at the battlefront "taking on the shape of a higher Thing, of great nobility."[98] It was an early instance of Teilhard's second universal component, the Human, and it eventually contributed to his own version of worlds within worlds. Although not a typical Teilhardian term, circumincession describes his understanding of current reality and of the future. Teilhard's memorable phrase, "union differentiates," captures this sense of the relation of the many and the one: the plurality of the cosmos converging to become personalized, not annihilated, in the Centric or Omega. Convergence does not mean that all become one, a monistic view, but a new kind of plurality is achieved at the very moment of union.

Omega wisdom is fundamentally about creativity. God's creation of the world is far from being a one-time event, but is an ongoing activity, and the cosmos participates in this process with creativity of its own. Cobb speaks of creativity as an ultimate reality manifested by God and world. For Teilhard, creation "is an act co-extensive with the duration of the World;" it "has never ceased."[99] Moreover, the human person must strive to create himself or herself as well as help create the world:

> Thus every man, in the course of his life, must not only show himself obedient and docile. By his fidelity he must *build* - starting with the most natural territory of his own self - a work, an *opus*, into which enters from all elements of the earth. *He makes his own soul* throughout all his earthly days; and at the same time he collaborates in another work, in

another *opus*, which infinitely transcends, while at the same time it narrowly determines, the perspectives of his individual achievement: the completing of the world.[100]

In his preferred version of John 1:1, Faust declares that activity, *der Tat*, is a first principle, and he commits his life to the pursuit of experience. His adventures seem without a moral purpose until near the play's end when he attempts to form a community of free individuals. Despite its capacity for evil, humanity in Goethe's drama nevertheless is valued for its "darkest urges" without which it could not realize its highest dreams. From God's perspective, Faust is "a good man" who "in his dark longings is well aware of the right path." (ll. 328-329; my own translation). Faust is free to create his own life.

Omega wisdom has the potential to reshape the scientific enterprise. Huston Smith's trenchant remark that Griffin's postmodern science will find little financial support from national funding sources may be accurate today, but perhaps not forever. It is far from clear that science, the kind that Griffin criticizes as subordinating quality and value in favor of quantitative measure, will proceed as it always has. Ferré argues that the ideals of modern science are accidental, appearing within a particular historical context, and by no means fundamental and irreplaceable. He quotes a physicist, Harold Schilling, who speaks of a "'new consciousness' breaking out in all the traditional disciplines, including his own field of physics."[101] Might not this "new consciousness" and recent scientific developments be signs of an emerging Omega wisdom?

But how could science begin to recognize the place of wisdom in its research methodology? A postmodern science may refer back to the Renaissance when hermetic and alchemical notions of nature were more acceptable to some scientists than objective, dualistic ideas. At the same time, it cannot disregard the solid achievements of scientific research based on mathematical precision and sophisticated instruments of observation. Postmodern science must include modern scientific methodology but also move beyond it by recapturing the holistic perspective of premodern science. According to Antoine Faivre, a *ratio hermetica*, a way of knowing based on hermetic ideas, may have something to offer:

> If, on the one hand, pure, official, exact science teaches objective disinterest, laic neutrality, the *ratio hermetica* teaches a pragmatic interest, a subjectifying interest. Medicine, astrology, magic must "operate" concretely since the Paracelsian type of High Science is the

186   *Landscapes of Wisdom*

knowledge of concrete facts, of *mirabilia*. There is no question of neglecting the other science, naturally, but of simultaneously using both: of not throwing out, as Kepler said, the baby with the bath water (that is to say, in its context, not to throw overboard astrological knowledge under the pretext that astronomical knowledge is being verified). The *ratio hermetica* also adds a principle of similitude, or participation in entity forces, to the causal determination of Aristotle.[102]

The "pragmatic interest" of a *ratio hermetica* is to pursue a knowledge which can benefit both spirit and mind. It is an acceptance of the information provided by "exact science" and its study of the realm of cause and effect, but it is also a need to know more about relationships beyond physical facts. According to the hermetic notion of participation, the cosmos is a web of interacting energies, and influences on human behavior can occur on levels of existence outside one's immediate consciousness. Science as practiced by Paracelsus and other Renaissance scientists attempted to study these relationships and energies for human benefit, and although their inexact methods and unsupportable theories often led to fruitless experimentation, their approach to research as a spiritual discipline may help redefine what science is all about.

Science may also find the glimmer of wisdom if it looks more closely at the dynamics of its own process of discovery. There is ample evidence from the lives of scientists and mathematicians that their work is profoundly creative. At times, solutions to difficult problems appear not simply from an orderly sequence of reasoning but from a far more mysterious process. The mathematician Henri Poincaré describes an experience during a period of intense mental activity when he was focusing on the development of a certain theorem:

> Just at this time I left Caen, where I was then living, to go on a geologic excursion under the auspices of the school of mines. The changes of travel made me forget my mathematical work. Having reached Coutances, we entered an omnibus to go to some place or other. At the moment when I put my foot on the step the idea came to me, without anything in my former thoughts seeming to have paved the way for it, that the transformations I had used to define the Fuchsian functions were identical with those of non-Euclidean geometry. I did not verify the idea; I should not have had the time, as upon taking my seat in the omnibus, I went on with a conversation already commenced, but I felt a certainty.[103]

Poincaré attributes the breakthrough to a period of "long, unconscious work" by a "subliminal self" where "reigns what I should call liberty, if we might give this name to the simple absence of discipline and to the disorder born of chance."[104] But before and after the illumination he engaged in periods of intense conscious work, the first period when he started the careful sifting of possibilities, the second when he verified the answer by disciplined calculation. The process of reasoning, according to Poincaré, may come in two stages, with an intervening "dance" of possibilities in the unconscious. Poincaré also believes that mathematics is more than a labor of the intellect; it also involves an emotional sensibility open to "the feeling of mathematical beauty, of the harmony of numbers and forms, of geometric elegance."[105] In the sciences, feelings based on aesthetic intuitions don't always pass subsequent intellectual verification, but when they do, scientists and mathematicians such as Poincaré begin sounding like artists describing the creative process.

Most essentially, Omega wisdom acknowledges the depth of the creative urge within humankind. We need to grow and develop. Indeed, we are most ourselves when we are growing and developing. We are defined not only by our own growth but also by the development of the community of beings around us. Our creativity draws inspiration and energy from the creative activity of the world. How we choose to interact with the world, both the given natural environment and the world of human culture and society, has an impact on the world and, consequently, on our own future actions. Our infinite capacity for destructive behavior, for misapplying our creative gifts, leads us to seek ways of purifying and sanctifying our efforts. We pray to a Creator God for guidance, or meditate on absolute emptiness which is the source of absolute fullness. In Omega wisdom, the prayer is for help in creating this world (and for some, paradoxically transcending it at the same time).

Feminist theologians remind us of the feminine face of God as the presence of the divine within the processes of the world. In Hebrew scripture, Wisdom is a feminine divine figure working in the world to assure order and promote life. Indeed, "she is life" (Prov. 4:13). Elizabeth Johnson proposes that we consider the third Person of the Trinity as Creator Spirit. The Holy Spirit in the Nicene Creed is *vivificantem*, vivifier or life-giver. For Johnson, this means a continuous involvement of the divine in creation: "The Spirit is the unceasing, dynamic flow of divine power that sustains the universe, bringing forth life."[106] Intimately involved in human history, guiding our creative impulses toward the realization of value, healing the brokenness that results from sinful acts, and luring the universe to new levels of development, Creator Spirit acts like the Eros of process thought "urging the world to new heights of enjoyment"[107] and the Universal Feminine of Teilhard impregnating "the gradual and majestic development of a Neo-cosmic, of an Ultra-human, and of a Pan-Christic."[108] Because hierarchy reinforces the sense of distance between Creator and creature, both feminist theology and the process school de-emphasize the role of hierarchy in the God-world relationship, preferring to focus on reciprocity and divine indwelling which, in Johnson's words, "weaves a genuine solidarity among all creatures and between God and the world."[109]

And if we were to describe the process of knowing that is the practice of Omega wisdom, we would emphasize the kind of *sapientia* that is always "on the way," never fully and finally formulated in a set of principles. Perhaps its only principle is openness, like the openness of the process God who receives whatever creatures have to offer. Like Alpha and Zero, it is a knowledge that reveals us to ourselves, and is one with our innermost core. Like the figure of Wisdom herself, it is ever moving, creating, sustaining. It requires a discipline, or its dynamic power will escape us. Hermetic masters, who may be counted among the forerunners of a contemporary Omega wisdom tradition, realized the difficulty of acquiring this knowledge. Perhaps, as the author of the *Asclepius* suggests, it can never be acquired, but only pursued:

> Now be completely present, give me your whole attention, with all the understanding that you are capable of, with all the subtlety you can muster. For the teaching about divinity requires a divine concentration of consciousness if it's to be understood. It's just like a torrential river, plunging headlong down from the heights so violently that with its rapidity and speed it outstrips the attention not only of whoever is listening but also of whoever is speaking.[110]

This is much like Faust's contemplation of the waterfall where Omega wisdom, the wisdom of *Wechseldauer*, lasting change or becoming, is as evanescent as the rainbow formed by the torrent's spray:

> But in what splendor from this storm evolving,
> Vaults up the shimmering arc, in variance lasting,
> Now purely limned and now in air dissolving,
> A cooling fragrance all about it casting.
> This mirrors all aspiring human action.
> On this your mind for clearer insight fasten:
> That life is ours by colorful refraction.
> (ll. 4721-4727)

Notes

1. Cobb and Griffin, *Process Theology*, 18.
2. Griffin, *God and Religion*, 9.
3. Ibid., 123.
4. Cobb and Griffin, 140. See also John Cobb, *Beyond Dialogue: Toward a Mutual Transformation of Christianity and Buddhism* (Philadelphia: Fortress Press, 1982), 114.
5. Griffin, *God and Religion*, 8.
6. David Ray Griffin and Huston Smith, *Primordial Truth and Postmodern Theology*, (Albany: State University of New York Press, 1989).
7. Ibid., 161, 167.
8. Ibid., 24, 95.
9. Ibid., 174.
10. Ibid., 159-60.
11. Ibid., 81.
12. See Griffin's summary of their points of agreement on p. 205.
13. Ibid., 153.
14. Ibid., 157-58.
15. Ibid.
16. Ibid., 83-84.
17. Ibid., 196.
18. Griffin, *God and Religion*, 23; italics are mine.
19. Cobb, "Two Types of Postmodernism," 152; italics are mine.
20. Griffin and Smith, 143.
21. Cobb and Griffin, 19-20.
22. Ibid., 101.
23. E.A. Burtt, "What Can Western Philosophy Learn from India?" *Philosophy East and West* 5 (1955): 202.
24. Ibid., 204.
25. E.A. Burtt, "Intuition in Eastern and Western Philosophy," *Philosophy East and West* 2 (1953): 283, 289.
26. Masao Abe, "Kenotic God and Dynamic Sunyata," in *The Emptying God: A Buddhist-Jewish-Christian Conversation*, ed. John B. Cobb, Jr. and Christopher Ives (Maryknoll, N.Y.: Orbis Books, 1990), 34. The dialogical exchange of essays between a number of writers which appeared in *The Emptying God* continued in *Buddhist-Christian Studies* 13 (1993) and *Divine Emptiness and Historical Fullness*, ed. Christopher Ives (Valley Forge, Pa.: Trinity Press International, 1995); the latter publication also reprinted Abe's essay.
27. Ibid., 35-36.
28. John B. Cobb, Jr., "On the Deepening of Buddhism," in *The Emptying God*, 101.
29. Griffin and Smith, 81. For Augustine's views on the difference between wisdom and ordinary knowledge, see *De Trinitate*, XII, 14.21-15.25.

30. Cobb and Griffin, 18, 68, 112-13, 116-17, 186; Griffin, *God and Religion*, 64.

31. Ewert H. Cousins, "Introduction: Process Models in Culture, Philosophy, and Theology," in *Process Theology: Basic Writings*, ed. Ewert H. Cousins (New York: Newman Press, 1971), 9.

32. Ian G. Barbour, "Teilhard's Process Metaphysics," in *Process Theology: Basic Writings*, 324.

33. Ibid., 324-25.

34. Teilhard de Chardin, quoted in Barbour, 326.

35. Ibid.

36. Barbour, 327.

37. Teilhard, quoted in Barbour, 327.

38. Barbour, 327.

39. Ibid., 328-29.

40. Teilhard, quoted in Barbour, 330.

41. Ibid., 331.

42. Ibid., 333.

43. Ibid., 334.

44. Ibid., 335.

45. Pierre Teilhard de Chardin, *The Phenomenon of Man*, (New York: Harper Colophon Books, 1965), 262.

46. Ibid., 294.

47. Barbour, 339.

48. Ibid., 341.

49. Barbour is referring to comments by Christopher Mooney, *Teilhard and the Mystery of Christ* (New York: Harper & Row, 1966).

50. Teilhard, quoted in Barbour, 344.

51. Ibid., 345.

52. Whitehead, quoted in Barbour, 346.

53. Barbour, 346.

54. Alfred North Whitehead, *Process and Reality*, corrected edition, ed. David Ray Griffin and David W. Sherburne (New York: Free Press, 1978), 21.

55. For example, see the articles which appeared in the March 1995 issue of *Zygon*.

56. Ursula King, *Spirit of Fire: The Life and Vision of Teilhard de Chardin* (Maryknoll, N.Y.: Orbis Books, 1996), 202.

57. N.M. Wildiers, "Foreword," in Pierre Teilhard de Chardin, *The Heart of Matter*, trans. René Hague (New York: Harcourt Brace Jovanovich, 1978), 7.

58. Pierre Teilhard de Chardin, quoted in Claude Cuénot, *Teilhard de Chardin: A Biographical Study* (London: Burns & Oates, 1965), 264f.

59. Pierre Teilhard de Chardin, *The Heart of Matter*, trans. René Hague (New York: Harcourt Brace Jovanovich, 1978), 15-16.

60. Ibid., 16.

61. Ibid., 18.

62. Ibid., 20.

63. Ibid., 23.
64. Ibid., 26.
65. Ibid., 28.
66. Ibid.
67. Ibid., 31-32.
68. Ibid., 31.
69. Ibid., 34.
70. For example, see Pierre Teilhard de Chardin, "The Mass on the World," in *The Heart of Matter*, 133. The choice of word is distinctively Teilhardian because *crucible*, derived from the Latin *crux* for "cross" or "trial," has the capacity to communicate meaning on both scientific and spiritual levels.
71. Teilhard, *The Heart of Matter*, 35.
72. Ibid., 38.
73. Ibid., 39.
74. Ibid., 43. While Teilhard was clearly attracted to a more cosmological form of Christ, he did not ignore or reject the importance of the historical Jesus. See Henri de Lubac, *The Religion of Teilhard de Chardin* (Garden City, N.Y.: Doubleday Image Books, 1968), 69-79. De Lubac also recognizes Teilhard's predilection for the Universal Christ beyond the Gospels and argues that this preference "would be more frequently endorsed by tradition than might be imagined" (72).
75. Ibid.
76. Ibid., 46.
77. Ibid., 47.
78. Ibid., 62. Subsequent quotations of Teilhard's vision of Christ are taken from 63-65.
79. Ibid., 66.
80. Ibid., 47.
81. Louis Bouyer, "Mysticism: An Essay on the History of the Word," in *Understanding Mysticism*, ed. Richard Woods (Garden City, N.Y.: Doubleday Image Books, 1980), 52-53.
82. "Perhaps it is Teilhard's main achievement to have sought a new formulation for a mysticism of the West, that is to say, a mysticism rooted in the Christian doctrines of creation and Incarnation, but expressed in a new manner." Ursula King, *Towards a New Mysticism: Teilhard de Chardin and Eastern Religions* (New York: Seabury Press, 1981), 203.
83. Teilhard de Chardin, "The Mass on the World," in *The Heart of Matter*, 119-20.
84. Teilhard, *The Heart of Matter*, 53.
85. Ibid.
86. Ibid., 55.
87. Ibid., 52.
88. Ibid., 49.
89. Ibid., 54.
90. Ibid., 59.

91. See King, *Spirit of Fire*, 144-54.
92. Ibid., 60-61.
93. On this topic, see King, *Towards a New Mysticism*, 123-49.
94. Even members of the Alpha school recognize the intellectual and spiritual affinities between Aurobindo and Teilhard; see Nasr, 241. My introduction to Kook as a potential dialogical partner comes from Jacob Agus, "Preface," in Abraham Isaac Kook, *The Lights of Penitence, Lights of Holiness, The Moral Principles, Essays, Letters, and Poems*, trans. Ben Zion Bokser (New York: Paulist Press, 1978), xiv. See also Margaret Chatterjee, "Rabbi Abraham Isaac Kook and Sri Aurobindo," in her *Studies in Modern Jewish and Hindu Thought* (New York: St. Martin's Press, 1997), 99-122.
95. Giulio Haas, *Die Weisheit von Teilhard und Jung: Gegensätze, die sich Vereinen* (Otten: Walter-Verlag, 1991), 40.
96. See essays by David Ray Griffin and John Cobb in *Archetypal Process: Self and Divine in Whitehead, Jung, and Hillman*, ed. David Ray Griffin (Evanston, Ill.: Northwestern University Press, 1989).
97. John B. Cobb, Jr., "Eternal Objects and Archetypes, Past and Depth," in *Archetypal Process*, 127.
98. Teilhard de Chardin, "Nostalgia for the Front," in *The Heart of Matter*, 179.
99. Teilhard quoted in De Lubac, 26.
100. Teilhard de Chardin, *The Divine Milieu* (New York: Harper Torchbooks, 1968), 60-61.
101. Frederick Ferré, *Hellfire and Lightning Rods: Liberating Science, Technology, and Religion* (Maryknoll, N.Y.: Orbis Books, 1993), 92-93.
102. Antoine Faivre, "The Children of Hermes and the Science of Man," in *Hermeticism and the Renaissance: Intellectual History and the Occult in Early Modern Europe*, ed. Ingrid Merkel and Allen G. Dubus (Washington, D.C.: The Folger Shakespeare Library, 1988), 433.
103. Henri Poincaré, "Mathematical Creation," in *The Creative Process*, ed. Brewster Ghiselin (New York: New American Library, 1952), 37.
104. Ibid., 42.
105. Ibid., 40.
106. Elizabeth A. Johnson, *Women, Earth, and Creator Spirit* (New York: Paulist Press, 1993), 42.
107. Cobb and Griffith, 26.
108. Teilhard, "The Heart of Matter," 60-61.
109. Johnson, 43.
110. From *Asclepius* 3, quoted in Peter Kingsley, "Knowing beyond Knowing: The Heart of Hermetic Tradition," *Parabola* (Spring 1997): 24.

Conclusion

Three Sacred Spaces[1]

Landscapes of wisdom can be found in areas and structures designed as symbolic expressions of spiritual worlds. To enter a sacred space is to step into a transformed and transforming environment for the spiritual journey. The shape of the space and the elements which it contains have special meaning and power to teach an inward kind of knowledge. For example, when entering Chartres Cathedral, its high vaulted ceilings and stained glass windows make an immediate visual and inward impact. Both features articulate Neoplatonic ideas concerning the hierarchy of being and the created world. In Neoplatonism, the spiritual journey is an ascent from the creaturely world of beings toward Being Itself, and similarly the cathedral's elevated ceilings invite the imagination to soar upward to God. The magnificently colored stained glass images illustrate Bonaventure's notion of creatures as vestiges of God: "Creatures . . . are vestiges, representations, spectacles proposed to us and signs divinely given so that we can see God"[2] and "the divine ray shines forth in each and every creature in different ways and in different properties."[3] Chartres depicts the Creator as lofty yet brightly present in his creation, but the cathedral does so without permitting any visual access to the natural world outside.

A Zen temple in the Daitoku-ji complex of temples in Kyoto, Japan, presents a landscape that is quite different. While Chartres emphasizes verticality, the Zen temple has a far more horizontal orientation. The long lines of the ceiling beams parallel floorboards and tatami mats. Brush paintings of Zen figures and natural subjects are hung here and there, but more significantly, a number of the rooms open out to a garden scenery composed of trees, shrubs, and large stones.[4] The spiritual journey here is not one of ascent but presence in this world. Walking and sitting meditation intensifies awareness of one's surroundings, and the sacred space of Daitoku-ji provides the stillness for practicing such awareness.

A third example, Thorncrown Chapel, designed by Fay Jones and completed in 1980,[5] combines aspects of Chartres and Daitoku-ji. Like

Chartres, it has a marked vertical dimension in its high peaked ceiling. Like a Zen temple, it allows views of the surroundings, in this case a forest in northwestern Arkansas. Because the chapel walls are made of glass held in place by thin wooden beams, persons sitting inside can meditate on God's mystery both above and within the natural world.

When I consider each of these three sacred structures as architectural representations of the three wisdom schools we have been examining, I enter them with my imagination in order to meditate on the mysteries they embody and to amplify my feelings about each of the schools. As a form of Alpha, Chartres Cathedral has an undeniable and profound grandeur. Its makers' mastery of symbolism is evident throughout its walls and windows. I stand small in a universe of stone and glass, and during the day, witness an extraordinary play of colored light on the walls and floor. In Chartres, wisdom speaks a symbolic language about the beauty of the earth, of human beings, and of the divine presence that irradiates and transcends all beings. The light veiled by the glass, the source of the windows' brilliance, is like the grace that nullifies gravity in attracting the soul toward realms of higher being. It is a powerful sensation, a lifting out of oneself that few other spaces can produce as effectively. Several hours in the cathedral and I begin to see a world in prayerful worship of its Creator.

After a few hours sitting motionlessly in zazen posture in a Zen temple, a place in which I experience the Zero school's teachings, I become acutely aware of everything around me, not as witnesses or symbols of a greater reality, but as they are in their own being and how they affect me. A fly lands on my hand - how annoying! A bird sings - how beautiful! A person near me coughs - another one like me struggling for insight! And after a week of sitting, my sensitivity to such moments has deepened to the point where I want to enjoy each moment for what it brings and nothing more. Here I have found a wisdom in stillness.

After sitting inside Thorncrown Chapel for an afternoon, I have seen the light shift slowly through the trees. The natural world is a realm of mystery as deep as the mystery articulated by the ceiling's upward thrust toward the heavens. I pray to the divinity which transcends us but I also let impressions of the surrounding forest penetrate my silence. Here is a wisdom that connects me to the earth but also invites me to contemplate the origin and foundation of my being. As the light fades into dusk, boundaries blur and the reality of the above appears to become more intimate with the reality around me. Perhaps this is the wisdom of Thorncrown.

Conclusion

Chartres Cathedral was both a spiritual and engineering achievement replicated in a number of Gothic churches during the Middle Ages with various degrees of success. Many architectural styles came before and after the Gothic mode, each embodying a different vision of Christian life and tradition, but none was more successful in expressing a spiritual metaphysics. Like the mystical texts composed during the same period, these sacred spaces still serve as resources of spiritual renewal, nourishing our inner selves whenever we turn to them and away from a world that seems empty of spiritual wisdom. But we also need a truly living wisdom communicated by contemporary teachers, and some of us turned eastward to Asian traditions for it.

The air of a Zen meditation hall can often seem vibrating with energy. Although everyone is still, the stillness is thunderous. Words are used in chants and *teishos*, talks on practice and Buddhist teaching delivered by the *roshi* or master. The sitter must use words to express his inner condition to the roshi during one-to-one interviews. But all sounds arise within a field of silence. When wisdom is spoken, practitioners are more prepared to hear it. For this reason, I am drawn to this tradition and its discipline of meditation. True insight, though hard to define, seems as near as moonlight or sitting on a cushion.

A certain number of Americans have become Buddhists; the number is small in comparison with other religions. A larger number of Americans have practiced Buddhism, and many of these have done so without becoming Buddhist. I count myself among the latter, and having had a taste of a vital spiritual practice in Zen, I now seek something similar in Western culture. Today, many in the West seek experiential knowledge of the earth and its relationship with the divine origin. Thorncrown Chapel offers a sacred space for encountering God in the natural world, and I can imagine it enabling a process or Teilhardian spirituality.

Living within an earth community of beings, we share a common yearning for the divine Eros who lures us toward further evolutionary growth. The challenge is in fully realizing that cosmic, human, and divine realities are becoming one and three, evolving toward union while becoming more and more themselves. On a human level, this requires a commitment to an active, creative life where, in Faust's definition of wisdom, personal freedom and existence are reconquered everyday (ll. 11574-11576). As I sit in Thorncrown Chapel, I have a glimpse of what this new form of wisdom might be, as I pray to the Creator Spirit above, within and all around me.

The Physicist and the Cardinal Revisited

In this concluding section, I would like to pose a final question: Can we identify a common thread of wisdom running through all three schools? I believe so. Ewert Cousins, a scholar of medieval mysticism and process thought, once during a conversation with Huston Smith responded to Smith's criticism of Teilhard by suggesting that both Dante and Teilhard were using the cosmology of their day to express their visions. According to Cousins, "In both cases the vision exceeds the cosmology, and is not endangered should the cosmology be superseded."[6] While Smith found the remark helpful to his understanding of Teilhard, the brevity of Cousins' suggestion permits at least two interpretations. The first interpretation finds Cousins to be in full agreement with Smith about the existence of a single, unchanging wisdom, but it leaves room for argument about the superiority of one cosmology over another. A question can be asked whether Dante's cosmos is a more profound description of reality than Teilhard's or the other way around.

The second interpretation is based on the phenomenological method described in the Introduction. Wisdom is ultimately indescribable, thus beyond such attributes as changing or unchanging. In fact, it is both, unchanging in its fundamental quality of being a holistic vision of reality, yet changing in the forms of its expression. The phenomenological method recognizes the two poles of wisdom, experience and expression, and their inseparability. Nasr used the metaphor of the hourglass to explain how perceptions of time changed over long periods of history.[7] The same metaphor can be applied to shifts in our understanding of wisdom. In the golden age of mystics and sages revered by the Alpha school, wisdom seemed like an unchanging body of sacred knowledge. Perhaps we are just beginning to recognize that wisdom's outer form may change while its inner essence remain the same.

Dante's canvas in the *Commedia* is vast. The colors on his palette and the figures in his imagination were derived from the mythology, philosophy, theology, history, and the science of his day. As a result, his poem presented a cosmos that was comprehensible to readers familiar with his sources of inspiration and knowledge. Teilhard has similarly drawn from the modes of knowing prevalent in his time. Importantly, his sources included scientific research as well as scriptural revelation. The greatness of both authors lies in their desire to experience and communicate wisdom using the types of knowledge which are the most universally accepted and have the greatest power to provide glimpses of sacred knowledge to their readers.

As an experience, wisdom includes an impulse for communication and sharing the vision with others. After his enlightenment, the Buddha wanted to remain silent, but when the god Brahma Sahampati begged him to teach others the way to liberation, he relented and became a teacher of the Dharma. Wisdom has never remained purely silent, even in the most silent of religious traditions. Wisdom doctrine is a message about the creative power of the absolute and the messenger reflects, indeed participates, in that power. The visionary experience of wisdom is an experience of possibility and potency in spiritual knowing-as-seeing.

Each of the three schools' doctrines presents a vision of great energy, a realization of wisdom's potency for communication, but the details differ greatly from vision to vision. For Alpha, the wisdom doctrine teaches a universal set of principles found at the heart of each tradition. The impersonal transcends the personal absolute, the Godhead beyond God. The doctrine speaks of levels of reality and the map of the spiritual journey describes a path from lesser to greater reality. For Zero, wisdom must be described in paradox, words pointing to a reality beyond words; "form is no other than emptiness, emptiness no other than form" according to the Great Prajna Paramita Sutra. The map is no-map, and the journey goes nowhere special, for every departure is an arrival. For the Omega school, wisdom is the unfinished story of the great cosmic journey. The shape of the final end, the Omega, is unknown. Teilhard's faith leads him to believe that its reality will be an intensification of the personal in the Person of Christ, but the features of the Omega can differ from religious tradition to religious tradition.[8]

Let us return to the two figures with which this book began, Nicholas of Cusa and Stephen Hawking. Both exhibit a desire to explore the heavens. Cusa achieves his understanding of the universe primarily through the use of his intellect, although he recognizes the significance of the sciences (and the arts) in pursuing knowledge of the world. For Cusa, the highest achievement is a spiritual insight, a learned ignorance, where all things, when examined, reply: "Of ourselves we are nothing, nor of ourselves are we able to give any other reply than nothing."[9] To the extent that our knowledge about things always has a boundary beyond which lies the unknown, all our attempts at knowing lead us to the ultimate source of things or the One which is beyond knowing. For the Cardinal, the unknown is both lure for intellectual and scientific inquiry and rooted in the Unknowable. Hawking also relies on his prodigious intellectual capacity, although he draws many of his conclusions from the data of scientific research. For Hawking, the highest achievement would be the discovery of "a complete theory," a rational and empirically verifiable explanation of reality. This, of course, is still far from being realized, and the unknown continues to stimulate further scientific query. For most scientists, the continuing presence of an unknown, however, need not point to an Unknowable, i.e., an incomprehensible Absolute, as it does for Cusa,

As an early Renaissance thinker, Cusa perceived the physical cosmos in a completely new way, but like many of his medieval predecessors, he believed that purely intellectual knowing was higher than knowing based on sense data.[10] However, both empirical and intellectual knowing are possible because of pure Possibility or *Posse* Itself, Cusa's name for God in his later works.[11] Cusa's message for the modern scientific community is that the very capacity of the mind for investigation, the very fact that it *can* explore the workings of the world, is grounded in *Posse* Itself. The realization of *Posse* Itself by the intellect is achieved by means of an inner ascent: "Hence, the simple vision of the mind is not a comprehensive vision, but it elevates itself from a comprehensive vision to seeing the incomprehensible,"[12] i.e., *Posse* Itself.

Contemporary scientific method precludes this sort of ascent, although individual scientists have given religious interpretations of their research experience or theories. A contemporary spirituality of knowing can emerge only if there is a universal recognition of the significance in our very desire or capacity to know, a significance that points to a reality larger than the rational mind though inclusive of it. Wisdom must speak and any success identifying a wisdom doctrine will require an experiential sharing of the vision together with an experience of the power or the *Posse* of the impulse behind the vision, the incomprehensible beyond the comprehensible. It will also mean the possibility of a plurality of visions, a succession of insights, as we gain new knowledge about ourselves and the universe, and thus new images and vocabularies with which to describe our physical and spiritual existence. The selection of criteria by which to judge the authenticity of experience will always be a difficult process, but spiritual traditions around the world can help identify authentic insights as well as provide the spiritual matrix within which such insights can arise. Of course, tradition can also attack new paradigms, and the process of growth can be and frequently is extremely painful.

The important first step in the reemergence of a sapiential perspective in our time will be for the modern world to realize that wisdom is sorely lacking as a universally accepted value. Wisdom must be cultivated and

Conclusion

supported as much as love and compassion, the virtues most readily identified with spirituality today. As the masters of spiritual discipline have often shown, wisdom and compassion are complementary. Love is deepened by knowledge, and at the deepest point of spiritual experience, knowing and loving are one.

Notes

1. In this section, I am borrowing material from my own essay, "A Rooted Flower, a Radiant Stone: Eckhart on Nature," in *An Ecology of the Spirit: Religious Reflection and Environmental Consciousness*, ed. Michael Barnes (Lanham, Md.: University Press of America, 1994), 111-23.
2. Bonaventure, *Collationes in Hexaemeron*, II, 11; quoted in Bonaventure, *The Soul's Journey into God. The Tree of Life. The Life of St. Francis*, trans. Ewert Cousins (New York: Paulist Press, 1978), 26.
3. *Hexaem.* 17 (V, 332); translation: Cousins, "Introduction," 26.
4. See plates 15, 23, 34, and 48 in John Covell and Yamada Sobin, *Zen at Daitoku-ji* (Tokyo, New York: Kodansha, 1974).
5. See Charles K. Gandee, "A Wayfarer's Chapel by Fay Jones," *Architectural Record* 169 (March 1981): 88-93.
6. Reported by Smith in Huston Smith, *Beyond the Post-Modern Mind* (New York: Crossroad, 1982), 127.
7. Nasr, 229.
8. I am thinking specifically of Kook and Aurobindo and their respective traditions, Judaism and Hinduism; see p. 175 and n. 94.
9. *De docta ignorantia* II, 13; Nicholas of Cusa, *Selected Spiritual Writings*, 166.
10. *De apice theoriae* 10; ibid., 297.
11. See H. Lawrence Bond, "Introduction," in Nicholas of Cusa, *Selected Spiritual Writings*, 56-70.
12. *De apice theoriae* 11; ibid., 297.

Bibliography

Augustine. *The Essential Augustine.* Ed. Vernon J. Bourke. Indianapolis: Hackett, 1964.
Abe Masao. "Kenotic God and Dynamic Sunyata." *The Emptying God: A Buddhist-Jewish-Christian Conversation.* Eds. John B. Cobb, Jr. and Christopher Ives. Maryknoll, N.Y.: Orbis Books, 1990.
_____. *Zen and Western Thought.* Honolulu: University of Hawaii Press, 1985.
Aitken, Robert. *A Zen Wave: Basho's Haiku and Zen.* New York: Weatherhill, 1978.
_____. *Encouraging Words: Zen Buddhist Teachings for Western Students.* New York: Pantheon Books, 1993.
Altizer, Thomas J. J. *The Genesis of God.* Louisville, Ky.: Westminster/John Knox Press, 1993.
Augustine. *Confessions and Enchiridion.* Trans. Albert C. Outler. The Library of Christian Classics 7. Philadelphia: Westminster Press, 1955.
Barbour, Ian G. "Teilhard's Process Metaphysics." In *Process Theology: Basic Writings.* Ed. Ewert H. Cousins. New York: Newman Press, 1971.
Barciauskas, Jonas. "A Rooted Flower, a Radiant Stone: Eckhart on Nature." In *An Ecology of the Spirit: Religious Reflection and Environmental Consciousness.* Ed. Michael Barnes. Lanham, Md.: University Press of America, 1994.
Barfield, Owen. *Saving the Appearances: A Study in Idolatry.* New York: Harcourt Brace Jovanovich, 1965.
Basho Matsuo. *The Narrow Road to the Deep North.* Trans. Nobuyuki Yuasa. Harmondsworth, Eng.: Penguin Books, 1966.
_____. *Narrow Road to the Interior.* Trans. Sam Hamill. Boston: Shambhala, 1991.
Berman, Morris. *The Reenchantment of the World.* Ithaca, N.Y.: Cornell

University Press, 1981.
Bhagavad Gita. Trans. Juan Mascaro. Harmondsworth, Eng.: Penguin, 1962.
Biser, Eugen. "Wisdom." *Sacramentum Mundi: An Encyclopedia of Theology.*
Bonavanture. *The Soul's Journey into God. The Tree of Life. The Life of St. Francis.* Trans. Ewert Cousins. New York: Paulist Press, 1978.
Boyde, Patrick. *Dante: Philomythes and Philosopher.* Cambridge: Cambridge University Press, 1981.
Brown, Jane K. "Mephistopheles the Nature Spirit." *Studies in Romanticism* 24 (Winter 1985): 475-490.
Burtt, E.A. "Intuition in Eastern and Western Philosophy." *Philosophy East and West* 2 (1953): 283-291.
Cassirer, Ernst. *The Individual and the Cosmos in Renaissance Philosophy.* Trans. Mario Domandi. New York: Barnes & Noble, 1963.
Cobb, John B., Jr. *Beyond Dialogue: Toward a Mutual Transformation of Christianity and Buddhism.* Philadelphia: Fortress Press, 1982.
_____. *Christ in a Pluralistic Age.* Philadelphia: Westminster Press, 1975.
_____. "Two Types of Postmodernism: Deconstruction and Process." *Theology Today* 47 (1990): 149-164.
_____, and David Ray Griffin. *Process Theology: An Introductory Exposition.* Belfast: Christian Journals, 1976.
_____, and Christopher Ives, eds. *The Emptying God: A Buddhist-Christian Conversation.* Maryknoll, N.Y.: Orbis Books, 1990.
Cousins, Ewert H. "Introduction: Process Models in Culture, Philosophy, and Theology." In *Process Theology: Basic Writings.* Ed. Ewert H. Cousins. New York: Newman Press, 1971.
Covell, John, and Yamada Sobin. *Zen at Daitoku-ji.* Tokyo, New York: Kodansha, 1974.
Dante Alighieri. *The Inferno.* Trans. John Ciardi. New York: Mentor Classic, New American Library, 1954.
_____. *The Paradiso.* Trans. John Ciardi. New York: Mentor Classic, New American Library, 1961.
_____. *The Purgatorio.* Trans. John Ciardi. New York: Mentor Classic, New American Library, 1957.
De Lubac, Henri. *The Religion of Teilhard de Chardin.* Trans. René Hague. Garden City, N.Y.: Doubleday Image Books, 1968.
Dionysius the Areopagite. *The Divine Names and The Mystical Theology.*

Trans. C.E. Rolt. London: SPCK, 1940.
Dupré, Louis. "Mysticism." *Encyclopedia of Religion.*
_____. *Religious Mystery and Rational Reflection: Excursions in the Phenomenology and Philosophy of Religion.* Grand Rapids, Mich.: Eerdmans, 1998.
Eckhart, Meister. *The Essential Sermons, Commentaries, Treatises, and Defense.* Trans. Edmund Colledge and Bernard McGinn. New York: Paulist Press, 1981.
Ferré, Frederick. *Hellfire and Lightning Rods: Liberating Science, Technology, and Religion.* Maryknoll, N.Y.: Orbis Books, 1993.
Franck, Frederick, ed. *The Buddha Eye: An Anthology of the Kyoto School.* New York: Crossroad, 1982.
Gandee, Charles K. "A Wayfarer's Chapel by Fay Jones." *Architectural Record* 169 (March 1981): 88-93.
Goethe, Johann Wolfgang von. *Faust, a Tragedy.* Trans. Walter Arndt. New York: W.W. Norton, 1976.
_____. *Faust: Parts 1 and 2.* Trans. Louis MacNeice. New York: Continuum, 1994.
Grafton, Anthony. *New Worlds, Ancient Texts: The Power of Tradition and the Shock of Discovery.* Cambridge: Belknap Press of Harvard University Press, 1992
Griffin, David Ray. *God and Religion in the Postmodern World: Essays in Postmodern Theology.* Albany: State University of New York Press, 1989.
_____. "Relativism, Divine Causation, and Biblical Theology." In *God's Activity in the World: The Contemporary Problem.* Ed. Owen C. Thomas. Chico, Calif.: Scholars Press, 1983.
_____, and Huston Smith. *Primordial Truth and Postmodern Theology.* Albany: State University of New York Press, 1989.
_____, ed. *Archetypal Process: Self and Divine in Whitehead, Jung, and Hillman.* Evanston, Ill.: Northwestern University Press, 1989.
_____, ed. *Physics and the Ultimate Significance of Time.* Albany: State University of New York Press, 1986.
Hawking, Stephen W. *A Brief History of Time: From the Big Bang to Black Holes.* New York: Bantam Books, 1988.
Jantz, Harold. *Goethe's Faust as a Renaissance Man: Parallels and Prototypes.* Princeton, N.J.: Princeton University Press, 1951.
Johnson, Elizabeth A. *Women, Earth, and Creator Spirit.* New York: Paulist Press, 1993.
Keene, Donald. *Travelers of a Hundred Ages.* New York: Henry Holt,

1989.

King, Ursula. *Spirit of Fire: The Life and Vision of Teilhard de Chardin.* Maryknoll, N.Y.: Orbis Books, 1996.

_____. *Towards a New Mysticism: Teihard de Chardin and Eastern Religions.* New York: Seabury Press, 1981.

Leclercq, Jean. *The Love of Learning and the Desire for God: A Study of Monastic Culture.* New York: Fordham University Press, 1974.

Lovejoy, Arthur O. *The Great Chain of Being: A Study of the History of an Idea.* Cambridge: Harvard University Press, 1936.

May, Rollo. *The Cry for Myth.* New York: W.W. Norton, 1991.

Miller, Jerome A. *In the Throes of Wonder.* Albany: State University of New York Press, 1992.

Nasr, Seyyed Hossein. *Knowledge and the Sacred: The Gifford Lectures.* New York: Crossroad, 1981.

Nicholas of Cusa. *Selected Spiritual Writings.* Trans. H. Lawrence Bond. New York: Paulist Press, 1997.

Nishitani Keiji. *Religion and Nothingness.* Trans. Jan Van Bragt. Berkeley: University of California Press, 1982.

Panikkar, R. *Myth, Faith and Hermeneutics: Cross-Cultural Studies.* New York: Paulist Press, 1979.

Pelikan, Jaroslav. *Faust the Theologian.* New Haven, Conn.: Yale University Press, 1995.

Poincaré, Henri. "Mathematical Creation." In *The Creative Process.* Ed. Brewster Ghilselin. New York: New American Library, 1952.

Rawlinson, Andrew. *The Book of Enlightened Masters: Western Teachers in Eastern Traditions.* Chicago: Open Press, 1997.

Santayana, George. *Three Philosophical Poets.* Cambridge: Harvard University, 1910.

Smith, Huston. "The View from Everywhere: Ontotheology and Post-Nietzschean Deconstruction of Metaphysics." In *Religion, Ontotheology and Deconstruction.* Ed. Henry Ruf. New York: Paragon House, 1989.

_____. *Beyond the Post-Modern Mind.* New York: Crossroad, 1982.

_____. *Forgotten Truth: The Primordial Tradition.* New York: Harper & Row, 1976.

_____. *The World's Religions: Our Great Wisdom Traditions.* San Francisco: HarperSanFrancisco, 1991.

Smith, Wilfred Cantwell. "Comparative Religion: Whither - and Why?" In *The History of Religions: Essays in Methodology.* Ed. Mircea Eliade and Joseph M. Kitagawa. Chicago: University of Chicago

Press, 1959.
Suzuki, Daisetz T. *Zen and Japanese Culture.* Princeton, N.J.: Princeton University Press, 1959.
Teilhard de Chardin, Pierre. *The Divine Milieu.* New York: Harper Torchbooks, 1968.
_____. *The Heart of Matter.* Trans. René Hague. New York: Harcourt Brace Jovanovich, 1978.
Ueda Makoto. *Basho and His Interpreters: Selected Hokku with Commentary.* Stanford: Stanford University Press, 1991.
Underhill, Evelyn. *Mysticism: A Study in the Nature and Development of Man's Spiritual Consciousness.* New York: E.P. Dutton, 1961.
White, Lynn. *Dynamo and Virgin Reconsidered: Essays in the Dynamism of Western Culture.* Cambridge: MIT Press, 1971.
Whitehead, Alfred North. *Process and Reality.* Corrected Ed. Ed. David Ray Griffin and David W. Sherburne. New York: Free Press, 1978.

Index

Abe Masao, ch. 4 *passim*, 164
Aquinas, Thomas, 50-51, 142-143
Aristotle, 108, 167, 186
Augustine, vii, 14-15, 31-32, 164, 189 n.29
Aurobindo, Sri, 182

Barbour, Ian, 165-170
Barfield, Owen, 137
Basho, 58-72, 82, 92-93, 98, 100-103, 105 n.61
Bergson, Henri, 173, 183
Bhagavad Gita, 44
Bohm, David, 37-38
Bonaventure, 12-13, 15, 28, 50-51, 193
Boyde, Patrick, 13-16
Buddha, 70, 78, 83, 197
Buddha-nature, 83-85
Buddhism, vii, xv-xvi, xviii, ch. 3 & 4 *passim*, 134, 136, 140, 159, 162, 182
Burtt, E.A., 163

Chartres Cathedral, 193-195
Christianity, vii-viii, xviii, 15, 17, 32-34, 43-44, 48, 51, 53, 123, 175
circumincession, 81-82, 183-184
Cobb, John B., Jr., ch. 6 *passim*, 159, 162, 164-165, 168-169, 182-184
coincidence of opposites, 126
cosmos, 7, 12-13, 21-23, 33, 25-26, 32-33, 35-36, 44, 50-51, 83-84, 86-88, 92, 95-96, 98-99, 101, 108, 111, 123, 196, 198; in process thought, 134, 137-140, 142-143, 149; in Teilhard, 165-170, 173, 180-181, 183-184, 186
Cousins, Ewert, 196
creatio ex nihilo, 89-90, 147, 168
creativity, 40, 108, 118, 125, 133-134, 138, 140-141, 156 n.5, 168, 182, 184, 187

Daitoku-ji, 193-194
Dante Alighieri, 2-3, 10, 58, 67, 72, 82, 93, 100, 107-109, 114, 117, 122-124, 128, 137, 143, 181, 196
Dionysius the Aeropagite, 11-12
Divine Comedy, 3-17, 196; landscapes in, 6, 7-10; metaphysics of, 11-17
Dogen, 84-85, 104 n.20
Dupré, Louis, xx

Eckhart, Meister, 2, 27-28, 32, 90, 118, 129 n.17
Eliot, T.S., 87-88
emptiness (see also nothingness and *sunyata*), 28, 38, 72-73, 77-81, 83-84, 91-92, 96-101, 117-118, 125, 134, 163, 182, 187, 197
Eros, 119, 134, 154, 195
esoteric/exoteric, 48-49
evil, 3, 5, 14, 35, 70, 79-81, 84, 95-96, 102, 111, 113,

121, 123-125, 128, 129
n.11, 134-135, 139, 154,
160-161, 164, 169, 185
evolution, 39, 44-46, 119,
131, 134, 144, 149-152,
165-170, 173-175, 178,
181, 195
exemplarism 11-13, 17, 26

Faust, 108-128, 134-135, 153,
180-185, 188, 195
Feminine, Universal or Eternal,
122, 126, 142, 172, 179,
187-188

God (see also Trinity), 6-7, 11-
17, 27-28, 78, 81-82, 85,
90-92, 94-95. 108, 110-
111, 114-115, 125-128,
159-160, 162, 167-170,
172, 175-185, 187-188,
193-195, 197-198; in
process thought, 133-139,
141-144, 150-152, 154
Godhead, 28, 90-92, 118, 125,
197
Goethe, Johann Wolfgang von,
108-128 *passim*, 134, 181,
184-185
Griffin, David Ray, ch. 6
passim, 159, 160-165, 168-
169, 182-183, 185

Hartshorne, Charles, 131-132
Hawking, Stephen, 1, 3, 197-
198
hierarchy, 13-17, 21-22, 24-30,
44, 46, 50-52, 86, 88, 92,
101, 123, 143, 188, 193

Hinduism, 23, 28, 34-35, 38,
40-41, 43, 48, 84, 97, 163,
173, 184
history & time, xvii; 164, 166-
168, 181-182, 187; in
Alpha, 40-46; in Zero, 93-
98; in Omega, 149-154

imagination, xvii, 17-18, 20-
21, 26, 30, 51-52, 68, 102,
112, 122, 124-125, 127,
183, 193-194, 196
intellect (*intellectus*), xiv, 7,
23-24, 27, 35, 49, 160-161,
164, 198
intuition, 40, 144, 160, 163,
187

Jesus Christ, 29, 32, 44, 48-49,
51, 82, 112, 153-155, 175-
177
Jungian psychology, 118, 125,
183

kalpa, 96-98
Kierkegaard, Soren, 95, 127
knowing, 15-16, 23-24, 28-29,
39, 48, 131, 136, 137-138,
147, 149 155, 159, 161-
164, 171, 180, 182, 185,
188, 196-199
Kook, Abraham Isaac, 182

landscape, xvii, 4, 6-7, 10, 51-
52, 72, 80, 84-85, 93, 101-
103, 107, 116, 121, 124,
127-128, 193
Leclercq, Jean, 50
love, 3, 7, 12, 14, 27, 31, 41,
79-80, 86, 96, 115-116,

121-122, 126, 135, 152, 154-155, 179-180, 199
matter, 13-14, 17, 22, 25, 30, 37-38, 45-46, 51, 88, 92, 138, 140, 142, 167-168, 170-174, 176, 179-180, 182-183
maya, 38, 40, 41, 47, 49
Mephistopheles, 108-128 *passim*, 134, 180
metaphysics, xvi-xvii, 4, 11-17, 78, 108, 123, 160, 166, 181; in Alpha, ch. 2 *passim*; in Zero, ch.4 *passim*; in Omega, ch. 6 *passim*
Mu/U, 78-9, 83-84
myth, xvii-xviii, 26, 33-35, 40, 44, 52, 58, 64, 93-4, 97-98, 104 n.46, 108-109, 117, 119, 122, 124, 127, 136, 142, 183, 196

Nasr, Seyyed Hossein, ch. 2 *passim*, 196
nature, in Alpha, 4, 11, 13, 17, 37, 41, 45, 49; in Zero, 57-58, 62-63, 69, 71-73; in Omega, 108-109, 111-113, 115-116, 120, 123-128, 137-138, 141-146, 148, 150, 161-162, 166, 170, 175
Neoplatonism, 11-13, 15-6, 21, 27, 29, 34, 41, 49-52, 78, 82, 108-109, 124, 127, 133, 193
Newton, Isaac, 37, 131, 138, 142

Nicholas of Cusa, 2-3, 49, 126, 197-198
Nietzsche, Friedrich, 31, 89-90, 139
Nishitani Keiji, ch. 4 *passim*
Noosphere, 169-170, 174-175
nothingness (see also *sunyata* and emptiness), 77, 80, 84, 89-92, 95, 97, 100, 102, 118, 125, 149, 182

participation, 24, 137, 141, 186, 197
Pelikan, Jaroslav, 127-128
perennial philosophy (see also Primordial tradition), 24-25, 34, 36-37, 46, 140
person (divine), 27, 29, 32, 44, 49, 81-82, 95, 187, 197
person (human), 7, 21, 28, 32-33, 36, 51, 82-83, 85-86, 88, 90-93, 125-126, 134, 137, 141
Pico della Mirandola, Giovanni, 126, 142
plurality, 47, 198
Poincaré, Henri, 186-187
Posse, 198
postmodern science, 144-148, 161, 185
postmodern worldview, 139-142, 144-148, 155, 162
prajna, 34, 46, 92, 136
Prajna Paramita Sutra, 197
prehension, 133, 161-163
Primordial Tradition (see also perennial philosophy), 22, 33, 38, 47, 136
process thought, 108-109, ch.6 *passim*, 160, 163-164,

180-183, 187-188, 195-196, 198

ratio hermetica, 185-186
reason, xiv-xv, 5, 15-16, 24, 30, 33, 47, 50, 88-89, 110, 124, 182-187, 198; in process thought, 136, 147, 155
redemption, 52, 93-95, 120-122, 125, 128, 180, 190
reenchantment, 136-137, 142, 148
relativity theory, 38, 131
Renaissance, 109, 111, 126-127, 142, 144, 185-6, 198

samsara, 82
sapientia (see also wisdom), xiv-xv, 15, 24, 33-35, 46-47, 50, 53, 188
Schuon, Frithjof, 35, 47
science, vii, xiii-xv, xvii, 161-162, 164-165, 182, 185-187; in Alpha, 36-39; in Zero, 85-93; in Omega, 142-149
scientia sacra, 24, 28, 34-35, 37, 40, 48-49,
sin, 4, 94-95, 169
Singer, Isaac Bashevis, viii
Smith, Huston, ch. 2 *passim*, 85, 140, 160-161, 164, 181-183, 185, 196
Smith, Wilfred Cantwell, xxi
soku, 81-2, 88, 96-7
soul, 3-9, 11, 14-16, 18, 25, 28-32, 35, 41-42, 46, 48-49, 53, 64, 110, 112, 114-115, 120-122, 138, 140,

142-144, 163, 170, 173-174, 178-179, 184
spirit, 13, 29, 32, 46, 48, 111, 113, 115, 119, 121, 124, 129 n.11, 140, 142-143, 167, 172-178, 180, 183, 186-187
sunyata (see also emptiness and nothingness), 72-73, 77-81, 83-84, 87, 90, 92, 96, 98, 100-101, 136, 163-164, 182
Suzuki, D.T., 57, 68, 70-71

Teilhard de Chardin, Pierre, 45-46, 132, 136, 164-184, 195-197
Thorncrown Chapel, 194-195
Tillich, Paul, 31, 78
time (see history & time)
Tradition (according to Alpha), 34
Trinity, 27, 29, 48, 51, 187
Tu Fu, 58, 69

Ulysses, 8-10, 107-108
unknowing, 28, 128
Urquell, 110, 125

Van Bragt, Jan, 100

Wechseldauer, 117, 125, 188
Whitehead, Alfred North, 131-133, 135-136, 140, 151, 153-155, 162, 164-167,
wisdom, vii, xx, 3, 5, 15-16, 160-161, 163-164, 171, 180-182, 184-188, 193-199; in Alpha, 21-25, 28, 33-36, 42, 46, 48-53; in

Zero, 82-83, 85, 92, 98-
   99, 101-103; in Omega,
   108, 111-112, 120-122,
   125-128, 132, 136, 142,
   149, 155

zazen, 57, 72, 99
Zen, 57, 72-73, 77, 80, 84, 87,
   93, 96-99, 102-103, 136,
   193-195; and Basho, 58,
   60, 68, 71

BD 111 .B18 2000
Barciauskas, Jonas Vladas.
Landscapes of wisdom